HOW AUTOCRATS ATTACK EXPERTISE

Chronicling and analyzing resistance to the threat that autocracy poses to American liberal democracy, this book provides the definitive account of Trump's assault on truth and his populist attacks on expertise, as well as scientific and legal opposition to them.

This book is about the threat of autocracy, which antedated Donald Trump and will persist after he leaves the stage. Pandering to populists, autocrats attack professional expertise in an Orwellian world, where "ignorance is strength" and where, as Hannah Arendt wrote, people "believe everything and nothing." Trump sought to inflame xenophobia by blaming China for the pandemic and closing U.S. borders, then declaring victory and, when that proved premature, wrongly blaming the number of tests for escalating cases. He sought to muzzle government scientists and denounced those who defied or evaded his directives as members of the "deep state," preferring to rely on inexpert buddies. He elevated obscure scientists who promoted quack cures and opposed effective preventive measures while sidelining the few reputable experts, who nevertheless courageously resisted political interference. In addition to these, as this book documents, independent scientists, scientific journals and professional associations also outspoken, often more so. Even the pharmaceutical industry sought to preserve the integrity of a federal bureaucracy that assured the public the drugs they consumed were safe and efficacious. Following Trump's numerous efforts to distort and undermine expertise, this book describes and evaluates the resilience of scientific and legal defenses of truth.

This definitive account and analysis of the Trump's populist rejection of truth and expertise will appeal to scholars, students and others with interests in politics, populism and the rule of law and, more specifically, to those concerned with resisting the threat that autocracy poses to liberal democracy.

Richard L. Abel is Michael J. Connell Distinguished Professor of Law Emeritus and Distinguished Research Professor, UCLA, USA.

Defending American Democracy

Other books included in the series:

How Autocrats Seek Power

How Autocrats Abuse Power
A GlassHouse book

HOW AUTOCRATS ATTACK EXPERTISE

Resistance to Trump and Trumpism

Richard L. Abel

Routledge
Taylor & Francis Group
a GlassHouse Book

Designed cover image: Ivan Marc/Shutterstock

First published 2024
by Routledge
4 Park Square, Milton Park, Abingdon, Oxon OX14 4RN

and by Routledge
605 Third Avenue, New York, NY 10158

Routledge is an imprint of the Taylor & Francis Group, an informa business

A GlassHouse book

British Library Cataloguing-in-Publication Data
A catalogue record for this book is available from the British Library

ISBN: 978-1-032-62909-4 (hbk)
ISBN: 978-1-032-62910-0 (pbk)
ISBN: 978-1-032-62912-4 (ebk)

DOI: 10.4324/9781032629124

Typeset in Sabon
by Apex CoVantage, LLC

CONTENTS

PREFACE

This book has a long genesis. In February 1989, after meeting South African lawyers in the U.S., Canada and England and securing the blessing of the African National Congress (because of the cultural boycott), I made my first visit to that country. Following two more extended field trips in 1990 and 1991, I published *Politics by Other Means: Law in the Struggle against Apartheid, 1980–1994* (Routledge 1995), documenting the extraordinary contributions of activists, lawyers, judges, journalists and NGOs to the creation of a nonracial liberal democracy.

A decade later—on Saturday morning, May 2, 2004—I was driving home to Santa Monica after several days of hiking in the Grand Canyon. To stay awake on the long, straight, empty stretches of Interstate-10, I turned on NPR's "Weekend Edition" and heard Seymour Hersh expose the torture of Iraqi detainees by American prison guards at Abu Ghraib. That broadcast had a particular resonance for me because I vividly remembered when, a quarter century earlier, Sy—my brother-in-law—had broken the news about Lt. William Calley's role in the massacre of My Lai villagers, a story that contributed to ending the Vietnam War. By the time I heard the interview repeated several more times, I resolved to examine how the U.S. would respond to this most basic violation of the rule of law—expecting that our nation's two-century-old democracy would be far more faithful to that ideal than South Africa's threatened white-minority regime had been. I spent the next 14 years analyzing the role of law and lawyers in torture, detention in Guantánamo Bay, electronic surveillance, civilian casualties of warfare, criminal prosecutions of alleged terrorists, courts-martial for war crimes, military commissions for Guantánamo detainees, habeas corpus petitions by those detainees, civil damages actions by victims of both terrorism and torture and civil liberties violations. The result was my two books *Law's Wars* and *Law's Trials* (Cambridge 2018).

When I gave talks about them, the most common question was whether I was going to write another about the Trump administration. I strongly demurred: Trump's shameless appeals to racism and his utter contempt for the law, professional expertise (in the administration's disastrous response to the COVID-19 pandemic) and the integrity of elections raised very different issues from the actions of the Bush and Obama administrations in the "war on terror" (however much I deplored them). But like so many others, I was transfixed and appalled by Trump's words and actions, first as a candidate and then in office. Therefore, I continued taking contemporaneous notes (as I had done for the "war on terror" books). After Trump lost the 2020 election, I read through the hundreds of pages I had accumulated and began to see deeply disturbing patterns. Because I believed then, and still do, that Trump and Trumpism represent the greatest threat to American liberal democracy in my lifetime, I wrote the present book and two others analyzing Trump's actions and the resistance they provoked with respect to immigration and criminal justice (Abel 2024a) and the 2020 election (Abel 2024b) and am completing a fourth book on the efforts to hold Trump accountable since the January 6 insurrection (Abel 2025).

If journalism is a first draft of history, this is a second. I have mined the writings of journalists, participants in the events and academics in order to offer the most comprehensive account I have been able to construct of the last seven years. I believe that the level of detail is necessary both to understand what Trump and his supporters did to undermine the essential elements of liberal democracy and to identify and evaluate the efficacy of the forms of resistance this provoked. Two great writers have eloquently explained their own reasons for immersing readers in a richly described world. In the preface to his novel *Roderick Hudson*, Henry James wrote:

> [R]elations stop nowhere, and the exquisite problem of the artist is eternally but to draw, by a geometry of his own, the circle within which they shall happily *appear* to do so. He is in the perpetual predicament that the continuity of things is the whole matter, for him, of comedy and tragedy; that this continuity is never, by the space of an instant or an inch, broken, and that, to do anything at all, he has at once intensely to consult and intensely to ignore it.[1]

A century later, Aleksandr Solzhenitsyn wrote in the preface to his historical novel *March 1917: The Red Wheel*: "I do understand that I am overloading the *Wheel* with detailed historical material—but it is that very material that's needed for categorical proof."[2] Rather than claiming to prove, I also offer readers as much evidence as possible to let them draw their own conclusions.

In the seven years I have been working on this book, I have been helped by many. Even though I have been emeritus for many years, the UCLA Law Library located elusive materials and generously provided student research assistants who identified the lawyers who brought the cases I discuss in the following chapters. I continue to benefit from an ongoing collaboration organized by Fabio Costa Morais de Sa e Silva and David Trubek, involving scholars from or writing about autocratic legalism in India, South Africa, Brazil, Hungary, Russia and China. And most of all, I am grateful to my wife, Emily, who listened to me rail against Trump's assault on liberal democracy through more than 2,500 dinners and unfailingly provided the encouragement I needed to persevere.

Notes

1 Henry James, "Roderick Hudson" (London: Macmillan, 1875).
2 Aleksandr Solzhenitsyn, "March 1917: The Red Wheel/Node III (8 March-31 March): Book 3" (translated by Marian Schwartz) (U Notre Dame Press 2017), quoted in Gary Saul Morson, "What Solzhenitsyn Understood" New York Review of Books 35, 37 (5.12.22).

ACRONYMS

AAPS	Association of American Physicians and Surgeons
ABA	American Bar Association
ACLU	American Civil Liberties Union
ADA	Americans with Disabilities Act
AFLDS	America's Frontline Doctors
ALA	American Library Association
AMA	American Medical Association
AP	Advanced Placement
BARDA	Biomedical Advanced Research and Development Authority
BMJ	*British Medical Journal*
BOP	Bureau of Prisons
CDC (or CDCP)	Centers for Disease Control and Prevention
CENTCOM	U.S. Central Command
CEO	Chief Executive Officer
CIA	Central Intelligence Agency
CMS	Centers for Medicare & Medicaid Services
CNBC	cable business news channel CNN: CNN Media Company (formerly Cable News Network)
COVID-19	severe acute respiratory syndrome coronavirus 2 (SARS-Cov-2)
CPA	Certified Public Accountant
CPAC	Conservative Political Action Coalition
CQ	chloroquine
CRT	Critical Race Theory
DHHS	Department of Health and Human Services

DHS	Department of Homeland Security
DJT	Donald J. Trump
DNA	Deoxyribonucleic Acid
DoD	Department of Defense
DoJ	Department of Justice
DoS	Department of State
DT	Donald Trump
EO	Executive Order
EPA	Environmental Protection Agency
EUA	Emergency Use Authorization
FBI	Federal Bureau of Investigation
FDA	Food and Drug Administration
FLCCCA	Front Line COVID-19 Critical Care Alliance
FSMB	Federation of State Medical Boards
GAO	Government Accountability Office
GHWB	George H.W. Bush
GM	General Motors
GOP	Grand Old Party (i.e., Republican Party)
GWB	George W. Bush
HCQ	hydroxychloroquine
HFHS	Henry Ford Health System
HHS	Health and Human Services Department
HIV	Human Immunodeficiency Virus
HJC	House Judiciary Committee
IC	Intelligence Community
ICU	Intensive Care Unit
IG	Inspector General
IRS	Internal Revenue Service
JAMA	Journal of the American Medical Association
LAFD	Los Angeles Fire Department
LAPD	Los Angeles Police Department
LG	Lieutenant General
LGBTQ	Lesbian Gay Bisexual Transexual Queer
MAGA	Make America Great Again (Trump slogan)
MMR	Measles Mumps and Rubella (vaccine)
MMWR	CDC's Morbidity and Mortality Weekly Report
mRNA	Messenger Ribonucleic Acid
MSNBC	NBC's television channel
NBC	National Broadcasting Company
NCMI	National Center for Medical Intelligence
NEC	National Economic Council
NEJM	*New England Journal of Medicine*

NIAID	National Institute of Allergy and Infectious Diseases (NIH)
NIC	National Intelligence Council
NIH	National Institutes of Health
NOAA	National Oceanic and Atmospheric Administration
NPR	National Public Radio
NSA	National Security Adviser or National Security Agency
NWS	National Weather Service
NYFD	New York Fire Department
NYPD	New York Police Department
NYS	New York State
ObGyn	Obstetrics and Gynecology
ODNI	Office of the Director of National Intelligence
OLC	Office of Legal Counsel
OMB	Office of Management and Budget
OWS	Operation Warp Speed
PEPFAR	President's Emergency Plan for AIDS Relief
RCT	Randomized Clinical Trial
RNA	Ribonucleic Acid
RNC	Republican National Committee
SAMHSA	DHHS Substance Abuse and Mental Health Services Administration
SARS-CoV-2	scientific name of COVID-19
SASC	Senate Armed Services Committee
SEL	Social Emotional Learning
SC	Senate Judiciary Committee
SSA	Social Security Administration
TCF	Long-Term Care Facilities
TRO	Temporary Restraining Order
VA	Veterans Administration
VAERS	Vaccine Adverse Event Reporting Scheme
WCWP	White Coat Waste Project
WHO	World Health Organization
WIV	Wuhan Institute of Virology
WMC	Washington Medical Commission

DRAMATIS PERSONAE

Jerome Adams Trump's Surgeon General

Paul Alexander Canadian health researcher and aide to Caputo

Scott Atlas Hoover Institution senior fellow; neuroradiologist

Alexander Azar DHHS Secretary

Stephen K. Bannon Trump adviser

William Barr Trump's Attorney General

Maria Bartiromo Fox News commentator

Jayanta Bhattacharya Stanford University professor of medicine, economics and health policy

Stephen Biegun Deputy Secretary of State

Deborah Birx White House Coronavirus Response Coordinator

Lauren Boebert Republican Colorado Representative

Albert Bourla Pfizer CEO

Rick Bright BARDA Director

Michael Caputo HHS Assistant Secretary for Public Affairs

Tucker Carlson Fox News commentator

Robert Charrow HHS general counsel

Chris Christie former NJ Governor

Francis S. Collins NIH Director

Kellyanne Conway White House counsellor

Kenneth Cuccinelli Senior Officer performing the duties of Trump's DHS Deputy Secretary

Joseph Cuffari DHS IG

Andrew Cuomo NY Governor

Ronald DeSantis Florida Republican Governor

Steve Doocy Fox News commentator

Ainsley Earhardt Fox News host

Larry Ellison Oracle CEO

Anthony Fauci NIAID Director

Thomas Frieden Obama's CDC Director

Matt Gaetz Republican Representative from Florida

George Gao head of China's CDC

Tedros Adhanom Ghebreyesus WHO Director General

Brett Giroir DHHS Assistant Secretary of Health and COVID-19 testing czar

Rudy Giuliani Trump lawyer

Simone Gold AFLDS doctor

Taylor Goodspeed CEA chair

Marjorie Taylor Greene Georgia Republican Representative

Sunetra Gupta Oxford University professor of epidemiology

Stephen Hahn FDA Commissioner

Sean Hannity Fox News commentator

Kevin Hassett CEA chair

Steven Hatfill Navarro adviser

Michael V. Hayden former Director of NSA and CIA

Hope Hicks White House Communications Director

Stella Immanuel doctor and HCQ advocate

Laura Ingraham Fox News host

Jay Inslee Washington State Democratic Governor

John Ionnidis Stanford University medical school professor

Ron Johnson Wisconsin Republican Senator

Robert Kadlec DHHS Assistant Secretary for Preparedness and Response

Robert F. Kennedy Jr. anti-vax advocate (and son of RFK)

Charlotte Kent chief, CDC scientific publications branch

Larry Kudlow NEC chair

Martin Kulldorff Harvard Medical School professor

Jared Kushner Trump's son-in-law and COVID-19 Task Force chair

Joseph Ladapo Florida Surgeon General

Rush Limbaugh conservative commentator

Peter Marks Director of FDA Center for Biologics Evaluation and Research

Roger Marshall Republican Kansas Senator

Kevin McCarthy California Republican House Minority Leader and then Speaker

Michael McCaul Texas Republican Representative

Kayleigh McEnany Trump's press secretary

Johnny McEntee Presidential Personnel Office Director

Kyle McGowan CDC chief of staff

Mark Meadows White House chief of staff

Cody Meissner Tufts University professor of pediatrics

Joseph Mercola anti-vax doctor

Nancy Messonnier CDC National Center for Immunization and Respiratory Diseases Director

Jason Miller Trump senior campaign adviser

Katie Miller Pence's communications Director

Stephen Mnuchin Treasury Secretary

Brian Monahan Congress's attending physician

Mick Mulvaney White House chief of staff

Peter Navarro Trump's trade adviser

Gavin Newsom California Democratic Governor

Jack Niklaus retired golf pro

Matthew Pottinger Deputy National Security Adviser

Robert O'Brien National Security Adviser

Jane M. Orient AAPS Executive Director

Mehmet Oz cardiothoracic surgeon and television celebrity

Rand Paul Republican Kentucky Senator

Nancy Pelosi Democratic House Speaker

Michael Pence Vice President

Michael Pompeo Secretary of State

Didier Raoult French scientist

Robert Redfield CDC Director

Gregory Rigano lawyer, HCQ advocate

Harvey Risch emeritus Yale public health and medical school professor

Geraldo Rivera Fox News commentator

Wilbur Ross Trump's Commerce Secretary

Christopher Rufo Manhattan Institute senior fellow

Anne Schuchat CDC Incident Manager

Marc Short Pence's chief of staff

Moncef Slaoui OWS Director

Stephen Smith NJ physician

Sean Spicer Trump press secretary

Sherri Tenpenny anti-vax doctor

Olivia Troye Pence's homeland security and counterterrorism adviser

Seema Verna CMS Administrator

Russell Vought OMB Director

Rochelle Walensky CDC Director

Chris Wallace Fox News host

Henry Walke CDC Director of the Center for Preparedness and Response

Herschel Walker unsuccessful Republican candidate for senator from Georgia

Gretchen Whitmer Democratic Governor of Michigan

Nina Witkofsky acting CDC chief of staff

Chad Wolf Acting DHS Secretary

Janet Woodcock Director of FDA's Center for Drug Evaluation and Research

Bob Woodward journalist and author

Michael Worobey University of Arizona evolutionary virologist

Xi Jinping China's President

Vladimir Zelenko doctor and HCQ advocate

1

THE AUTOCRATS' WAR ON EXPERTISE

Nearly 250 years ago, Adam Smith extolled the virtues of the division of labor.[1] Today, we all enjoy its benefits to an extent Smith could not possibly have imagined. But specialization also makes each of us depend on others—experts—and dependence can breed fear and resentment. Richard Hofstadter once observed that "intellect is resented as a form of power or privilege" because it is "needed too much."[2] Most of the time, this resentment has few obvious human targets—when we are frustrated by our computers, cell phones, cars, household appliances, mass transit, the Internet. But some forms of specialization arouse particular ire, as shown by numerous historical examples.[3] In early 19th-century England, Luddites protested machines replacing handweaving.[4] In the 1970s, Ivan Illich criticized formal education, professional medicine and specialized knowledge more generally.[5] Feminists attacked medicine for its patriarchal practices.[6] AIDS activists urged better medical care for HIV and demanded that pharmaceutical companies share their patents.[7]

Many of these movements expressed legitimate grievances, and their campaigns often improved and humanized expertise. Autocrats, by contrast, view <u>all</u> expertise as a threat to the absolute power to which they aspire. They insist that they alone control truth. George Orwell's Ministry of Truth pronounced: "War is peace. Freedom is slavery. Ignorance is strength."[8] Hannah Arendt elaborated this in her account of *The Origins of Totalitarianism*.[9]

> In an ever-changing, incomprehensible world the masses had reached the point where they would, at the same time believe everything and nothing, think that everything was possible and nothing was true. . . . The totalitarian mass leaders based their propaganda on the correct psychological

DOI: 10.4324/9781032629124-1

> assumption that, under such conditions, one could make people believe the most fantastic statements one day, and trust that if the next day they were given irrefutable proof of their falsehood, they would take refuge in cynicism; instead of deserting the leaders who had lied to them, they would protest that they had known all along that the statement was a lie and would admire the leaders for their superior tactical cleverness.

More than most, Trump had no choice but to rely on experts, given his woeful ignorance and refusal (or inability) to read. But he demanded that they be his experts. He wrote in 2007: "I value loyalty above anything else—more than brains, more than drive, and more than energy."[10] As both candidate and president, Trump regularly indulged in scattershot attacks on experts, appealing to his supporters' status anxieties. Reviling experts generally, he told a rally: "We are smarter than they are. They say [they are] the elite. We are the elite. You are the elite."[11] He boasted about relying on his gut instincts while simultaneously insisting that he knew more than experts in any field. As a candidate, he said: "I never have" time to read.[12] He claimed to reach the right decisions "with very little knowledge other than the knowledge I had, plus the words 'common sense,' because I have a lot of common sense and I have a lot of business ability." (Trump hotels filed for bankruptcy six times.[13] Several commentators estimated he would have made more money had he simply invested his substantial inheritance conservatively.)[14] "Every time I say I had an uncle who was a great professor at MIT for 35 years . . . and then they say, Is Donald Trump an intellectual? Trust me, I'm like a smart person."[15] On a visit to the Centers for Disease Control and Prevention (CDC) on March 6, 2020, he again cited genetics as evidence for his own brilliance: his uncle "taught at MIT for, I think, like a record number of years. He was a super genius." "I like this stuff. I really get it. People are surprised that I understand it. Every one of these doctors said, 'How do you know so much about this?' Maybe I have a natural ability."[16] "A lot of people said" of his decisions: "Man, he was more accurate than guys who have studied it all the time." When his fitness for office was questioned in January 2018, he retorted:

> throughout my life, my two greatest assets have been mental stability and being, like, really smart. . . . I went from VERY successful businessman, to top T.V. Star to President of the United States (on my first try). I think that would qualify as not smart, but genius . . . and a very stable genius.[17]

His intellectual arrogance (like his sexual behavior) was promiscuous. Issuing an executive order "Promoting Beautiful Federal Civic Architecture," he praised "Greco-Roman architecture," deriding modernism as "ugly and inconsistent" (thereby unconsciously parroting the prejudices of England's future King Charles III).[18] When Trump's foreign policy (or lack thereof) was criticized, he said:

> the experts are terrible. Look at the mess we're in. . . . If our presidents and our politicians were on vacation for 365 days a year and went to the beach, we'd be in much better shape right now in the Middle East.[19]

(He practiced what he preached, visiting one of his leisure properties three out of every ten days in his first three years and spending 307 days of his presidency playing golf.[20] The verdict is still out about whether this was better for the country.) Trump compared his meeting with North Korean President Kim Jong-un to his sexual conquests:

> You meet a woman in one second, you know whether or not it's going to happen. It doesn't take you 10 minutes and it doesn't take you six weeks. It's like, whoa. OK. You know? It takes somewhat less than a second.[21]

(As a result of that bromance, Kim secured four more years to develop weapons and missiles with nuclear warheads, some now threatening the continental U.S.) Trump even vaunted his contempt for the military, who "want to do nothing but fight wars so that all of those wonderful companies that make the bombs and make the plans and make everything else stay happy." (This was a misreading of the warning against the military-industrial complex issued by President Eisenhower—a former general who knew what he was talking about.)[22]

Challenged about his comprehension of pending legislation, Trump replied: "I know the details of taxes better than anybody. Better than the greatest C.P.A. I know the details of health care better than most." He claimed to understand more about "the big bills" in Congress "than any president that's ever been in office."[23] In October 2018, Trump accused scientists who blamed climate change on human agency of pursuing "a very big political agenda."[24] (This was a typical Trump ploy: attributing to others his own misconduct. It was he who was pursuing a political agenda—appeasing fossil fuel interests—by opposing efforts to reduce carbon emissions.) Dismissing the disastrous wildfires aggravated by climate change, he confidently assured the secretary of the California Natural Resources Agency: "it'll start getting cooler . . . you just watch." When the secretary demurred, saying, "I wish science agreed with you," Trump just blew him off: "I don't think science knows, actually."[25] He cavalierly rejected his own administration's Fourth National Climate Assessment—"I don't believe it"—later asserting that "people like myself" with "very high levels of intelligence" were "not necessarily such believers" while adding irrelevantly: "You look at our air and our water, and it's right now at a record clean."[26] Trump's acolytes followed suit. His second EPA Administrator, Andrew Wheeler (a former coal lobbyist), said he placed "little weight on quantitative estimates" of soot standards.[27] Trump casually condemned the Federal Reserve for raising interest rates. "They're making a mistake because I have a gut, and my gut tells me more sometimes than anybody else's brain can ever tell me." Trump's contempt for expertise pervaded his administration. Half of the scientists surveyed at 16 federal agencies in 2018 reported attacks by political appointees and said politics had "hindered the ability of their agencies to make science-based decisions."[28] A House Committee on Science, Space, and Technology found that the Trump administration had shown "open hostility towards federal scientists."[29]

Trump sought to fill policymaking positions with ideologues. His nominee for Undersecretary of Defense for Policy, Anthony Tata, had resigned from the Army after having affairs with at least two women and calling Obama a "terrorist leader."[30] Joseph L. Votel (former CENTCOM commander), Gen. Tony Thomas (former Special Operations commander) and LG David A. Deptula (former top Air Force general) removed their names from a letter supporting the nomination. SASC Chair Inhofe canceled the hearing on the nomination (realizing he lacked the votes). Trump responded by simply naming Tata "the official performing the duties of the Deputy Undersecretary of Defense for Policy," which did not require confirmation—a strategy he used when other nominations were blocked. Trump named as head of the U.S. Agency for Global Media (which oversees six entities) Michael Pack, a Stephen Bannon ally, who had said that being a journalist was "a great cover for a spy" (thereby compromising the credibility of his entire operation) and promptly fired or forced out the Directors of the Voice of America and the Open Technology Fund.[31] The Government Accountability Office (GAO) found that the appointments of Acting DHS Secretary Chad Wolf and his deputy, Kenneth Cuccinelli, violated the Vacancies Reform Act.[32] DHS IG Joseph Cuffari agreed that the GAO report disclosed "troubling aspects" in the appointments but said it would be "pointless" to intervene in an "inter-branch disagreement" because neither GAO nor the DHS OIG "can issue a binding determination on that issue." Trump never appointed a science adviser and failed to fill more than a third of senior DoD and DHS positions with confirmed appointees.[33]

Trump waged open warfare on the career civil service.[34] The day after issuing an executive order making it easier to fire federal employees, he complained to donors:

> Somebody said, President, what's the toughest country to deal with? Is it Russia? Is it China? Is it North Korea? No, the toughest country by far is dealing with the United States. It's true. These people are sick. . . . [Y]ou have a lot of people from past administrations, and they're civil service.

> I fired some. I say some, just get rid of them. We had a lot of them come to the floor during the impeachment hoax. You see them coming in with their bow ties and everything. It's a weird deal. We have some pretty deep-set, deep-seated people—we got a lot of them and we got rid of them.

(The reference to bow ties recalled Nixon's 1952 attack on his Democratic presidential opponent Adlai Stevenson—who wore them—as an "egghead," an epithet for an intellectual.) *The Washington Post* said: "the cadre of dedicated civil servants whom he calls the 'deep state' . . . are really the greatest strength of the U.S. government." The National Treasury Employees Union, representing 150,000 members, sued to block the order. When Scott Foster refused to identify ten underachievers at the Department of Veterans Affairs—so Trump could fire them dramatically at the ceremonial signing of the EO—he himself was fired; and when the Office of Special Counsel blocked that action, Foster was transferred to a lower-profile job with lesser pay. OSC had received 26 percent more complaints under Trump than during Obama's first term. Secretary of State Pompeo said that "when we identify" "deep-staters" "we move them out of the way." Interior Secretary Zinke complained: "I got 30 percent of the crew that's not loyal to the flag." The principal scientist at the National Park Service was pressured not to mention human-induced global warming. At the end of his term, Trump issued an executive order creating a new category of "Schedule F" employees, who could more easily be hired and fired. He also sought to embed his own political employees in high civil service positions so they could not be removed by Biden, making Michael Ellis (a White House staffer) NSA general counsel. (He later resigned after NSA Director Nakasone placed him on leave during a DoD IG investigation.)

Trump's response to Hurricane Dorian presents the clearest example of his solipsism. After National Weather Service (NWS) Birmingham tweeted: "Alabama will NOT see any impacts from #Dorian," Trump tweeted erroneously: "Alabama will most likely be hit (much) harder than anticipated," thereby spooking Alabamans.[35] When the Bureau corrected this, Trump just doubled down on his own forecast, directing his chief of staff to complain to Commerce Secretary Ross—"the NWS intentionally contradicted the president . . . we need to know why"—and demanding "a correction or an explanation or both." After Ross ordered his political staff to act, NOAA Acting Director Neil Jacobs warned employees: "we could definitely lose our jobs." This prompted an abject (and false) apology: NOAA had "spoke[n] in absolute terms that were inconsistent with probabilities from the best forecast products available at the time" and was "motivated by a desire to embarrass the president more than a concern for the safety of people in Alabama." NOAA's acting chief scientist then compounded the damage by assuring employees that this intervention "was not based on science but on external factors including reputation and appearance, or simply put, political." The NWS Director defended his subordinates, declaring that Birmingham had done "what any office would do." Jacobs insisted hypocritically: "there is no pressure to change the way you communicate or forecast risk in the future." In June 2020, the National Academy of Public Administration found there had been a violation of NOAA's integrity policy, and the Commerce Department IG concluded that "the Department and NOAA acted contrary to the apolitical mission of NWS." Nevertheless, that summer, Ross limited public statements by career employees (a parallel to the muzzling of government scientists during the COVID pandemic, discussed in Chapter 2).

These attacks on science, truth, expertise and the media by the Trump administration were far from unprecedented. Spiro Agnew, Nixon's disgraced Vice President (later forced to resign by charges of political corruption), railed against the media's "nattering nabobs of negativism"—"the hopeless, hysterical hypochondriacs of history" (in speechwriter William Safire's awesome alliterations). An aide to George W. Bush allegedly disparaged "the reality-based community," whose members naively "believe that solutions emerge from your judicious study of discernible reality. . . . We're an empire now, and when we act, we create our own reality."[36] (That was a great success in Bush's wars in Afghanistan and Iraq.) But Trump far surpassed his predecessors, displaying utter contempt for facts and a willful inability to discriminate between truth and falsehood. Thirty years before becoming president, he had "written" in *Trump: The Art of the Deal*:[37]

> I play to people's fantasies. People may not always think big themselves, but they can still get very excited by those who do. That's why a little hyperbole never hurts. People want to believe that something is the biggest and the greatest and the most spectacular. I call it truthful hyperbole. It's an innocent form of exaggeration—and a very effective form of promotion.

He embraced the "birtherism" lies about Obama as early as 2013 and never recanted.[38] *The Washington Post* itemized more than 16,000 falsehoods during his presidency.[39] After a campaign built on lies (including many about the size of his rallies), Trump began his administration by lying about the size of his inauguration crowd, claiming a "million and a half people" and blaming the networks for showing "an empty field."[40] (A professor of crowd science estimated 300,000–600,000 based on aerial photographs.) After Trump complained to the National Park Service Director and White House Press Secretary Sean Spicer followed up with repeated phone calls, NPS edited its photos to crop the empty spaces. At a press conference that evening, Spicer falsely stated that "this was the largest audience to ever witness an inauguration—period." (No: an estimated 1.8 million people attended Obama's first inauguration—three to six times as many as those at Trump's.) When this was challenged,

Spicer accused the media of "dishonesty," and Trump warned: "they're going to pay a big price." (Trump repeatedly railed against the "FAKE news media," calling them "the enemy of the American people," shamelessly boasting he did this "to discredit you all and demean you all, so when you write negative stories about me no one will believe you.")[41] White House counselor Kellyanne Conway explained that Spicer was using "alternative facts" (a phrasing that stuck). Rudy Giuliani later went further, declaring that "truth isn't truth."[42] Retired Gen. Michael V. Hayden (who had been Director of both the NSA and CIA) wrote in his memoir that "we in the intelligence world . . . have never served a president for whom ground truth doesn't really matter."[43]

As this chapter shows, the Trump administration's propagation of "alternative facts" both expressed and further blurred the distinction between truth and falsehood.[44] Chapter 2 describes and analyzes the administration's assault on expertise. Chapter 3 examines how the politicization of science persisted as Republicans sought to undermine the Biden administration's pandemic mitigation measures. Because federal courts played a central role in the war against science, I identify the party of the president who appointed the judge (as a proxy for the judge's political preference) and analyze the relationship between party and whether the judge did or did not support science in Chapter 4.

Notes

AP:	Associated Press
CNN:	Cable News Network
G:	Guardian
NPR:	National Public Radio
NYT:	New York Times
WP:	Washington Post

1 Smith (1776).
2 Hofstadter (2020: 39); quoted in Sadurski (2022: 186).
3 Chowkwanyun (2022: 328–329).
4 Bailey (1998).
5 Illich (1971, 1973, 1974).
6 Boston Women's Health Book Collective (1973).
7 Epstein (1998).
8 Orwell (1949).
9 Arendt (1951).
10 Trump and Zanker (2007: 160), quoted in Dean and Altemeyer (2020: 93); cf. Holmes (2018: 422–423).
11 Burgin (2022: 69); Brown (2020).
12 Fisher, "Donald Trump doesn't read much. Being president probably wouldn't change that," WP (7.17.16).
13 Lee, "Fact Check: Has Trump declared bankruptcy four or six times?" WP (4.26.16).
14 Grosen, "Donald Trump would be richer if he'd have invested in index funds," Fortune (8.20.15); Alexander, "It's official: Trump would be richer if he had just invested his inheritance into the S&P 500," Forbes (10.11.21).
15 Wolff (2018: 49).

16 Benen, "Trump thinks he may have a 'natural ability' to address viral outbreaks," MSNBC (3.9.20); Wright (2021: 79)
17 Rucker and Leonnig (2020: 9).
18 Small, "Trump makes classical style the default for federal buildings," NYT (12.23.20); Murphy, "Prince Charles's 10 principles for architecture—and 10 much better ones," G (12.27.14).
19 Gass, "Trump: 'The experts are terrible,'" Politico (4.4.16).
20 Bump, "Nearly a third of the days he's been president, Trump has visited a Trump-branded property," WP (12.30.19); Bump, "Trump's presidency ends where so much of it was spent: A Trump Organization property," WP (1.20.21); Burke, "Donald Trump spent almost a year playing golf during presidency," Seattle Medium (1.4.21).
21 Haberman, "Trump attacked generals as weak and too focused on allies, Woodward's book says," NYT (9.10.20).
22 Parker, "Trump says he's open to investigation of DeJoy's campaign fundraising," WP (9.8.20); President Dwight D. Eisenhower's Farewell Address (1961) www.archives.gov/milestone-documents/president-dwight-d-eisenhowers-farewell-address.
23 Edwards (2021: 219).
24 Edwards (2021: 125).
25 Bump, "The President who says the coronavirus will go away makes the same prediction about global warming," WP (9.14.20).
26 Benen, "Trump says his 'gut' is more reliable than everyone else's 'brains,'" MSNBC (11.28.18); Edwards (2021: 125).
27 Skowroneck et al. (2021: 109, 111–113).
28 Badger, Bui and Parlapiano, "The government agencies that became smaller, and unhappier, under Trump," NYT (2.1.21).
29 U.S. House Committee on Science, Space, and Technology (2021).
30 O'Brien, "Trump taps retired general and Fox News regular as Pentagon policy chief," Politico (6.10.20); Lamothe and Kim, "Senate hearing for controversial Pentagon nominee Anthony Tata canceled just before it was set to begin," WP (7.30.20); Cooper, Edmondson and Haberman, "Inflammatory comments delay confirmation of retired general to Pentagon post," NYT (7.31.20); Jones (2020).
31 Wong, "V.O.A. directors resign after Bannon ally takes over," NYT (6.16.20); Hansler and Stelter, "'Wednesday night massacre' as Trump appointee takes over at global media agency," CNN (6.18.20); "Voice of America and other U.S. Government media never engage in propaganda. Is that about to change?" WP (6.20.20); Folkenflik, "Citing a breached 'firewall,' media leaders sue U.S. official over firings," NPR (6.24.20); Hsu, "Appeals court blocks Trump administration takeover of organization fighting digital censorship and surveillance," WP (7.22.20); Borger, "Voice of America journalists condemn Trump-backed boss over 'spy' remarks," G (8.31.20); Folkenflik, "At Voice of America, Trump appointee sought political influence over coverage," NYT (9.2.20); Farhi, "Voice of America interim director pushed out by Trump-appointed overseer in final flurry of actions to assert control," WP (12.9.20); Bannett, "I was Voice of America's director. Trump's latest pick to run the organization is dangerous," WP (12.12.20).
32 Werner, "Top DHS officials Wolf and Cuccinelli are not legally eligible to serve in their current roles, Congressional watchdog agency finds," WP (8.14.20); Fox, "Trump administration defends Homeland Security leadership," AP (8.17.20); Sands, "DHS watchdog won't investigate Wolf and Cuccinelli appointments, says courts will have to decide," CNN (9.15.20); Itkowitz, Wagner, Firozi, Sonmez and Miroff, "Acting Homeland Security Secretary Wolf to step down, nine days ahead of Biden's inauguration," WP (1.11.21).

33 "Four more years of Trump's contempt for competence would be devastating," WP (9.8.20).
34 Rein, Dawsey and Olorunnipa, "Trump's historic assault on the civil service was four years in the making," WP (10.24.20); "Trump's newest executive order could prove one of his most insidious," WP (10.24.20); Rainey, "Federal Employee Union sues over Trump civil service executive order," Politico (10.28.20); Rein, Hamburger, Eilperin and Freedman, "How Trump waged war on his own government," WP (10.29.20); Lipton, "Trump issues order giving him more leeway to hire and fire federal workers," NYT (10.23.20); Hohmann, "Lame-Duck Trump burrows loyalists inside government, starting with NSA," WP (11.10.20); Nakashima, "Former GOP operative Michael Ellis placed on administrative leave from NSA's top lawyer job," WP (11.21.20); Klehm, "Senators asking Acting DoD IG to investigate appointment of NSA general counsel," Lawfare (11.17.20); Rein, "Trump moves to strip job protections from White House budget analysts as he races to transform civil service," WP (11.28.20); Wang and Nakashima, "Pelosi calls for halt in efforts to install Trump loyalist as NSA's top lawyer," WP (1.19.21); Nakashima, "NSA official installed as Trump left office resigns after he was sidelined," WP (4.18.21); Barnes, "Report finds no wrongdoing in hiring of Trump loyalist as N.S.A.'s top lawyer," NYT (10.22.21).
35 Diaz, "Trump: I'm a 'very stable genius,'" CNN (1.6.18); Benen, "Trump shows how not to answer questions about mental stability," MSNBC (1.8.18); Benen, "Trump claims to be an 'extremely stable genius,' then proves otherwise," MSNBC (5.24.19); Cummings, "Trump says he's 'so great looking and smart, a true Stable Genius' in a tweet bashing 2020 Dems," USA Today (7.11.19); Rizzo (2020a: 97–99); Skowroneck et al. (2021: 103–107); Karl (2021: 310–311).
36 Suskind, "Faith, certainty, and the Presidency of George W. Bush," NYT (10.17.04).
37 Trump and Schwartz (1987), quoted in Lemire (2022: 23).
38 Karl (2021: 8–11).
39 Kessler et al. (2020).
40 Lee, "Trump claims 1.5 million people came to his inauguration. Here's what the evidence shows," Vox (1.23.17); Swaine, "Trump inauguration crowd photos were edited after he intervened," G (9.8.18); Farley and Robertson, "The facts on crowd size," FactCheck.org (1.23.17); Frostenson, "A crowd scientist says Trump's inauguration attendance was pretty average," Vox (1.24.17); Karl (2021: 41, 104).
41 Karl (2021: 135, 143, 245).
42 Morin and Cohen, "Giuliani: 'Truth isn't truth,'" Politico (8.19.18).
43 Hayden (2018).
44 D'Ancona (2017); Patterson (2019); Rosenblum and Muirhead (2020); Nichols (2017); Farkas and Schou (2019); Carpenter (2018); Prado (2018); Ball (2017); Karl (2021: 117, 121); McIntyre (2018, 2022).

2

POLITICIZING PROFESSIONAL EXPERTISE

The Trump Administration's Response to the COVID-19 Pandemic

1. Acknowledging the COVID-19 Pandemic

Throughout the COVID-19 pandemic, Trump and his apparatchiki sought political advantage by exploiting the festering, inchoate resentment of expertise (just as they did fear of immigrants, see Abel 2024a). China publicly reported COVID-19 on December 31, 2019.[1] On January 3, George Gao, head of China's CDC, spoke with CDC Director Robert Redfield, who passed the information to HHS Secretary Alexander Azar. Gao phoned Redfield again three days later, crying because the situation in Wuhan was so bad. A week later, the CDC issued an official health advisory. On January 20, the World Health Organization (WHO) and China confirmed human-to-human transmission, and the U.S. reported its first case. Trump declared confidently at the World Economic Forum in Davos on January 21: "We have it totally under control. It's one person coming in from China, and we have it under control. It's going to be just fine." The President's Daily Brief on January 23 advised that COVID was "just like the flu." (Trump recalled in May that he had been told "it was of no real import . . . it wasn't, 'Oh, we got to do something.' ") On January 24, Redfield assured a Senate committee: "We are prepared for this." NIAID Director Anthony Fauci said COVID "isn't something the American people need to be worried or frightened by" but acknowledged it was "an evolving situation." (Yet the same day, the DoD's National Center for Medical Intelligence [NCMI] concluded that the virus had "a roughly even chance of becoming a global pandemic during the next four months." However, an NSC official said the Council "did not follow" NCMI's warning.) The same day, Trump tweeted: "China has been working very hard to contain the Coronavirus. The United States greatly appreciates

DOI: 10.4324/9781032629124-2

their efforts and transparency. It will all work out well. In particular, on behalf of the American people, I want to thank President Xi." (HHS Secretary Azar had warned that this "is a big give to Xi. You should not do that lightly. His response has not been going well.") On January 28, Deputy National Security Adviser Matthew Pottinger briefed his boss, National Security Adviser Robert O'Brien, about a phone call he had just received from a doctor in China, warning that COVID was spreading across many provinces, and half the cases were asymptomatic. At the President's Daily Brief, O'Brien told Trump: "this will be the biggest national security threat you face in your presidency"; and Pottinger repeated his warning and urged a ban on travel from China. After the briefing, Trump's chief of staff Mick Mulvaney was "incandescent with anger," accusing Pottinger of acting as though he were head of HHS or the CDC. Nevertheless, Pottinger convened an interagency meeting that afternoon, renewing his call for a ban on travel from China. Larry Kudlow, National Economic Council (NEC) chair, objected, pointing to the buoyant stock market as proof there would be no pandemic: "Is all the money dumb?" (No—just slow: the Dow Jones Industrial Average fell from over 29,000 to less than 20,000 over the next few weeks.) Mulvaney told Pottinger his proposal "was totally inappropriate. You won't come to another one of these" meetings. But Peter Navarro, Trump's trade adviser, also advised the NSC to impose "an immediate travel ban on China." The next day, Mulvaney created the White House coronavirus task force under Azar. After Pottinger and Navarro reiterated their warnings at its first meeting, Mulvaney asked O'Brien to "get Pottinger under control" and removed Navarro from the Task Force.

On January 27, Biden (seeking the Democratic presidential nomination) wrote in a *USA Today* op ed that "Trump's demonstrated failures of judgment and his repeated rejection of science make him the worst possible person to lead our country through a global health challenge."[2]

> The outbreak of a new coronavirus, which has already infected more than 2,700 people and killed over 80 in China, will get worse before it gets better. Cases have been confirmed in a dozen countries, with at least 5 in the United States. There will likely be more.

The next day, National Security Adviser O'Brien concurred: the virus would be "the biggest national security threat you face in your presidency." But the day after that, Press Secretary Stephanie Grisham said: "the risk of infection for all Americans remains low."

On January 30, Mulvaney, Azar and Deputy Secretary of State Biegun told Trump the U.S. needed to repatriate several thousand diplomats and permanent residents from Wuhan.[3] He angrily resisted: "We're not letting them come back. You risk increasing numbers. You won't increase my numbers."

"The first flight was a mistake. Those people should not have been in China in the first place." (Where else should diplomats be?) But he finally capitulated. The same day, WHO declared a public health emergency of international concern, the highest level of alarm, and the U.S. confirmed the first person-to-person transmission. Yet Trump delivered an upbeat speech in Michigan:

> We think we have it very well under control. We have very little problem in this country at the moment—five—and those people are all recuperating successfully. But we're working very closely with China and other countries, and we think it's going to have a very good ending for it, so that I can assure you.

The next day, the U.S. declared a public health emergency: the government restricted entry by foreigners and required Americans returning from China to quarantine for 14 days. On February 2, it banned travel to and from China. But Trump remained publicly optimistic: "We pretty much shut it down coming in from China."

The first U.S. death occurred in Santa Clara County, California, on February 6 (although the CDC did not confirm it for six weeks, after 29 more had died).[4] That day, Trump told Chinese President Xi that he hoped warmer weather would reduce the threat. Xi agreed that temperature played a large role. Once it reached 50 degrees, the virus would lose strength. The next day, Trump repeated this baseless claim three times, with characteristic hyperbole: "When it gets a little warmer, it miraculously goes away. I think it's going to work out good. We only have 11 cases and they're all getting better." He said the same to Bob Woodward that day: "I think that that goes away in two months with the heat." (At the same time, he acknowledged it was an air-borne disease and "maybe five times more . . . deadly than even your strenuous flus.") Fox News echoed Trump's reassurance on February 24. One host said, "the thing that's going to end this is the warmer weather," prompting the other to indulge in black humor, "thank God for global warming." Attorney General Barr was easily persuaded: "Many, including me, were hoping that it would behave much like the flu and abate somewhat during the summer months." Trump confessed to Bob Woodward a month later: "I always wanted to play it down. I still like playing it down because I don't want to create a panic." Indeed, on February 8, the president called the chances of getting COVID "miniscule." On February 10, he told Fox Business that China would "have it under control fairly soon. You know in April, supposedly, it goes [away] with the hotter weather. And that's a beautiful date to look forward to." "A lot of people think that goes away in April with the heat—as the heat comes in. Typically, that will go away in April." On February 11, he said: "right now we have 13 people," and "the risk is relatively low" that it would become a global pandemic. Two days later, he called into

Geraldo Rivera's Fox News program: "We think and we hope, based on all signs, that the problem goes away in April" because "heat kills the virus." "It's a problem in China" but "has not been spreading very much." In late February, Kayleigh McEnany said confidently: "we will not see diseases like the coronavirus come here." As the pandemic continued to intensify in April, Trump's complacent self-confidence remained undiminished: "So what do I know? I'm not a doctor. I'm not a doctor. But I have common sense."

On February 26, Trump said:

> The flu in our country kills from 25,000 people to 69,000 people a year. . . . And so far, if you look at what we have with the 15 people and their recovery . . . one is pretty sick but hopefully will recover, but the others are in great shape.[5]

On March 1, he said there would be a vaccine "relatively soon." The next day, he told a large rally that COVID was "very safe" and promised therapies—"sort of another word for cure." The day after, he repeated his false reassurance—"a lot of people will have this, and it's very mild"—and displayed his woeful combination of scientific ignorance and arrogance: "You take a solid flu vaccine—you don't think that would have an impact . . . on corona?" He told a Fox interviewer that the WHO death rate was "really a false number." He also falsely claimed that "anybody that wants a test can get a test." (The first U.S. test failed. The administration refused to use the WHO test because it had been developed in Germany.) "I met with the leaders of health insurance industry, who have agreed to waive all co-payments for coronavirus treatments." (That was false; the waiver applied only to tests.) On March 9, he repeated his false comparison:

> So last year 37,000 Americans died from the common Flu. It averages between 27,000 and 70,000 per year. Nothing is shut down, life & the economy go on. At this moment there are 546 confirmed cases of CoronaVirus with 22 deaths. Think about that!

On March 10, he said: "We're prepared and we're doing a great job with it. And it will go away. Just stay calm. It will go away." The day after that, he declared: "the virus will not have a chance against us." The following day, he compared his own actions to then–Vice President Biden's response to H1N1 Swine Flu: "one of the worst on record. Our response is one of the best." (CDC estimated that 7,070–13,930 died from swine flu in the U.S. in 2009; there were 1,642 official confirmed deaths.)[6] Seeking to persuade North Carolina's governor to let the RNC meet in his state, Trump said of COVID fatalities on May 29: "What people don't realize, it's a tiny percentage of 1 percent of the people that really get hit, and they're generally older people and older people with a bad heart problem or diabetes or something." Trump's rationale for maintaining this Pollyanna façade became clear after Chris Christie criticized him: "You tell people that we've got it under control, but it's clear that we don't." Trump explained: "I'm not going to scare people. It's not my job. My job is to reassure people and not scare them." When Christie insisted that "it's not just going to go away magically one day," Trump said he would rather "tell them it's going to go away. Chris, when the weather gets warm, it's going to go away." In April, the White House canceled a plan to send five masks to every household to avoid causing "concern or panic."

Trump repeatedly enacted his symbiotic relationship with and dependence on Fox News.[7] The day after Sean Hannity estimated the death rate as "way under 1 percent," Trump echoed him on the same show: "it's, you know, a very, very small number in this country. And we're going to try and keep it that way as much as possible." Fox host Trish Regan said that coronavirus warnings from Democrats were "yet another attempt to impeach the president." The same day, Hannity tweeted: "CORONAVIRUS IMPEACHMENT SCAM." Geraldo Rivera offered false comfort: "if you can hold your breath for ten seconds, then you don't have this disease." When a *Fox & Friends* host said now was "actually the safest time to fly," her guest promptly concurred that people were "overreacting." Cohost Ainsley Earhardt bragged that "our numbers are down compared to other countries that are really having a major problem with this"; she was seconded by Rep. Gaetz: "America has had the best response to coronavirus in the world." When a reporter asked what Trump would "say to Americans who are watching you right now and are scared?" the president made it clear that the media's only role was to be a cheerleader: "I say that you're a terrible reporter . . . that's a very nasty question and I think it is a very bad signal that you're putting out to the American people." Other right-wing commentators minimized COVID. Rush Limbaugh pronounced confidently: "the coronavirus is the common cold, folks." "I'm dead right on this." These messages had their intended effect: in early March, Republicans were less than half as likely as Democrats to believe COVID-19 was an "imminent threat to the United States." At the end of the month, a poll found that 79 percent of those who got most of their news from Fox said the media had "greatly" or "slightly" exaggerated the risk, compared with 35 percent who watched MSNBC. That month, Democrats consistently reported taking more COVID precautions than Republicans (even after controlling for sociodemographic and geographic variables), and these divisions increased over time. Democrats also wanted the government to take more precautions, while the Republicans wanted fewer. Democrats blamed Trump first, and Republicans blamed him last (among four alternatives).

From the outset, the administration politicized disputes over the origin of COVID-19.[8] After weeks of investigation, nearly a dozen top international experts on viral genome evolution unanimously concluded on February 1, there was no evidence the virus had been created in a lab. Five of those scientists published an article in *Nature Medicine* in March 2020: "analyses clearly show that SARS-CoV-2 is not a laboratory construct or purposefully manipulated virus." But Trump trade adviser Peter Navarro, who had no scientific background but was a fierce adversary of China, said it "created that virus, and they sent over hundreds of thousands of Chinese citizens here to spread that . . . around the world. Whether they did that on purpose, that's an open question." "That virus was a product of the Chinese Communist Party." Miles Yu, the senior China policy official at DoS (also not a scientist), wrote Secretary of State Pompeo in April that circumstantial evidence pointed to the Wuhan Institute of Virology (WIV) as the source. Pompeo then grossly exaggerated this, declaring there was "enormous evidence" that the virus came from WIV. Although ODNI said on April 30 that the intelligence community "concurs with the wide scientific consensus that the covid-19 virus was not manmade or genetically modified," Trump declared (without bothering to read their report) his own "high confidence" that WIV was the origin of the virus, citing unnamed "scientific people, intelligence people, and others." Asked why he had high confidence, he said cryptically: "I'm not allowed to tell you." Three days later, Pompeo repeated that "there is a significant amount of evidence that this came from that laboratory in Wuhan." Trump wanted to declare his conviction publicly in May or June but was discouraged by advisers. Seeing other ways to stoke xenophobia, however, he repeatedly referred to the "Chinese virus," "China flu" and even "Kung flu." On June 11, National Security Adviser O'Brien flatly asserted:

> whatever happened the Chinese have repurposed [COVID] into a bioweapon. And they're using it, they're attempting to take advantage of Covid to gain a geopolitical advantage over the United States and the free world, and to displace the United States as the leading power in the world.

Trump's assertion that President Xi "didn't want to contain [covid] from the rest of the world because it would've put him at a big disadvantage" was "an absolutely reasonable hypothesis." In his 2021 memoir, Chief of Staff Meadows flippantly asserted that "the mystery" of COVID's origins "didn't seem all that hard to solve" because "it had probably leaked from the nearby Wuhan Institute of Virology." "In April [2020], Tucker [Carlson] shocked many of us as he reported 'Fauci-directed' taxpayer dollars were still flowing to the Wuhan Virology Lab. I called Secretary Azar immediately to order him to stop this lunacy." (As of August 11, 2022, a plurality of IC elements had low confidence that the virus was of zoonotic origin, one element had medium confidence it originated in a lab leak, and three elements said the evidence was insufficient to decide. In October 2022, Sen. Burr, the senior

Republican on the Senate Health Committee, published a minority report [of which he was the only signatory] suggesting a lab leak but offering no new evidence. After 18 months of work, Republican senators released a 300-page report conceding they could not determine the origin of the pandemic, although Sen. Marshall claimed: "there's enough evidence, if this was a civil case, that we would convince a jury" it was an unintentional lab leak. (He was a doctor, not a lawyer.) But he concluded: "Wuhan's early covid cases are a mystery.")

On February 23, Navarro wrote a memo to the president, accurately predicting that "there is an increasing probability of a full-blown COVID-19 pandemic that could infect as many as 100 million Americans, with a loss of life of as many as 1–2 million souls."[9] Yet the same day, Trump assured reporters: "We have it very much under control. Very interestingly, we've had no deaths." (The first actually had occurred on February 6 but was kept secret.) However, the Task Force had taken a far more pessimistic view, which Redfield communicated to his deputy, Nancy Messonnier (who had directed the CDC National Center for Immunization and Respiratory Diseases since 2016). On February 25, she told a press conference:

> As more and more countries experience community spread, successful containment at our borders becomes harder and harder. Ultimately, we expect we will see community spread in this country. It's not a question of if this will happen, but when this will happen, and how many people in this country will have serious illnesses. Disruptions to everyday life may be severe, but people might want to start thinking about that now. . . . We are asking the American public to prepare for the expectation that this might be bad.

Watching this on television in the middle of the night, as his plane returned from India, Trump woke the press corps to demand: "Who is this woman! Who is she? She's going to scare people!" He immediately tweeted: "The Coronavirus is very much under control in the USA. We are in contact with everyone and all relevant countries. CDC & World Health have been working hard and very smart." (Talking to Bob Woodward two weeks earlier, he had contradicted this: "You just breathe the air and that's how it's passed . . . and so that's a very tricky one. That's a very delicate one. It's also more deadly than even your strenuous flu.")[10] Trump added: "Stock Market starting to look very good to me!" But when WHO agreed with Messonnier it was unclear whether COVID could be stopped from spreading, the Dow dropped more than 1,000 points.

Nevertheless, Trump stayed firmly on message—with typical incoherence: "Other than yesterday, which was something pretty bad, with respect to the virus, and we'll see what happens." "Things like that happen where . . . it had nothing to do with you. It's an outside source that nobody would have ever predicted. . . . I think it's going to be under control." At the same time, he furiously phoned Azar: "What the hell is this woman doing? What are these statements? The market has collapsed." The Secretary responded: "What she said is true and we're actually planning to meet with you at five p.m. the day you get back to go through all of this." Trump retorted: "You gotta keep her away from the microphone. You gotta get out there and clear this up. Get the market calm again."

At the press conference after he landed, Trump continued to minimize the pandemic: only ten in the U.S. were sick, and "most of the people are outside of danger right now."[11] (His figure deliberately excluded the 35 on the cruise ship *Diamond Princess*, discussed later.) Larry Kudlow said on CNBC: "We have contained this. I won't say airtight, but pretty close to airtight. We have done a good job in the United States." The next day, however, *The New York Times* headlined: "Viral Crisis in U.S. Is Deemed Likely"; and *The Washington Post* said: "Threat to Americans called 'inevitable.'" On February 25, the CDC issued its first warning about COVID-19. And the stock market lost 12 percent of its value in a week.

Azar reprimanded Messonnier.[12] (It did not help that her brother was Deputy Attorney General Rod Rosenstein, who had earned Trump's everlasting ire by appointing Robert Mueller as special counsel.) CDC Incident Manager Anne Schuchat said Azar had called her ten minutes after Messonnier's briefing, leaving her "upset." She added (in an understatement): "the reaction to the morning briefing was quite volatile." Azar assured the public: "In the United States, thanks to the president and this team's aggressive containment efforts this disease . . . is contained." Schuchat backed him up: "We believe the immediate risk here in the United States remains low, and we're working hard to keep that risk low." But she also warned it was inevitable that COVID would come to the U.S. Trump retorted: "I don't think it is inevitable." "In some ways it is easier [than the flu], in some ways it is a little tougher."

Trump replaced Azar as head of the Task Force with Pence, whose chief of staff, Marc Short, directed it not to use the word "pandemic" or say the situation could "change rapidly."[13] Mulvaney ordered that all communications be approved by Short or Pence's Communications Director Katie Miller (Stephen's wife). Messonnier and Redfield were rarely allowed to issue statements. When the CDC proposed to issue a statement—"*While the situation could change rapidly*, at this time, Americans don't need to change their day-to-day-lives, but should stay informed and practice good hygiene"—Miller eliminated the italicized phrase. Pence confirmed that he saw the problem as "a communication discipline issue. My number one issue is getting a handle on communications." There were no further CDC telebriefings until mid-June. Olivia Troye (Pence's homeland security and counterterrorism adviser) said Short instructed her to block Dr. Robert Kadlec (DHHS Assistant Secretary for Preparedness and Response) from Task Force meetings because he wanted to distribute supplies based on need rather than population. (Subsequent reports by the State Department and GAO found evidence that politics had compromised science.)[14]

On February 26, Trump tweeted:

> Low Ratings Fake News MSDNC [sic—he is mocking MSNBC] (Comcast) & @CNN are doing everything possible to make the Caronavirus [sic] look as bad as possible, including panicking markets, if possible. Likewise their incompetent Do Nothing Democrat comrades are all talk, no action. USA in great shape @CDCGov.[15]

In a news briefing, he offered an even rosier picture: "when you have 15 people—and the 15 within a couple of days is going to be down to close to zero—that's a pretty good job we've done. This is a flu. This is like a flu." Fox Business host Kennedy Montgomery parroted him: "No one's talking about the flu. The flu is so much worse." So did Hannity, whose doctor guest said on his show: "worst case scenario, it could be the flu." (This constant repetition seems to have had the desired effect: 57 percent of those who regularly watched conservative news believed COVID was no more deadly than the flu.) Trump said: "I don't think" schools will close, "especially with the fact that we're going down, not up. We're going very substantially down, not up." (Within a month, there would be 1,300 deaths.) He failed to mention that the CDC had identified the first case of domestic transmission. And he minimized Messonnier's warning in typically (deliberately?) incoherent language: "Well, I don't think it's inevitable. It probably will it possibly will. I could be a very small level or it could be a larger level. Whatever happens, we're totally prepared."

On February 27, Trump said to a meeting of African American leaders, "it's going to disappear. One day—it's like a miracle—it will disappear."[16] Azar told a House Committee the same day: "The immediate risk to the public remains low. It will look and feel to the American people more like a severe flu season." Trump addressed a rally the next day: "The Democrats are politicizing the coronavirus, you know, that, right?" It was "their new hoax" and "single talking point." He told Hannity on March 9 that Democrats were "scaring the living hell out of people, and I see it again as like, 'Oh, let's bludgeon Trump with this new hoax.'" When New York Gov. Cuomo asked for 30,000 ventilators, Trump complained to Hannity on March 26: "a lot of the numbers that are being said in some areas are just bigger than they're going to be." Fox News echoed this on March 29: "people are driving by their hospitals and . . . they're not seeing anybody in the parking lots." Mulvaney told CPAC on February 28 that Democrats "think this is going to be what brings down the president. That's what this is all about." Trump asked the next day: "Why isn't there this huge panic every single year over flu?" He acknowledged that some schools would close and public transportation would be affected. "But we do this [sic], we know how to handle this." "Right now, at this moment, there is no need to change anything you're doing on a day-to-day basis." "I hope [Americans] don't change their routine." And CDC Director Redfield concurred: "The American public needs to go on with their normal lives. The risk is low."

On February 29, Trump again boasted about the administration's "pretty amazing" response.[17] "We have 15 people [infected] in this massive country, and because of the fact that we went early, we went early we could have had a lot more than that." Democrats were "politicizing the coronavirus. . . . This is their new hoax." Hours later, Steven Hatfill (a virologist awarded nearly $6 million after being cleared of suspicion in post-9/11 anthrax attacks) emailed Navarro, whom he was advising:

> In truth we do not have a clue how many are infected in the USA. We are expecting the first wave to spread in the US within the next 7 days. This will be accompanied by a massive loss of credibility and the Democratic accusations are just now beginning. This must be countered with frank honesty about the situation and decisive direct actions that are being taken and can be seen in the broadcast news.

Navarro warned Trump on March 1 that the response to this "very serious public health emergency" was "NOT fast enough." On March 2, experts in public health and law wrote a letter (later signed by more than 800) to Pence and other officials urging a comprehensive response.[18] The same day, Fauci said, "We're dealing with clearly an emerging infectious disease that has now reached outbreak proportions and likely pandemic proportions" (although he had not cleared the word "pandemic" with Short and Miller). Short ordered Azar's chief of staff: "You've got to get Fauci on message. He is saying things that are too extreme." When Dr. Deborah Birx (White House Coronavirus Response Coordinator) was introduced to Trump on March 2 (in a meeting lasting less than 30 seconds), he told her that "the people I'm talking to say that this isn't going to be any worse than the flu." Birx replied that she had "evidence to fully support the conclusion that this outbreak is not going to be like the seasonal flu or even pandemic flu. This virus is very deadly." But Trump was unmoved: "these are good people. Smart people.

I trust these people. They know what they're saying." The same day, Surgeon General Jerome Adams tweeted: "Seriously people. STOP BUYING MASKS! They are not effective in preventing the general public from catching #Coronavirus." He said reassuringly on March 6: "the risk to the average American of coronavirus at this time remains low."

On March 5, Azar said public laboratories would conduct 400,000 tests a week.[19] Visiting the CDC the next day, Trump maintained that 5 million tests would be available by the end of the month: "We are, really, really, very highly prepared for anything . . . anybody that wants a test can get a test." (A year later, Brett Giroir, Trump's testing czar, admitted: "When we said there were millions of tests available, there weren't.") CDC Director Redfield told Trump obsequiously: "I want to thank you for your decisive leadership in helping us . . . put public health first." But on March 18, Trump (characteristically) reversed himself, screaming at Azar: "Testing is killing me! I'm going to lose the election because of testing! What idiot had the federal government do testing?" Azar explained that five days earlier, Jared Kushner had taken charge of testing. Trump called it "gross incompetence to let CDC develop a test." "We should have left this to the states and the private sector." He reiterated his gripe on June 15:

> the downside of having good testing is you find a lot of cases that other countries who don't even test don't have. . . . If we stop testing right now, we'd have very few cases, if any . . . we will show more cases . . . when other countries have far more cases than we do.

(Birx recalled ruefully a year later that "people really believed in the White House that testing was driving cases, rather than testing was a way for us to stop cases.") In July, the White House press secretary (inconsistently) boasted that "we have the most testing in the world" and claimed that "we're very low and beating most countries, if not all, in Europe" on "our case fatality rate." (The U.S. rate was close to the global average but higher than Brazil's and twice that of South Korea.) Trump complained that testing was a "double-edged sword . . . when you test, you create cases." In early July, he declared that many positives just "are kids that have the sniffles. Or somebody else who has gotten better already. Actually, [tests] are very inaccurate. Now, it shows you location, but outside of that all it does is give the news fodder." The administration later sought to block money for testing, tracing and the CDC in the Coronavirus Relief Bill.

On the March 6 CDC visit, Trump also said: "most of those [240 infected] people are going to be fine. . . . We've had 11 deaths, and they've been largely old people . . . who were susceptible to what's happening." He opposed evacuating passengers from the *Diamond Princess*—"I would be inclined to say leave everybody on the ship for a period of time"—despite the fact that many were elderly, receiving inadequate medical care and spreading infection. He complained:

> a lot of people . . . [would] rather quarantine people on the land. Now when they do that our numbers are going to go up. I like the numbers where they are. I don't need to have the number double because of one ship that wasn't our fault.

After the passengers were evacuated, Trump directed Azar "to fire whoever made that decision." Advised that it was Pompeo's subordinate, Trump retorted: "fire him anyway," ordering Mulvaney to find a way. When the Department of State repatriated 14 infected passengers, Trump complained: "that doubles my numbers overnight" and urged that they be reported separately. Days later, he said to Azar, Fauci, Redfield and Kadlec: "We import goods. We are not going to import a virus. No, why don't we send it somewhere. Don't we have an island that we own? What about Guantánamo?" He raised that absurd idea again at a later meeting. (Imagine quarantining elderly Americans suffering from COVID in the same facility where the U.S. had imprisoned alleged terrorists without trial for two decades.)

On March 9, Trump retweeted a tweet accusing his opponents of exaggerating COVID to make the stock market fall and hurt him.[20] He also tweeted:

> Last year 37,000 Americans died from the common Flu. It averages between 27,000 and 70,000 per year. Nothing is shut down, life & the economy go on. At this moment there are 546 confirmed cases of CoronaVirus, with 22 deaths. Think about that!

A day later, he promoted the antimalarial drugs hydroxychloroquine (HCQ) and chloroquine (CQ) as COVID treatments, explaining: "I'm a smart guy" and "I feel good about it." When an NBC reporter noted Fauci's skepticism about those drugs and asked why Trump disagreed, the president cut him off: "I say that you're a terrible reporter . . . it's a very nasty question." On March 10, WHO declared a pandemic, but Trump still told Republican senators: "We're doing a great job with it. And it will go away. Just stay calm." Defense Secretary Esper recalled Trump saying: "I'm taking" HCQ. "I feel great. It's a miracle." "You'd be surprised at how many people are taking it. . . . I've heard a lot of good stories about it."

At a White House meeting on March 11, Birx urged a suspension of all travel to the U.S. so as not to overwhelm hospitals. Treasury Secretary Mnuchin resisted: "You can't do that, Mr. President. We're not talking about the r-word [recession] here. We're talking about the d-word. This will be a depression; you'll never get out of it throughout your presidency." Birx pushed back: "I present all of my data based on evidence of what I'm seeing globally. Where's your evidence?" When Mnuchin offered none, Trump surprisingly told him: "We can always rebuild the economy. We can't get these lives back. We can make the money back. We've got to shut it down." He barred travel from Europe but assured:

> the vast majority of Americans: The risk is very, very low. Young and healthy people can expect to recover fully and quickly if they should get the virus. . . . Wash your hands, clean often-used surfaces, cover your face and mouth if you sneeze or cough, and most of all, if you are sick or not feeling well, stay home.[21]

He said nothing about social distancing or masks. "This is not a financial crisis, this is just a temporary moment of time." "The virus will not have a chance against us. . . . Our future remains brighter than anyone can imagine." On March 13, he declared a national emergency, claiming there would be testing sites at Walgreens and CVS and a Google website explaining how to access them. But none of this existed. Trump admitted two days later (in typically contradictory language): "this is a very contagious virus. It's incredible. But it's something that we have tremendous control over." A day after that, he just compounded the confusion: "the virus, no, that's not under control for anyplace in the world. I was talking about what we're doing is under control"—whatever that meant. On March 15, the Task Force recommended a nationwide shutdown.[22] Trump reluctantly agreed the next day, declaring: "We will be stronger than ever before!" But three days later, he privately admitted to Woodward that "it's a nasty situation." (These flip-flops—not coincidentally—were paralleled on Fox News: Sean Hannity had said on March 10 that "healthy people, generally, 99 percent recover very fast, even if they contract it"; but he praised Trump's March 13 decision as "a massive paradigm shift in the future of disease control and prevention" and "a bold, new precedent.")

Trump also told governors to obtain the necessary equipment themselves. Washington Gov. Jay Inslee called this "equivalent to Franklin Delano Roosevelt on December 8, 1941, saying, 'Good luck . . . *you* go build the battleships.'" Five northeastern states (Connecticut, New York, New Jersey, Massachusetts and Rhode Island) agreed to act together. The governors of Kansas, Michigan and Colorado complained that the federal government was getting equipment before them. On March 18, Trump told reporters that a federal quarantine of New York, New Jersey and Connecticut had been suggested by "a lot of states that are infected but don't have a big problem." (It was hardly coincidental that the first group of states were blue and the second red.)[23] "They're having problems down in Florida" (another red state) with "heavily infected" people coming from other states. New York Governor Cuomo said this would be "a declaration of war." (It was also unconstitutional.)

On March 21, Scott Atlas (a neuroradiologist and senior fellow at the Hoover Institution, with no expertise in virology or epidemiology) wrote CMS Administrator Seema Verma that the government response was "a massive overreaction . . . inciting irrational fear." Covid "would cause about 10,000 deaths," a number that "would be unnoticed" in a normal flu season. (It has since caused more than 100 times as many.) "The panic needs to be stopped." On March 30, Trump said: "Stay calm. It will go away. . . . you know it is going away, and it will go away. And we're going to have a great victory." On April 2, Dr. Stephen Smith (a New Jersey physician who also lacked expertise in virology and epidemiology) assured viewers watching Laura Ingraham's Fox News program: "I think this is the beginning of the end of the pandemic." (He made exaggerated claims based on a few of his patients and no controls.)[24] She arranged for him to visit Trump in the White House, who told Smith admiringly: "I've been watching you." Four days later, Trump again echoed Fox, tweeting: "LIGHT AT THE END OF THE TUNNEL!" (evoking Lyndon Johnson's tragically false optimism during the Vietnam War). Four days after that, he said the prediction of "the minimum number [of deaths] was 100,000 lives, and I think we'll be substantially under that number." On April 13, William Bennett (Reagan's Secretary of Education) channeled Atlas, declaring on *Fox & Friends*: "We're going to have fewer fatalities from this than from the flu." Stephen Moore (a conservative economist advising the Trump administration) said: "Fauci is the villain here. He has the Napoleon complex and thinks he is the dictator who could decide how to run the country."[25] "We were saying, 'Why does Trump keep Fauci around?' " On April 12, Fauci told CNN:

> If you had a process that was ongoing and started mitigation earlier, you could have saved lives. If we had, right from the beginning shut everything down it may have been different. But there was a lot of pushback for [sic—he means against] shutting everything down back then.

Hours later, Trump retweeted a message with the tag #FireFauci.

2. Hydroxychloroquine (HCQ)

On Laura Ingraham's Fox News show on March 16, Gregory Rigano (a lawyer who had launched a blockchain fund to "cheat death" and "end Alzheimer's") and James Todaro (a Columbia medical school graduate turned cryptocurrency investor) touted a self-published document citing a French preprint by Didier Raoult of a non-randomized study of 36 subjects, which claimed that "within a matter of six days, the patients taking hydroxychloroquine tested negative for coronavirus . . . the patients that took the control tested positive."[26] They also asserted that HCQ could be used as a prophylactic, having learned this via Twitter from Adrian Bye, a self-styled philosopher (and white supremacist) living in China's Wudang Mountains. Rigano said confidently: "we have strong reason to believe that a preventative dose of hydroxychloroquine is going to prevent the virus from attaching to the body and just get rid of it completely." Ingraham related on Fox that she had taken HCQ in Africa and did not get sick. (Post hoc ergo propter hoc?) She emailed Rigano's document to Kushner. The same day, Elon Musk tweeted: "maybe worth considering chloroquine for C19," with a link to the Rigano document, which falsely boasted it had been written "in consultation with Stanford University School of Medicine, UAB [University of Alabama at Birmingham] School of Medicine and National Academy of Science researchers." Two days later, Rigano told Tucker Carlson (who falsely identified his guest as an adviser at Stanford University School of Medicine): "What we're here to announce is the second cure to a virus of all time," claiming the paper was "a well-controlled peer-reviewed study that showed a 100% cure rate against coronavirus."

On March 19, Trump endorsed the drugs, exposing his ignorance and confusion while aping academic respectability by citing a scientific journal.[27]

> Now a drug called chloroquine—and some people would add to it "hydroxy-." Hydroxychloroquine. So chloroquine or hydroxychloroquine. Now, this is a common malaria drug. It is also a drug used for strong arthritis. If somebody has pretty serious arthritis, also uses this in a somewhat different form. But it is known as a malaria drug, and it's been around for a long time and it's very powerful. . . . Hopefully they will BOTH (H works better with A, International Journal of Antimicrobial Agents) be put to use IMMEDIATELY. PEOPLE ARE DYING, MOVE FAST, and GOD BLESS EVERYONE. . . . The FDA has moved mountains—Thank You!

(Raoult—a notorious contrarian—had published the study on March 20, having halted his trial of HCQ and azithromycin early because all six patients were "virologically cured." On March 24, a San Francisco microbiologist and fraud buster blogged that peer review of the article had taken only a day, the control and treatment groups revealed significant differences and the population was not random. Furthermore, six of the 26 patents had dropped out: two were transferred to intensive care, one died and one had stopped taking HCQ because of nausea. On April 3, the journal publisher said the study "does not meet the Society's accepted standards.")

On Ingraham's show on March 17, Dr. Fauci had warned against "anecdotal" studies that "were not controlled." Asked at a March 30 Task Force meeting if HCQ was promising, Fauci answered: "no." But Trump simply brushed off Fauci's objection: "I think, without saying too much, I'm probably more of a fan of that than—maybe than anybody. But I'm a big fan, and we'll see what happens. I feel good about it." (He treated drugs like sports teams.) Kadlec's manager of strategic innovation and emerging technology emailed Christopher Houchens, acting Director of BARDA's Division of Chemical, Biological, Radiological and Nuclear Medicine Countermeasures: "This can be a BIG immediate win." Troubled by such pressure, Houchens wrote BARDA Director Rick Bright, warning of "safety liabilities" and insisting on a fuller "understanding on the clinical utility of the drug." Bright said HHS general counsel Robert Charrow had told him to "drop everything and make the chloroquine donated by Bayer widely available to the American public."

The next day, Trump ordered the FDA to grant emergency use authorizations (EUAs) to CQ and HCQ, calling them "a game changer" (a phrase he picked up from Ingraham, who reported one doctor bragging that it saved patients "like Lazarus, up from the grave"). Trump followed up with a tweet insisting that "hydro" "be put in use IMMEDIATELY." Fox promoted it nearly 300 times between March 23 and April 6. On March 23, Dr. Mehmet Oz (a retired cardiothoracic surgeon and television celebrity) asked Kushner to urge Trump to "push academic centers to move more expeditiously" on HCQ. On March 28, Oz wrote Birx that the French study showed that "the treatment appears safe and results are better than expected."

On March 21, Janet Woodcock, director of the FDA's Center for Drug Evaluation and Research, wrote HHS: "We must be really carefully [sic] not to be seen as endorsing an off label use. We prosecute companies for this. It is CDCs job to give advice on medical practice decisions."[28] On March 24, a man died after eating CQ, which was used to clean fish tanks; his wife, who survived a stay in the ICU after taking it, said she had seen the press conference at which "Trump kept saying it was pretty much a cure." When Trump ordered Azar to approve the drugs, the HHS Secretary cautioned that there had to be trials. Trump was dismissive: "It doesn't matter. These are very smart people, Larry Ellison [co-founder and CEO of Oracle] and Laura Ingraham, and they say they work, so just approve them." "Larry Ellison called me. He tells me remdesivir works. So get the FDA to approve it today." "Larry's the smartest person I know. He says it's safe." "And Laura says chloroquine works as a cure. So the FDA has to approve it also." (Trump clearly preferred influencers to scientists.) When Azar warned that antimalarial drugs had side effects, Trump retorted: "No, these products are safe. Laura says she takes it all the time and nothing happens. . . . I want these approved today." Azar complained to Meadows, who replied: "you gotta do something to show the president we're making therapies available. The media is showing all these people being cured from these therapies. Even zinc. We should approve all these products that the media says work."

After the FDA granted EUAs to both drugs on March 28, usage rose dramatically, doubling in the month following Trump's comments.[29] The

American Association of Poison Control Centers reported misuse. But Trump told *Fox & Friends* on March 30:

> [H]ydroxychloroquine is something that I have been pushing very hard. I got the very early approval from the FDA. It was going to take a long time, and Dr. Stephen Hahn, the head of the FDA, gave us an early approval, a very quick approval, a 24-hour approval . . .. and I got it done, because I said: "look, some of these people are very sick and they're not going to make it. Let's do it. Let's get it done."

HHS Assistant Secretary of Health Giroir said the White House "really want to flood Ny [sic] and NJ with treatment courses." The Deputy Director of the Strategic National Stockpile told Giroir (correctly) that the EUA applied only to hospital use. Giroir (who often wore his military-style uniform as a Public Health Service admiral) retorted peremptorily: "NOPE. Needs to go to pharmacies as well. The EUA matters not. The drug is approved therefore can be prescribed per doctor's orders. This is a FINAL ANSWER." At an April 4 White House meeting, Hahn discussed the importance of clinical trials of HCQ. Navarro interjected: "I'm hearing that people are saying that [the evidence about HCQ was] only anecdotal. I have, in my hand, fifteen articles, which prove the efficacy of hydroxychloroquine." (Was he unconsciously channeling Sen. Joseph McCarthy's infamous claim: "I have here in my hand a list of 205 that were known to the Secretary of State as being members of the Communist Party"?)[30] Fauci replied: "I've read those articles, and they are all noncontrolled, non-placebo-controlled nonrandomized, anecdotal cohort studies that most of the scientific community doesn't believe." Insisting "that's science, not anecdote," Navarro yelled at Fauci: "You're ignoring all the data, and it's killing people!" Navarro objected:

> mainstream media . . . appears incapable of reading anything more than study headlines. To date, almost 40 studies have reported apparent usefulness of hydroxychloroquine or chloroquine in shortening length of hospital stay, improving symptoms, and resolving lung lesions as seen on X-rays.

Rudy Giuliani echoed him: critics had "thrown cold water on it because they were academics." Randomized trials were "silly." Giuliani had taken the drug three times without side effects, as had a police officer friend and others. Doctors "don't know what they're talking about." Trump spoke in the White House briefing room: "I'll say it again: What do you have to lose? Take it."

On April 5, he told Woodward:

> I am a big fan of hydroxy. It may not work, by the way, and it may work. If it does work, I will get no credit for it, and if it doesn't work, they'll blame the hell out of me . . . we've ordered millions of doses of hydroxy.

The next day, Navarro said on CNN:

> Doctors disagree about things all the time. My qualifications in terms of looking at the science is [sic] that I'm a social scientist. I have a Ph.D. And I understand how to read statistical studies, whether it's in medicine, the law, economics or whatever.

The same day, Trump met Hahn, Ingraham and the two guests from her show. On April 13, NIAID published a report calling for Phase Three clinical trials for anti-COVID drugs, including HCQ. Meadows warned Azar: "if this goes out, the president will fire you." "The president wants this drug approved now, Alex. It works." About the same time, Navarro gave Hahn the retrospective reviews of HCQ. Hahn was unconvinced: "this is not high-level evidence to support what you want to do. We have to wait for the clinical trials to be done." Navarro insisted that "I know the literature." On April 18, Trump said he was using HCQ prophylactically, declaring "it certainly didn't hurt me. I feel good" and claiming it had received "tremendous, rave reviews." But on April 24, the FDA warned against use outside hospitals or clinical trials.

Dr. Rick Bright had obtained the EUA. But in April, he was removed as BARDA Director and HHS deputy assistant secretary for preparedness and response and transferred to a less responsible position in NIH.[31] He said he had been pressured to fund research on HCQ.

> I believe this transfer was in response to my insistence that the government invest the billions of dollars allocated by Congress to address the Covid-19 pandemic into safe and scientifically vetted solutions, and not in drugs, vaccines and other technologies that lack scientific merit. I am speaking out because to combat this deadly virus, science—not politics or cronyism—has to lead the way.

His whistleblower complaint accused Kadlec (his superior) of being a "danger to public health," abusing his authority, wasting funds and censoring scientific research. Trump brusquely dismissed Bright: "I don't know him. I never met him. I don't want to meet him . . . he looks like an angry, disgruntled employee who, frankly, according to some people, didn't do a very good job." Navarro called him a "deserter in the war on the China virus." Azar said, "everything [Bright] was complaining about was achieved." "This is like someone who was in choir trying to say he was a soloist back then." On May 14, Bright testified before a hearing of the House Energy and Commerce Committee's Subcommittee on Health on "scientific integrity in the COVID-19 response," declaring that "lives were endangered, and I believe lives were lost." His lawyers disclosed that the Office of Special Counsel had found "reasonable grounds" to believe Bright had suffered retaliation, and it had asked Azar to reinstate him while OSC investigated. OSC also made a preliminary determination of a "substantial likelihood of wrongdoing," namely, "cronyism," in the award of contracts. DHHS said it "strongly disagrees with the allegations and characterizations in the complaint." Republican committee members criticized Bright. Rep. Gus Bihrakis (R-Fla) knew a veteran who was "cured" by HCQ.

On May 11, a study found that those who took HCQ with an antibiotic were twice as likely to suffer cardiac arrest.[32] On May 19, Hatfill emailed Navarro that Fauci, Hahn and Bright "have blood on their hands"; Navarro repeated that to White House officials and sent them a petition drafted by the business manager of the Association of American Physicians and Surgeons (AAPS), a fringe group with just 5,000 members (0.5 percent of the nearly one million American doctors), which opposed all government involvement in health care, promoted a variety of conspiracy theories and claimed Obama had used hypnosis to win the 2008 election. It accused Fauci and the Task Force of "crimes against humanity" and "mass murder" for being "insubordinate to POTUS" by opposing HCQ. On May 27, Fauci said, "the scientific data is really quite evident now about the lack of efficacy." On June 2, the AAPS sued the FDA, claiming that "officials from prior administrations acted contrary to the wishes of President Donald Trump, by arbitrarily limiting use of HCQ from the Strategic National Stockpile." On June 8, Trump listened approvingly as the famous golfer Jack Nicklaus told a White House assemblage (on speaker phone) how he and his wife had had COVID in March, took HCQ at Trump's suggestion and recovered. NIH Director Collins objected that "anecdotes where people draw a cause-and-effect conclusion are dangerous." "The data, when you look at it in a rigorous way, do not support this."

On June 16, the FDA revoked the EUA, finding the drugs were ineffective and had multiple side effects, some fatal.[33] Trump responded by retweeting a video of "very respected doctors" calling HCQ a "cure" and declaring that masks were unnecessary. Dr. Stella Immanuel "was spectacular in her statements about it, and she's had tremendous success with it." When it was reported that she had made videos claiming doctors created medicines using DNA from aliens, Trump said with typical incoherence: "I thought she was very impressive, in the sense that, from where she came—I don't know what country she comes from—but she said that she's had tremendous success with hundreds of different patients." (Immanuel was born in Cameroon and got her medical degree at the University of Calabar in Nigeria. She founded a charismatic religious sect and claimed that endometriosis, infertility, miscarriage and STDs were caused by spirit spouses.)[34] At a demonstration by Tea Party Patriots and America's Frontline Doctors on the Supreme Court steps on July 24, Immanuel proclaimed that "nobody needs to get sick. This virus has a cure . . . you don't need a mask." Doctors who refused to prescribe

HCQ were like "good Germans who allow the Nazis to kill Jews." After Facebook and Twitter deleted her speech, she threatened: "if my page is not back up face book [sic] will be down in Jesus name." In October 2021, the Texas Medical Board fined her $500 and required her to obtain informed consent from patients before treating them with off-label medications.

Trump tweeted angrily about the EUA revocation: "Many doctors and studies disagree with this!" Navarro called it "one of the great tragedies of this pandemic that the anti-Trump mainstream media demonized a cheap and effective medicine that could have saved tens of thousands of American lives." He complained to Hahn: "The FDA has had a tremendous negative effect on the ability to do clinical trials and advance the use of CQ as a prophylactic and therapeutic. The latest proposed action is OUTRAGEOUS." "This is a Deep State blindside by bureaucrats who hate the administration they work for more than they want to save lives." On June 24, Hatfill bragged to the AAPS Executive Director: "I've got a backchannel to DJT. We see the Vice President on Friday and have a knife fight scheduled with the FDA." Hatfill suggested to a cardiologist at the Henry Ford Health System that a "prison might be a good place for a clinical prophylaxis trial" of HCQ while cautioning HFHS: "PLEASE—NEVER mention the White House together with my name." On July 1, the FDA found the drugs caused "serious heart rhythm problems and other safety issues, including blood and lymph system disorders, kidney injuries, and liver problems and failure." Undeterred, Trump tweeted the FDA on July 7: "The highly respected Henry Ford Health System just reported based on a large sampling that HYDROXYCHLOROQUINE cut the death rate in certain sick patients very significantly. The Dems disparaged it for political reasons (me!) Disgraceful. Act now." He complained that "hydroxy has tremendous support, but politically it is toxic. If I would have said, 'Do not use hydroxychloroquine under any circumstances,' they would have come out and said it's a great thing."

On July 16, Hatfill drafted an online petition urging the FDA to reauthorize HCQ and sent Navarro a supportive "Letter with 370 physician signers" (claiming a month later it had 8,000). The same day, Hatfill wrote to a Navarro aide: "Peter and the DT need some ammunition. I'm currently in the process of specifically outlining what Fauci and Hahn did wrong and the havoc it has caused." He was working with "underground cardiologists" to "put more direct pressure shortly on the FDA and Fauci." On July 24, Trump tweeted the video of America's Frontline Doctors, claiming HCQ was a "cure for Covid." On August 4, Hatfill emailed AAPS leaders that he and others would engage in "a sit-down drag out face-to-face fight with Fauci." A day after the August 5 meeting of the NIH COVID-19 Treatment Guidelines panel, Hatfill told Navarro: "we were fed a load of bullshit." He wanted an "outside panel to review the Fauci Panel" and "give ammunition for the AG to start an investigation of the Fauci Panel. . . . That would shut them up for a bit." He explicitly connected his "scientific" advice with its anticipated political payoff: "Within 10–14 days of the start of HCQ outpatient treatment—figures should start to decrease. . . . Is that not about the same time that some sort of voting goes on?" On August 8, he asked a Texas cardiologist (this must be the "underground cardiologist" mentioned earlier; he had been disavowed by his former employer, Baylor University, for spreading covid misinformation) to argue for HCQ but added again: "Best if I keep in the background for the time being" and "work in the shadows."

The FDA denied the EUA reapplication on August 10. Hatfill also sent documents about HCQ to Sen. Johnson (chair of the Homeland Security and Governmental Affairs Committee), leading him and Sens. Lee and Cruz to write Hahn about the EUA revocation (in a letter Hatfill edited). On August 27, Johnson wrote Dr. Harvey Risch (emeritus professor at Yale Public Health and Medical Schools): "Meadows said he would ask Secretary Azar to issue whatever approval HHS can issue." (Risch and three other doctors wrote an "Open Letter to Fauci Regarding the Use of Hydroxychloroquine for Treating COVID-19"; but his Yale colleagues were "seriously alarmed" by his promotion of HCQ on Ingraham's and Bannon's shows. Risch had also enlisted Dr. Vladimir Zelenko, who promoted HCQ based on treating his own patients.) On September 22, Hatfill urged Meadows to fire Fauci and Hahn for having "grossly misadvised" Trump. In his 2021 memoir, Meadows continued to maintain that HCQ "had hundreds of testimonials from doctors and patients, indicating that it worked."

3. Taking Precautionary Measures

In March, after the top CDC doctor refused to issue a directive under Title 42 of the U.S. Code closing both U.S. land borders as a pandemic precaution, Pence overruled him and called Redfield, who ordered senior staff to do this and signed the order on March 20.[35] Olivia Troye, Pence's homeland security and counterterrorism adviser, said Stephen Miller (deeply hostile to immigration) was behind the decision. Trump announced: "the CDCP has decided to exercise its authority to give CBP the tools it needs to prevent the transmission of the virus coming through both the northern and the southern borders." But Dr. Anthony So, an international public health expert at Johns Hopkins Bloomberg School of Public Health, said the decision "is not based on science or evidence. This order directly endangers tens of thousands of lives and threatens to amplify dangerous anti-immigrant sentiment and xenophobia." (COVID-19 was so firmly established in the U.S. by then that border restrictions were far less important.) Dr. Martin Cetron, Director of CDC's Division of Global Migration and Quarantine, said the directive "came from outside the CDC subject matter experts" and was not justified by the evidence.[36] CDC Principal Deputy Director Schuchat agreed. Citron asked to be excused from working on the order, telling a colleague: "It's just morally wrong to use a public authority that has never, ever, ever been used this way. It's to keep Hispanics out of the country."

On March 23—just hours after Fox host Steve Hilton said: "You know that famous phrase, 'the cure is worse than the disease'? That is exactly the territory we're hurtling towards"—Trump tweeted: "WE CANNOT LET THE CURE BE WORSE THAN THE PROBLEM ITSELF."[37] He wanted to reopen the country on Easter Sunday (April 12). Kellyanne Conway warned him this would be "a huge mistake. You don't own the deaths right now, but you'll own all the deaths if you do this." Trump replied: "We have to open. It's killing people." But on March 25, *The New York Times* published a dramatic story about Elmhurst, Queens, where Trump had grown up, entitled "'People Are Dying': 72 hours inside a N.Y.C. hospital battling coronavirus." When Birx said, "You could, right off the bat have a thousand Elmhursts," Trump backed down.

On March 26 Birx gushed on the Christian Broadcasting Network that Trump had been so attentive to the scientific literature and the details and the data. I think his ability to analyze and integrate data that comes out of his long history in business has really been a real benefit during these discussions about medical issues.[38] (A year later, after leaving government, she repeated that Trump had "understood the data.") She added that "19 out of our 50 states . . . have persistently low level [sic] of cases. And at this point have less than 200 cases. So that's almost 40% of the country with extraordinary [sic] low numbers." (Those 19 were 34 percent of states but contained just 7 percent of the population.) "38 of our states have less than 50 cases" per 100,000 people. (Actually, just 28 states had that few.) On April 6 and 16, she told Trump: "we have seen declines in cases across the country," and nine states "have less than 1000 cases and less than 30 new cases per day." (But case numbers began rising in June, and Birx omitted the data necessary to calculate case/population ratios.) She claimed confidently that the administration was "putting out the embers."

On April 2, at Trump's direction, the Centers for Medicare & Medicaid Services (CMS) and the CDC urged all nursing home workers to wear masks and create separate COVID-19 units.[39] But the next day, the president undercut CMS:[40]

> The C.D.C. is advising the use of nonmedical cloth face covering as an additional voluntary public health measure. So it's voluntary. You don't have to do it. . . . I don't think I'm going to be doing it . . . somehow sitting in the Oval Office behind that beautiful Resolute Desk . . . as I greet presidents, prime ministers, dictators, kings, queens.

He followed that up by saying: "they've learned about face masks—the good and the bad . . . it's not a one-sided thing, believe it or not." (Masks do have two sides: an outside to protect the wearer and an inside to protect others.) When Azar urged him to wear a mask, Trump retorted: "wearing a mask is a sign of weakness." No one at that meeting except Pottinger wore a mask, and Short declared at the next meeting: "No masks will be worn." On a May 21 tour of a Ford plan, Trump wore a mask only "in the back area. I didn't want to give the press the pleasure of seeing it." On July 19, he told Fox News's Chris Wallace: "I don't agree with the statement that if everybody wears a mask everything disappears." (No one ever said that.) At the White House on August 13, he compounded the confusion with a statement so contradictory, it could be neither understood nor disproved: "We have urged Americans to wear masks and I emphasized this is a patriotic thing to do. Maybe they're great, and maybe they're just good. Maybe they're not so good." (A June poll found that 94 percent of Democrats always or very often wore a mask, compared to 46 percent of Republicans. The gap in support for six precautionary measures between the two parties grew dramatically from March to October. In November 2022, a study of a natural experiment comparing Boston schools that did and did not require masks found they significantly reduced the number of cases.)[41]

Birx reported constant White House opposition to her recommendations.[42] "Some roaming the halls of the West Wing believed that the less we did, the less we would be accountable for whatever was about to happen." Taylor Goodspeed, a conservative lawyer heading the Council of Economic Advisers, wrote on April 8 that only 26,000 would die by Memorial Day. Birx predicted 100,000–240,000. (There were 107,233 deaths.[43] Birx later complained: "in every internal senior advisor discussion, the president was reminded of just how wrong I had been in my projections. It never mattered that my projections were right then and continued to be right.") Stephen and Katie Miller cited the false, totally unsubstantiated claim by Wendy Bell, a conservative radio host, that "there's a huge chance the Covid death numbers are exaggerated, to the tune of 94 percent."

On March 24, Trump had announced on Fox News that he wanted the nation "opened up and just raring to go by Easter" because "it was a beautiful time."[44] He declared on April 3: "We will never shut down the country again. Never." On April 10, he explained how he made this "biggest decision I've ever had to make" by pointing to his head and saying: "that's my metrics." But three days later, when East and West Coast governors (mostly Democrats) explored lifting pandemic restrictions, Trump declared: "the authority of the president of the United States" on the subject "is total. The president of the United States calls all the shots." "I have ultimate authority." "And that's the way it's got to be." Pence agreed: "in the long history of this country, the authority of the President of the United States during national emergencies is unquestionably plenary." New York Gov. Cuomo denounced Trump: "We don't have a king. We have an elected president." Biden used the occasion to assure voters he was "not running for office to be King of America." Constitutional law scholars backed the governors. Even Sens. Paul and Rubio said states should regulate themselves. Jonathan Turley, a George Washington University law professor who had testified for Trump during the first impeachment, said: "the president had no authority to order a national lockdown and certainly does not have authority to now order the lifting of such orders by the governors." John Yoo (author of the notorious OLC torture memos) concurred: "only the states can impose quarantines, close institutions and businesses, and limit interstate travel." Rep. Liz Cheney tweeted the text of the Tenth Amendment: "The powers not delegated to the United States . . . are reserved to the States." A day later, Trump capitulated—"the governors are responsible"—but then added inconsistently: "If we disagree with [their decision], we're not going to let it open." Alexander Lazar, professor of pathology and genomic medicine at University of Texas, recalled that at "a ton" of meetings of up to 35 states, "almost everyone was within a standard deviation of what everyone else was doing. It was more of a purple bell curve than a bimodal distribution of red and blue peaks."[45] Yet Democratic governors were more likely than Republican to mandate masks; and though advisers told him 81 percent of Republicans supported mask requirements, Trump rebuffed them after his chief of staff, Meadows, warned, "The base will turn on you."

In March, Michigan Gov. Whitmer announced a three-week "pause to save lives," closing colleges, high schools, workplaces and indoor dining.[46] But on April 17, a day after the CDC issued reopening guidelines, protesters held Operation Gridlock in Michigan, which was featured on Fox News. Two minutes later, Trump tweeted: "LIBERATE VIRGINIA, and save your great 2nd Amendment. It is under siege," "LIBERATE MICHIGAN," "LIBERATE MINNESOTA." Garrett Soldano, a chiropractor, launched Michiganders Against Excessive Quarantining, whose website got as many as 380,000 visits at its peak. On April 30, thousands protested in the state capital, chanting "Lock Her Up," waving Confederate flags, calling Whitmer Hitler and hanging her in effigy. Men armed with assault weapons stormed the Capitol. Protesters continued demonstrating for weeks, some at the governor's mansion with assault weapons, and Whitmer received death threats. Trump said: "the Governor of Michigan should give a little, and put out the fire. These are very good people, but they are angry . . . make a deal." Scott Atlas tweeted: "the only way this stops is if people rise up. You get what you accept. #FreedomMatters #StepUp." Whitmer replied: "I'm not going to be bullied into not following reputable scientists and medical professionals." Michigan Attorney General Nessel called Atlas "disappointing, irresponsible, and the reason why the United States finds itself in such desperate circumstances." Atlas insisted: "I NEVER was talking at all about violence." (Nine men had been arrested a month earlier in a plot to kidnap Whitmer, for which they were later convicted.) Even Trump's Surgeon General said Americans should strive to be "patriots" by wearing masks and staying home. *The Washington Post* said: "Scott Atlas's rabble-rousing will lead to illness and death. He should be fired."

On April 15, Trump said of the pandemic: "We're going to have an amazing year next year." "We'd love to see if we could" have a vaccine available "prior to the end of the year."[47] Moncef Slaoui (former head of the GlaxoSmithKline vaccines department, now leading Operation Warp Speed, charged by Trump with developing the vaccine) expressed confidence that "we will be able to deliver a few hundred million doses of vaccine by the end of 2020." On April 21, Redfield told *The Washington Post*: "There's a possibility that the assault of the virus on our nation next winter will actually be even more difficult than the one we just went through." Two days later, Trump accused CNN of misquoting Redfield (although it had just repeated the Post story) and declared that Redfield would issue a correction. But the CDC Director acknowledged he had been quoted accurately.

On April 23, William N. Bryan, DHS undersecretary for science and technology, presented the Task Force and Trump with two preliminary studies showing that the COVID virus on a surface could be killed by exposure to the sun or cleaning agents like bleach.[48] Trump said at a news conference immediately thereafter that the coronavirus "dies quickest in sunlight." He speculated:

> So supposing we hit the body with a tremendous—whether it's ultraviolet or just a very powerful light—and I think you said that hadn't been checked because of the testing. And then I said, supposing you brought the light inside the body, which you can do either through the skin or some other way, and I think you said you're going to test that, too. I see the disinfectant that knocks it out in a minute, one minute. And is there a way we can do something like that by injection inside or almost a cleaning? As you see, it gets in the lungs, it does a tremendous number on the lungs, so it would be interesting to check that.

Standing next to the president, Birx's only contribution was to say: "not as a treatment." (She later explained: "You can see how extraordinarily uncomfortable I was. Those of you who have served in the military"—she had been an Army colonel—"know that there are discussions you have in private with your commanding officers and there's discussions you had in public.") In the following days, the Kansas Poison Control Center reported a 40 percent increase in cases of people drinking cleaning fluid; two men were hospitalized after doing so in Georgia. Lysol declared that "under no circumstance" should its bleach be ingested; Clorox said: "bleach and other disinfectants are not suitable for consumption or injection under any circumstances." Trump later claimed (falsely) that he had only been "asking a question sarcastically to reporters."

On April 29, Trump assured industry executives that COVID was "gonna go. It's gonna leave. It's gonna be gone. It's gonna be eradicated."[49] A week later, he repeated this to a meeting of Congressional Republicans:

> This is going to go away without a vaccine. I just rely on what doctors say. They say it's going to go . . . eventually, it's going to go away. The question is will we need a vaccine. At some point, it will probably go away by itself.

A week after that, however, he bragged at the launch of Operation Warp Speed that it was "the most aggressive vaccine project in history." Then he confusingly belittled it: "I just want to make something clear. It's very important: Vaccine or no vaccine, we're back. . . . In many cases, they don't have vaccines, and a virus or a flu comes, and you fight through it." Before the launch, Trump had said to his officials: "we're not going to go out there and have our masks on. I don't think the masks are a good look." Fauci, Birx and Collins wore them but not Trump or the military. At a Task Force meeting the first week of May, Birx assailed the maldistribution of remdesivir, which was "killing people." Meadows replied: "we understand." But the next day, he effectively accused her of leaking "damaging" information to the press. "In case you don't understand, hear me now. You will never say anything like that again in any meeting." The daily meetings ended, and she was dropped from future invitations. On May 15, Trump said:

> Don't forget, we have more cases than anybody in the world. But why? We do more testing. . . . When you test, you find something wrong with people. If we didn't do any testing, we would have very few cases.

He repeated that on June 15 and was echoed by some governors.

Beginning in June, Meadows pressured the FDA to give convalescent plasma an EUA as a covid treatment.[50] He proudly recounted this in his memoir:

> [Hahn] had been quite accommodating. Then the National Institutes of Health, led by Dr. Fauci, had begun speaking with the press about how the FDA was moving "too fast" on getting Covid-19 drugs approved. The NIH said that the FDA should not have approved certain treatments such as convalescent plasma due to a miniscule amount of risk. . . . [FDA Commissioner Hahn] transitioned into a full-blown bureaucrat, determined to slow things down rather than to help people. . . . [Meadows told Hahn]

> This is of national importance. You are going to issue the emergency use authorization *now*. . . . It's for the president of the United States.

Trump talked weekly to Hahn, who said the president "express[ed] dismay over NIH potentially putting up roadblocks." Dr. John C. Fleming (an anti-abortion activist who was Assistant to the President for Planning and Implementation) also met weekly with Hahn and his staff. The FDA had been ready to issue an EUA on August 12, but NIH wanted a clinical trial. On August 19, Dr. Paul Alexander sent Hahn a summary of studies "to help give us cover in our decisions." (Alexander's background and other interventions are described later.) The same day, *The New York Times* reported that NIH was objecting to approval. Furious that NIH had talked to *The Times*, Trump ordered Director Francis Collins to "get it done" in two days. Birx and others also criticized Collins.

On August 20, the FDA was told it had to approve the EUA by August 23 because Trump was going to announce it at the Republican National Convention on August 24 and did not want the approval to seem politically motivated. But the Mayo Clinic data on which the approval was based lacked key entries. Trump assailed the FDA: "you have a lot of people over there that don't want to rush things. They want to do it after November 3rd." The FDA responded that it was following the procedures used in other public health emergencies. Hahn also objected. (He later called the decision a "line in the sand" because Trump's pressure was putting patients at risk.) The FDA's chief counsel emailed Hahn's chief of staff on August 21: "would like to be able to tell Meadows it's done." Trump called Collins: "You know, my polling numbers are looking really good. But you doctors are killing me!" "People are dying." Collins replied: "You don't want to make a decision on data that turns out to be wrong. It'll come back to haunt you." "We are within a week of having a much larger data set where I know I can trust the antibody levels. Can we please just put this off until next week?" Trump retorted: "No. Absolutely not. We've got to have the data on Friday [August 21], or it doesn't matter." The data were available the next day.

On August 22, Trump tweeted:

> The deep state, or whoever, over at the FDA is making it very difficult for drug companies to get people in order to test the vaccines and therapeutics. Obviously, they are hoping to delay the answer until after November 3rd. Must focus on speed, and saving lives! @SteveFDA

Hahn assured him that "we either were nearing a decision or had made a decision." But Trump angrily phoned Azar: "Did you see my tweet? Why hasn't the FDA approved convalescent plasma? Is it that fucking Hahn again?" Azar responded: "For the love of God, stop doing this! [i.e., posting tweets visible to the public] We talked about this." Trump was making the FDA look politicized. "The FDA are bureaucrats and are not going to react well." But when Azar said the EUA might be ready by August 25, Trump was delighted: "oh, good, good. I want to announce it. . . . We're going to set up a press conference." Meadows blamed the delay on "a fumble by a number of people in the federal government." "Sometimes you have to make them feel the heat if they don't see the light."

Before the press conference to announce the EUA, the FDA told Trump that COVID patients who were under 80, not intubated and received plasma with a high level of antibodies within three days of diagnosis were 35 percent more likely to be alive a month later compared with those who received plasma with a low level of antibodies.[51] He asked: "Why'd you pick thirty-five percent? Why don't we say fifty?" Azar warned: "that would make us a target for criticism." Trump persisted: "I like fifty. Doesn't fifty just sound better to you? Five-zero. Fifty." Hahn explained: "we can't say fifty because that's not what the data show." At the press conference, Trump called convalescent plasma "a very historic breakthrough in the fight against the China virus," "a powerful therapy" made possible "by marshaling the full power of the federal government." But he misrepresented the data as saying plasma was "proven to reduce mortality by 35 percent," which he called a "tremendous number." Collins had to stand there without demurring. Azar also called plasma a "major advance"; "we dream in drug development of something like a thirty-five percent mortality reduction." Then Hahn compounded Trump's error, claiming "a thirty-five percent improvement in survival": 35 out of every 100 patients "would have been saved because of the administration of plasma." But an FDA spokesperson pointed to a graph showing only that the 30-day survival rate was 76 percent among those getting a high level of antibodies and 63 percent among those getting a low level. After Dr. Peter Marks (Director of the FDA Center for Biologics Evaluation and Research) erroneously said there was "roughly a 35 percent <u>relative</u> improvement in the survival rates of patients" (emphasis added), he was invited to the Oval Office to celebrate with Trump.

Robert M. Califf (Obama's FDA Commissioner) urged Hahn "to publish a correction . . . to correctly state the translation from relative to absolute effect." Scott Gottlieb (Trump's former FDA Commissioner) said: "the Mayo observational study indicates that would be 3 people [out of 100] saved at 7 days or 5 at 30 days." Hahn's figure was "not only blatantly wrong" but also "an egregious public statement." Margaret Hamburg (another former FDA Commissioner) and Joshua Sharfstein (former Principal Deputy FDA Commissioner) said that calling plasma a "breakthrough" was "a wild overstatement." The assertion that it reduced mortality by 35 percent was "flatly untrue." "The president turned a question of medical science and policy into a political hot potato that has damaged the agency's reputation for independence and science at a critical time for Americans."

A shamefaced Hahn admitted the criticism was "entirely justified. What I should have said better is that the data show a relative risk reduction, not an absolute risk reduction." Nevertheless, an FDA spokeswoman incorrectly tweeted: "Convalescent plasma has shown to be beneficial for 35% of patients," citing the Mayo Clinic study. One of that study's main authors replied: "Do I know where the 35 percent comes from? No." *The New York Times* said the figure "is much closer to three to five out of every 100, and even that lower estimate is questionable." Hahn:

> should be familiar with basic statistics. The trouble is, Dr. Hahn is serving a president who routinely demonstrates an overt hostility to science . . . and he's being pressed by that president to clear drugs and vaccines for use as quickly as possible.

On August 31, Eric Topol, founder and Director of the Scripps Research Transnational Institute, wrote Hahn: "Tell the truth or resign." "We cannot entrust the health of 330 million Americans to a person who is subservient to President Trump's whims, unprecedented promotion of unproven therapies, outrageous lies, and political motivations." Hahn's chief of staff emailed senior HHS political appointees: "potus said a lot of false remarks with Hahn today about what this was so we need to make sure POTUS talkers are correct." Hahn fired the FDA's chief spokeswoman (who had previously worked for Ted Cruz and *One America News* and been appointed just 11 days earlier) and terminated a contract with a man who had advised him to apologize. The DHHS chief of staff claimed these actions were "100 percent coincidence." That evening, Marks told Hahn: "the EUA should be signed off" by the next morning. The FDA issued the EUA on August 23, the day before the RNC, calling it "Another Achievement in Administration's Fight Against the Pandemic."

4. Paul Alexander, Michael Caputo and Reopening

On May 11, Dr. Paul Alexander (senior adviser to Michael Caputo, Assistant Secretary for Public Affairs in DHHS, which oversees CDC) wrote Azar's speechwriter: "We have to now 'unscare' people while as we reopen, we will see blips and spikes in cases and deaths." "We must school them that we will respond to the spikes and hotspots as needed."[52] (Alexander had a Ph.D. in Health Research Methods, Evidence and Impact from McMaster University in Ontario, where he was a part-time unpaid assistant professor. In September, the university distanced itself, saying Alexander was only a "consultant" and "not speaking on behalf of McMaster University or his Department."[53] Caputo had been mentored by Roger Stone and worked with Oliver North in Central America and on behalf of Vladimir Putin for Gazprom.)[54]

Although the Supreme Court upheld state limitations on religious gatherings, Trump said: "Today, I'm identifying houses of worship—churches, synagogues and mosques—as essential places that provide essential services. The governors need to do the right thing and allow these very important, essential places of faith to open right now, for this weekend. If they don't do it, I will override the governors." (He could not do so.) Attorney General Barr said on May 17: "if a government allows movie theaters, restaurants, concert halls, and other comparable places of assembly to remain open and unrestricted, it may not order houses of worship to close, limit their congregation size, or otherwise impede religious gatherings." Ten days later, he directed all U.S. Attorneys to be "on the lookout for state and local directives that could be violating the constitutional rights and civil liberties of individual citizens." On May 21—days after the CDC released a report that COVID had killed three and infected dozens at church events in Arkansas and infected 87 percent of those at a choir practice in Washington state—White House officials removed a Centers guidance that churches should consider virtual religious services. Paul Ray (administrator of the White House Office of Information and Regulatory Affairs) had proposed deleting several passages that "raise religious liberty concerns."

> Each faith tradition—not the federal government—is best situated to understand the demands of its own beliefs and therefore to choose among the multiple effective means of preventing the virus's spread, those means that best comport with its beliefs.

Jay Butler, a senior CDC official, objected to colleagues on May 23: "this is not good public health."

At an April 23 HHS briefing, Pence claimed, "truly remarkable progress in moving our nation forward." But Birx presented more than 20 slides showing numbers of cases across the country, and Fauci said some states had opened too early and needed to "drop back a few yards." Nevertheless, Azar echoed Pence's claim of "remarkable progress." On an April 28 visit to the Mayo Clinic, Pence refused to wear a mask because a photo could be used by Democrats against Trump (who also refused to wear one).[55] Marc Short, Pence's chief of staff, asked Redfield to relax the CDC recommendations concerning Smithfield Foods meat processing plants (located in states crucial to the forthcoming election). Pence and Kellyanne Conway pushed the CDC to relax its guidance on church reopening. Katie Miller, Pence's head of communications, said all agency guidelines, recommendations and statements about the pandemic had to be cleared with her. (In his memoir, Meadows railed against "ill-considered and random" guidances. Federal agencies "had been using bad data to come up with their rules, and then handing those rules down to the public as if they had come straight from heaven." "When they *didn't* know something for sure, they made a guess, then issued compulsory guidance.")

On May 8, when the CDC press office asked permission for Redfield to be interviewed about the pandemic's impact on childhood vaccinations, Alexander responded:

> the key is to highlight that we are all not equally at risk and children at minimal risk based on how the virus has been characterized thus far. . . . In US, CDC data suggests children 0–19 years old have risk of 0%.[56]

(As of June 23, 2023, there had been 1,839 deaths in this age group.)[57] He sent this to Caputo with a typically self-serving comment: "this is how I am supporting the messaging. . . . Any way to help you and showcase your work for this great President." The same day, Alexander boasted to Caputo that he had diluted a CDC press statement about the disproportionate impact of the pandemic on people of color by emphasizing that such disparities were "endemic and long-standing." He assured Caputo:

> I will always know the words to use or discussion to blend the medicine with the politics . . . saying the economic issues are longstanding and endemic points to the past administrations and democratic govn [sic—he means Democrat control of the government].

On May 30, he acknowledged that the "the statement that minoring [sic—"minority"] groups are at higher risk . . . is very accurate" but warned that "in this election cycle that is the kind of statement coming from CDC that the media and Democrat antagonists will use against the president," whose enemies were already accusing him "directly of the deaths in the African American community from COVID." "[E]ach time we talk about these deaths we need to" explain that "this was due to decades of democrat [sic] neglect." (The CDC statement on racial disparities was never released.)

When an HHS senior adviser expressed concern that a CDC press release could be seen "as a reason not to open up America in red states," Alexander suggested they declare that "the risk in US or even globally of persons 60 years and less is less than seasonal influenza, the data shows this." (As of June 21, 2023, there had been 276,412 COVID-19 deaths of those under 65; CDC estimated a total of 30,000 flu deaths for <u>all</u> ages in the 2019–20 and 2021–22 flu seasons, 19,000–58,000 in the 2022–23 flu season and "minimal influenza activity" in 2020–21.)[58] He wrote Caputo: "we need also to tout the good stories as we know of elderly with serious conditions who get it and survive." On June 20, Alexander asked Caputo if a CDC press release about extending the cruise ship ban was "supposed to frighten readers?" and assured his boss he had "toned it down" to "constantly showcase the good work and hope, etc." (Florida Gov. DeSantis remained angry even after the ban was watered down to a "conditional sail order"; but Redfield said later he had been determined to issue that order if it was "the last thing I did as CDC director" before being fired.) When a DHS official wrote a guidance recommending asymptomatic testing in correctional and detention facilities, OMB Director Russell Vought sent it to Meadows, complaining: "it never ends." The recommendation was eliminated. The Domestic Policy Council successfully removed references to face coverings, virtual services and choral singing in a CDC guidance on places of worship. After failing to eliminate CDC's reference to social distancing in restaurants and bars, OMB changed a recommendation of six feet to the meaningless "encourage social distancing."

On June 12, at CDC's first telebriefing since the backlash against Messonnier's February 25 warning, Dr. Jay Butler, the Center's Deputy Director of Infectious Diseases, cautioned that the government would have to reinstate mitigation measures "if cases begin to go up again, and particularly if they go up dramatically."[59] (Deaths soon began increasing, more than doubling within a month.)[60] Caputo immediately wrote Butler he was "very displeased" and directed him not to do any more briefings.

On June 16, Pence wrote in a *Wall Street Journal* op ed that "panic" over a second wave of COVID infections was "overblown."[61]

> With testing, treatments and vaccine trials ramping up, we are far better off than the media report. . . . While talk of an increase in cases dominates cable news coverage, more than half of states are actually seeing cases decline or remain stable. . . . In the six states that have reached more than 1,000 new cases a day, increased testing has allowed public health officials to identify most of the outbreaks in particular settings . . . and contain them . . . today less than 6% of Americans tested each week are found to have the virus. Cases have stabilized over the past two weeks, with the daily average case rate across the U.S. dropping to 20,000—down from 30,000 in April and 25,000 in May. And in the past five days, deaths are down to fewer than 750 a day, a dramatic decline from 2,500 a day a few weeks ago—and a far cry from the 5,000 a day that some were predicting.

The next day, Trump assured Hannity that the virus was "fading away." (In fact, new cases/day increased twelvefold to almost 240,000 in mid-January, and daily deaths increased nearly sixfold to 4,433 on January 21, 2021.)[62] Trump said at a rally three days later:

> We've tested now twenty-five million people. When you do testing to that extent, you're going to find more people, you're going to find more cases. So, I said to my people, "Slow the testing down, please." It's a disease, without question, has more names than any disease in history. I can name "Kung flu."

Navarro later said Trump was speaking "tongue in cheek." But asked about this, Trump made a rare candid admission: "I don't kid."

On June 30, Alexander sent Caputo a two-page critique of CDC Principal Director Schuchat, who had 32 years of experience at the Center.[63] "Her aim is to embarrass the president." "She is duplicitous." "She is implying that prior to now, the administration, including her, have not taken [covid] seriously. This is false." "The risk of death in children 0–19 years of age is basically 0 (zero) . . . PERIOD . . . she has lied. . . . It is very false her statement that it causes death in children." (Meadows repeated this lie in his 2021 memoir.) Alexander also disseminated other far more dangerous disinformation.

> Importantly, having the virus spread among the young and healthy is one of the methods to drive herd immunity. This was not the strategy but all must be on deck now and it is contributing positively at some level. What is at issue is the politics by people like her. . . . She is basically committing hari kari [sic], saying they at CDC have failed for this is their job. She failed. But they are saying this to damage the president here [for not wearing a mask] but it is his decision. Moreover, he is tested more than anyone in the entire world several times a day rapid testing as we know . . . so he does not need a mask to be honest.

Caputo forwarded this to Redfield (Schuchat's boss). Then Catherine Grantio (in the White House Liaison Office health department) called CDC to complain about Schuchat. At the same time, Caputo tried to punish the CDC communications team for speaking to NPR and helping a CNN reporter reach him, asking the CDC official—"in what world do you think it was your job to announce an administration public service announcement campaign to CNN?"—and demanding the name of the CDC press officer who approved NPR interviews.

Alexander emailed Caputo on July 3:[64]

> Americans "must go on with life." So the bottom line is if it is more infectiouness [sic] now, the issue is who cares? If it is causing more cases in

> young, my word is who cares . . . as long as we make sensible decisions, and protect the elderely [sic] and nursing homes, we must go on with life . . . who cares if we test more and get more positive tests.

The next day, he emailed Caputo and six other officials:

> [T]here is no other way, we need to establish herd [immunity], and it only comes about allowing the non-high risk groups [to] expose themselves to the virus. PERIOD. . . . Infants, kids, teens, young people, young adults, middle aged with no conditions etc. have zero to little risk . . . so we use them to develop herd . . . we want them infected . . . and recovered . . . with antibodies.

(As of June 21, 2023, there had been 1,839 deaths ages 0–18 and 44,656 ages 19–44, for a total of 46,495.)[65] He successfully pressured the CDC to alter the title of a report and remove words like "pediatric" to refer to those 18 and older (even though Centers often adopted that usage, as did the American Academy of Pediatrics) and replace "children, adolescents, and young adults" with "persons." He wrote Caputo, Hahn and eight other senior officials on July 24: "It may be that it will be best if we open up and flood the zone and let the kids and young folk get infected" to achieve "natural immunity . . . natural exposure." The next day, Caputo asked: "How can this be researched and proven true or false?" Alexander offered data, saying, "I did not want to look like a nut ball and if as they think and as i [sic] think this may be true. Several hard hit areas may have hit heard [sic] at 20% like NYC." He wrote Redfield on July 27:

> We essentially took off the battlefield the most potent weapon we had . . . younger healthy people, children, teens, young people who we needed to fastly [sic] infect themselves, spread it around, develop immunity, and help stop the spread.

Kyle McGowan, CDC chief of staff, resigned in August because of "a series of multiple decisions that showed a lack of desire to listen to the actual scientists." He later said: "It was understood that [Alexander] spoke for Michael Caputo, who spoke for the White House." In his 2021 memoir, Meadows demonstrated the administration's dangerous incomprehension.

> President Trump knew that eventually, the virus was probably going to come for us all; it didn't matter how many masks we wore or how many hours we spent sitting inside on our couches. It was only through "herd immunity" as Dr. Fauci and his colleagues reminded us several times, that pandemics die out.

(Fauci consistently denied that encouraging herd immunity was an appropriate response to the pandemic.)

Trump tweeted on July 9:

> for the 1/100th [sic—"hundredth"] time, the reason we show so many Cases, compared to other countries that haven't done nearly as well as we have, is that our TESTING is much bigger and better. We have tested 40,000,000 people. If we did 20,000,000 instead, Cases would be in half, etc. NOT REPORTED.[66]

In July, he accused the CDC of "very tough & expensive guidelines for opening schools." "The Democrats think it would be bad for them politically if U.S. schools open before the November Election, but it is important for the children and families. May cut off funding if not open!" (He could not do this.) Pence explained: "we just don't want the guidance to be too tough. And that's the reason next week the CDC is going to be issuing a new set of tools." CDC Director Redfield insisted Trump and he were "totally aligned." "[T]he advantage of everybody not doing it in the exact same way is you begin to learn what aspects are more effective than others." Two weeks later, CDC declared that children were at low risk of infection or transmission but cited little evidence. The statement came from the DHHS Substance Abuse and Mental Health Services Administration (SAMHSA)—with no expertise in infectious diseases and with little CDC involvement. An anonymous official reported that the new guidelines had been substantially edited by the White House. Redfield said there should be exceptions for "hot spots," where more than 5 percent tested positive, which would include parts of at least 33 states. A CDC document marked "for internal use only" classified the full reopening of schools as "highest risk" and urged testing of students and teachers and contact tracing.

Olivia Troye, Pence's representative on the coronavirus task force, later reported she was repeatedly asked by Marc Short to get the CDC to produce more reports showing a decline in covid among the young.[67] Before a Task Force briefing in late June, White House officials asked top CDC officials for "a snazzy, easy-to-read document" demonstrating that schoolchildren had a low risk of infection and death. Birx wanted the CDC to use the SAMHSA paper warning that school closures would have a long-term effect on the mental health of schoolchildren and asserting that "very few reports of children being the primary source of Covid-19 transmission among family members have emerged" and asymptomatic children "are unlikely to spread the virus." In a July 19 email, Birx asked Redfield to incorporate that document "as background in the introduction section" of the CDC guidance. After CDC scientists pointed to numerous errors and expressed concern that the guidance minimized risks, the Centers eliminated the claim about asymptomatic children, but the introduction still warned about children not attending school. The White House added a preamble on the benefits of children returning to school and retitled the document: "The Importance of Reopening America's Schools This Fall." Before it was published, the White House sent it to Meadows, Kushner, Larry Kudlow and Stephen Miller (among others), asking for "critical edits." The published version said covid could be less deadly to children than the seasonal flu—a claim to which the CDC had objected. (There were 188 deaths of children under 18 from flu during the 2019–20 season and only one the next flu season because of pandemic precautions.[68] As of June 21, 2023, 1,839 children under 18 had died of covid.)

Alexander wrote Redfield to complain that a report about covid risks for pregnant women "reads in a way to frighten women . . . as if the President and his administration can't fix this and it is getting worse."[69] "The CDC is undermining the President by what they put out" through "subtle and direct hits." The Center's record was "spotty" and "questionable." "Who says the CDC is the sole font [sic—"fount"] of wisdom when it comes to detecting and fighting deadly pathogens." In June, the chairs of the House Energy and Commerce Committees had written Azar to complain that CDC usually had just one political appointee—its Director—but now had five. "Now more than ever, the American people need a robust and effective CDC that is not repeatedly undermined by others in the administration, including the president and the vice president." On July 7, nearly 350 public health organizations urged Azar to advocate for the CDC, which should be allowed to speak "with an unfettered voice."

After Trump criticized Harvard for holding classes online, Harvard and MIT sued to block a rule denying visas to foreign students who could not take in-person classes.[70] Johns Hopkins and several California universities did the same, and at least 18 states joined the lawsuits. More than a dozen tech companies supported the Harvard/MIT lawsuit. Trump tweeted: "Too many Universities and School Systems are about Radical Left Indoctrination, not Education. Therefore, I am telling the Treasury Department to re-examine their Tax-Exempt Status." (That clearly unconstitutional proposal resembled Nixon's weaponization of the IRS against his enemies.)[71] D Mass Judge Allison D. Burroughs (Obama) approved a settlement in which the regulation was withdrawn.

5. Killing the Messengers—and Defending Them

On July 11, after *The Washington Post* published a story about worsening relations between Trump and Fauci, the White House declared that "several White House officials are concerned about the number of times Dr. Fauci has been wrong on things" and enumerated his many alleged errors, such as "at this moment [February 28], there is no need to change anything that you're doing on a day-by-day basis."[72] But the administration omitted what followed: "When you start to see community spread, this could change and force you to be much more attentive to doing things that would protect you from spread." Fauci warned later that COVID-19 could become "a major outbreak." When he observed that "I don't think you can say we're doing great" compared to other countries, an angry Trump retorted that Fauci had "made a lot of mistakes," called him "a little bit of an alarmist" and claimed that "large portions of our country" were "corona-free." Told there were high levels in California, Arizona, Texas and Florida, Trump replied: "that's starting to head down in the right direction. And I think you'll see it rapidly head down very soon." (Instead, new cases per day increased from less than 20,000 in June to more than 900,000 in January.)[73] Trump complained that Fauci had "this high approval rating, so why don't I have a high approval rating with respect . . . to the virus? So it sort of is curious." (A poll found that 67 percent trusted Fauci, while only 26 percent trusted Trump.) When Meadows told Fauci the administration was sick of his "talking out of turn" and contradicting Trump, Fauci replied: "All I'm doing is describing what's really happening out there. You can't expect me not to do that."

DHHS Assistant Secretary Giroir said: "Dr. Fauci is not 100 percent right, and he also doesn't necessarily . . . have the whole national interest in mind. He looks at it from a very narrow public health point of view."[74] (Five years earlier, Texas A&M Health Science Center had forced Giroir to resign as CEO for being "more interested in promoting yourself" than the Center.) The day after Giroir's critique, Trump retweeted Chuck Woolery: "the most outrageous lies are the ones about Covid 19. Everyone's lying. The CDC, Media, Democrats, our Doctors, not all but most. . . . I think it's all about the election and keeping the economy from coming back." Trump retweeted another Woolery post that there was "worldwide and overwhelming" scientific evidence that schools should reopen. (Woolery is a musician and game show host who had been accused of anti-Semitism.[75] When his son tested positive the next day, Woolery experienced an instantaneous conversion, tweeting that the "COVID-19 pandemic is real.")

Dan Scavino (Trump's Director of Social Media) posted a cartoon on Facebook of "Dr. Faucet" with a Pinocchio nose dripping water into a sink drowning Uncle Sam; the water temperature was set to "extra cold," and drops had public health warnings: "Indefinite lockdown!" "Schools stay closed this fall!" "No NFL Season" and "Shut up and obey!"[76] The next day, Navarro published a *USA Today* op ed headlined: "ANTHONY FAUCI HAS BEEN WRONG ABOUT EVERYTHING I HAVE INTERACTED WITH HIM ON." But Trump surprisingly criticized Navarro for making "a statement representing himself. He shouldn't be doing that."

And the White House tweeted: "The Peter Navarro op-ed didn't go through normal White House clearance processes and is the opinion of Peter alone. @realDonaldTrump values the expertise of the medical professionals advising his administration." After being criticized, *USA Today* said Navarro's op ed did not meet its standards. Fauci called the White House attacks "bizarre." "I think they realize now that that was not a prudent thing to do because it's only reflecting negatively on them." Undaunted by the president's reaction, Alexander wrote 11 senior DHHS officials on August 11: "Dr. Fauci has no data, no science to back up what he is saying on school reopening, none . . . he is scaring the nation wrongfully."

The day of Navarro's op ed, Fauci said in a speech: "this is a pandemic of historic proportions . . . comparable to what we saw in 1918." Meadows promptly told Collins: "You've got to get Tony to back down on that. That is not based on any facts. He's extrapolating. He's scaring people." A day later on Fox News, Meadows condemned Fauci's comparison: "not only is that false, it is irresponsible." In his memoir, Attorney General Barr called Fauci "a consummate bureaucrat—one with a huge ego and penchant for self-promotion." Trump complained to Barr that Fauci:

> likes to predict the worst outcomes. That way you'll end up looking good when the worst case doesn't happen. You'll get credit for preventing it. . . . I can't do that as President. I have to be the optimist—keep the country's spirit up.

Barr replied: "I think you guys are giving him too much prominence. . . . Think about broadening the circle and bringing in an outsider to take the point." And indeed, Scott Atlas started playing a prominent role in the White House about that time (discussed later). Barr deplored "the tiresome cant that decision-making on the virus ought to just 'follow the science'—'science' defined by public health officials like Fauci. This is absurd. 'Science' in a situation like this is rarely fixed, but uncertain and shifting."

Sen. Rand Paul joined the chorus of Fauci detractors, perhaps feeling that his M.D. degree qualified him as an expert.[77] (But it was in ophthalmology; he had no expertise in infectious diseases or epidemiology, did not practice medicine and did not renew his American Board of Ophthalmology certification when it expired in 2005.) When he accused Fauci of praising New York Gov. Cuomo, who "had one of the worst death rates in the world," Fauci bristled: "you misconstrued that, senator, and you've done that repetitively in the past." "In New York, it's about 22 percent" who tested positive. "If you believe 22 percent is herd immunity, I believe you're alone in that." When Paul claimed that another third of the population had cross-reactivity, Fauci exposed Paul's ignorance, pointing to a recent study finding that the other coronaviruses causing the common cold "do not cross-react with the covid-19." In December, the conspiracy theorist Jack Posobiec tweeted: "Dr. Fauci owes @RonPaul an apology." Paul seconded that "he owes one to every single parent and school-age child in America."

Thomas Frieden, Jeffrey Koplan, Savid Satcher and Richard Besser (former CDC Directors under both parties) said: "no president ever politicized its science the way Trump has."[78] "We cannot recall over our collective tenure a single time when political pressure led to a change in the interpretation of scientific evidence." The chief health care officer of the Association of American Medical Colleges called Trump's attack "shocking. When you begin to discredit scientists like Fauci, who are national treasures, you are in serious trouble." But Trump was unrepentant, declaring: "I don't think [Redfield] knows if the pandemic would be worse in the fall." Covid was "going to disappear and I'll be right. Because I've been right probably more than anybody else." The White House prohibited Redfield and other CDC officials from testifying about school reopening before a House Education and Labor Committee hearing, just as it had earlier prohibited Fauci and other Task Force members from testifying before a House Appropriations Committee subcommittee because Congress was full of "Trump haters" and had "all these committees looking for trouble."

Deborah Birx became a punching bag for both parties. On July 27, she said in support of the Virginia governor's pandemic restrictions that people "have gone to the Virginia Beach area . . . and unknowingly bring that virus back."[79] Marc Short angrily texted her that his relatives often vacationed there and accused her of "taking away the livelihoods of people his family knew and cared about." Democrats were no happier with Birx. On July 30, Nancy Pelosi privately told Meadows and Mnuchin: "Deborah Birx is the worst," accusing her of flattering the administration. On CNN's "State of the Union" on August 2, Birx defended her performance, declaring that COVID-19 was "extraordinarily widespread. To everybody who lives in a rural area, you are not immune or protected from this virus." A furious Trump called her the next day:

> What do you think you're doing? Don't you ever do that again. "Extraordinarily widespread"! Do you know how those words scare Americans? . . . Who in Comm[unication]s let you do this. . . . You should be paying more time and attention to listening to what we know instead of spreading reckless lies.

When she maintained that "the virus is widespread," he exploded: "That's it. Do you understand me? Never again! The virus is under control." She refused to back down, warning: "If we don't take action now then the rest of the summer, the fall, and the winter are going to be far worse than what we saw in the spring." However, the president had hung up. (There had been

155,000 deaths when she spoke; there were 550,000 by the end of the following March.)[80] Trump said later that day:

> So crazy Nancy Pelosi said horrible things about Dr. Deborah Birx, going after her because she was too positive on the very good job we are doing on combatting the China Virus, including Vaccines and Therapeutics. In order to counter Nancy, Deborah took the bait & hit us. Pathetic!

(In March 2021, Birx recalled: "I got called by the president. It was very uncomfortable, very direct and very difficult to hear." Trump had "felt very strongly that I misrepresented the pandemic in the United States, that I made it out to be much worse than it is. I felt like I didn't even make it out as bad as it was.")

On July 8, Trump told Bob Woodward, "We're in great shape. Most of the country is headed absolutely away from the virus. We're totally set with our hospitals."[81] When Woodward objected that "it's on fire," Trump retorted:

> Because we did [i.e., tested] 40 million people, anybody that has the sniffles—any kid that has a little bit of a cold, they test positive. And it's going to go away in two days. It's frankly . . . ridiculous.

But two weeks later, he admitted to the first meeting the coronavirus task force had held in three months: "It will probably, unfortunately, get worse before it gets better." He continued to contradict this publicly, however, saying at an August 7 press conference that the pandemic "is disappearing." "It's going to disappear."

On August 3, HBO aired an interview in which Trump told Axios journalist Jonathan Swan: "Take a look at some of these charts. . . . The United States is lowest in numerous categories. We're lower than . . . the world . . . lower than Europe."[82] But Trump did not actually know what the numbers meant. (At the end of June 2020, the U.S. had more than 2.5 million cases and more than 125,000 deaths and was experiencing more than 40,000 new cases a day; Canada had 100,000, 8,500 and 200; UK 300,000, 40,000 and 800; and France 150,000, 30,000 and 700.)[83] He said unspecified "books" and "manuals" claimed the U.S. tested too much and had higher cases "because of the testing." Earlier in the interview, he had said, "they are dying, that's true. . . . it is what it is. But that doesn't mean we aren't doing everything we can. It's under control as much as you can control."

In early August, Fauci told Congress that the summer surge was caused by the failure to shut down.[84] Trump shouted: "wrong! We have more cases because we have tested far more than any other country, 60,000,000. If we tested less, there would be less cases. How did Italy, France & Spain do? Now Europe sadly has flare ups." "With the exception of New York & a few other locations, we've done MUCH better than most other countries in dealing with the China virus." (U.S. cases per capita, which had consistently exceeded those in the rest of the world, quickly soared above those in Europe and far above those in the rest of the world between October 2020 and March 2021, peaking in January 2021.)[85]

When the coronavirus task force was sidelined, Fauci, Birx, Hahn and Redfield formed a "doctors group" to resist the intensifying politicization of the government's handling of the pandemic, agreeing they would resign if anyone was fired.[86] Birx said:

> All of the doctors [on the task force] received death threats. My daughters got the same rude text messages. I mean, you can't even imagine what those text messages looked like. A lot of sexual references, saying, "the country would be better off if you were dead." "You're misleading the country." "Your tongue should be cut out."

She was getting 10–20 death threat letters a week at home. Trump told Azar, Fauci and Birx:

> I am sick and tired of how negative you all are. I am sick and tired of your speculations. I spend half of my day responding to what Tony Fauci has to say, and I'm President of the United States!

He told Fauci, "you've got to stop being so negative!" and said to Birx, "Every time you talk, I get depressed. You have to stop that."

In July, the editorial board of *The Lancet* (one of the world's oldest and most respected medical journals) urged Americans to elect a president "who will understand that public health should not be guided by partisan politics."[87] The editor accused Trump of a "crime against humanity" for cutting WHO funding. The Lancet Commission on Public Policy and Health in the Trump Era later issued a scathing critique of all the administration's policies.[88] In October, for the first time in its 175 years, *Scientific American* made a political endorsement—of Biden.

> The evidence and the science show that Donald Trump has badly damaged the U.S. and its people—because he rejects evidence and science. The most devastating example is his dishonest and inept response to the COVID-19 pandemic, which cost more than 190,000 Americans their lives by the middle of September. He has also attacked environmental protections, medical care, and the researchers and public science agencies that help this country prepare for its greatest challenges.

That month, the *New England Journal of Medicine* also waded into politics for the first time in its 208 years, in an editorial entitled "Dying in a

Leadership Vacuum," signed by all 34 U.S. editors. It called the administration "dangerously incompetent." U.S. "leaders" had "taken a crisis and turned it into a tragedy." "We should not abet them and enable the deaths of thousands more Americans by allowing them to keep their jobs."

> The Centers for Disease Control and Prevention, which was the world's leading disease response organization, has been eviscerated. . . . The National Institutes of Health . . . have been excluded from much crucial government decision making. And the Food and Drug Administration has been shamefully politicized, appearing to respond to pressure from the administration rather than scientific evidence. Our current leaders have undercut trust in science and in government. . . . Instead of relying on expertise, the administration has turned to uninformed "opinion leaders" ' and charlatans who obscure the truth and facilitate the promulgation of outright lies.

That month, *Nature* also endorsed Biden.

> No US president in recent history has so relentlessly attacked and undermined so many valuable institutions, from science agencies to the media, the courts, the Department of Justice—and even the electoral system. Trump claims to put "America First." But in his response to the pandemic, Trump has put himself first, not America.

The journal *Science* published about a dozen editorials criticizing the Trump administration's response to the pandemic and its contempt for science.

The presidents of the National Academy of Sciences and the National Academy of Medicine condemned "the politicization of science, particularly the overriding of evidence and advice from public health officials and the derision of government scientists." 81 Nobel Laureates endorsed Biden: "At no time in our nation's history has there been a greater need for our leaders to appreciate the value of science in formulating public policy." 1,044 current and former CDC Epidemic Intelligence Service officers sent a letter to the administration deploring "the ominous politicization and silencing of the nation's health protection agency."[89] In November, epidemiologists at the Harvard School of Public Health and other institutions wrote:

> ineffective national policies and responses, especially compared to those of other wealthy nations or compared to the intricate preparation and planning by previous administrations of both parties, have been driving the terrible toll of COVID-19 and its inequities in the United States.[90]

Seeking to control public access to the worsening numbers, the administration ordered hospitals to send pandemic data to the politically dominated DHHS instead of the more independent CDC.[91] It was planning to ask governors to "consider" sending the National Guard to hospitals to "help improve data collection." After the President of the American Hospital Association said, "this makes no sense," and the National Governors Association objected, the administration backed down. But CMS said the administration had already ordered hospitals to send it data or risk funding. Nearly three dozen current or former members of the federal Healthcare Infection Control Practices Advisory Committee criticized the action.

6. Alexander and Caputo–Again

On August 8, Alexander emailed Caputo that a forthcoming CDC report about the risk to children was "garbage," "so false" and "so misleading," an attempt "to hurt the public and the administration."[92] "[T]his is about scaring parents and women to hide in the basement and to impact the election." "CDC needs to be schooled and cleaned up." Its officials were "rouge [sic—"rogue"] and up to mischief." Redfield "gots [sic] to start firing people in large numbers there! This agency is working against the President daily!" Alexander wrote Redfield the same day that the Morbidity and Mortality Weekly Reports (MMWRs) were "hit pieces on the administration," "very misleading" and "designed to hurt this Presidnet [sic]." Redfield should do the following:

> put an <u>immediate stop</u> on all CDC MMWR reports due to the incompleteness of reporting. . . . Nothing to go out unless I read and agree with the findings how they [sic] CDC, wrote it and I tweak it to ensure it is fair and balanced and "complete" (emphasis in original).

When Dr. Christine Casey (editor of MMWR Serials) received this, she immediately phoned Dr. Michael Iademarco (who supervised her boss, Dr. Henry Walke) and Redfield, waking them at 2 a.m. Later that morning, Iademarco assured her that "the action of doing nothing was what we were going to do" and directed her to delete Alexander's email. She did so but first printed a hard copy because the exchange had made her "uncomfortable."

MMWR Editor in Chief Charlotte Kent recounted that while on vacation in August, she, too, had been told to delete her copy of Alexander's email to Caputo and Azar and learned that other copies had been deleted on Redfield's order.[93] In March 2021, Redfield confirmed that "I was on more than one occasion called by the [DHHS] secretary [Azar] and his leadership, directing me to change the MMWR. He may deny that, but it's true." Azar did deny it, claiming Trump "has always been receptive to the data and science presented by me and other members of the task force." But CDC publication of a ten-state study of COVID-19 infection numbers was delayed for weeks; and another study suggesting COVID-19 had been present in the U.S. as early as December 2019 was ready for publication in June but still not out in September.

Alexander recommended edits of 19 MMWRs and managed to alter or delay at least five. Schuchat recalled being criticized for publishing an MMWR about efforts to contain covid in early 2020 because it "did not draw the conclusion sought by the Administration—i.e., that everything that could have been done was done." An angry phone call from Meadows left her "very shaken." Azar and his chief of staff also called Redfield to "express their disappointment with this MMWR." Azar warned that "if the CDC would not get in line, then HHS would take control of approving the publication of the MMWRs." After Redfield refused to make changes, Azar and HHS General Counsel Charrow "directed CDC to change the MMWR process and added that if CDC did not follow the direction, then HHS would take MMWRs away from the CDC or stop their publication." CDC capitulated. Starting in May, Alexander, Caputo and others were added to the distribution list of advance summaries. Casey said this "unprecedented" action "breached" the "production firewall." Walke called it "ridiculous and such an overreach." Charlotte Kent, chief of the CDC scientific publications branch, threatened to resign publicly. Redfield told Caputo that Alexander's emails were "inappropriate" and should stop. But nothing happened until *Politico* sought an HHS comment about Caputo. Within two days, Nina Witkofsky (a nonscientist political appointee who was named acting CDC chief of staff after Kyle McGowan resigned) told Kent to remove Alexander from the distribution list "because of all the comments and crazy stuff he wrote." Nevertheless, two days after that, Alexander told Caputo he was "making a formal request for CDC to provide us with complete reports when asking for our clearance and input" and demanding "ample time to review before publishing." He asked HHS to review "all CDC MMWR reporting in the last 6 months." The same day, an appalled Caputo replied:

> Are you watching the news today? Your email demands of the CDC are leading every network news program and will lead the Sunday shows. Every major newspaper too. This is not a good place for you to be—and you put me there too. Do you think this is a job well done? Don't send any emails to anyone outside APSA until further notice.

Three days after that, HHS announced that Alexander had left the Department and Caputo would take medical leave.

Emails published in September revealed that Alexander directed NIH press officers and others to tell Fauci what to say to the media because Alexander "vehemently" disagreed with Fauci about "kids getting tested . . . and even university students in a widespread manner."[94] He told Fauci's press team:

> ensure Dr. Fauci indicates masks are for the teachers in schools. Not for children. There is no data, none, zero, across the entire world, that shows children, especially young children, spread this virus to other children, or to adults, or to their teachers. None. And if it did occur, the risk is essentially zero.

Fauci had been unaware of Alexander's actions but insisted: "no one tells me what I can say and cannot say. I speak on scientific evidence." His spokesperson added: "I don't feel it is correct to say there is 'no evidence. . . . ' Or that 'they take influenza home but do not take covid home.'" Alexander replied that there is "little, if any evidence" of transmission by children and wearing masks would be "traumatic" for them. "I am saying that rct [randomized controlled trials] evidence should not be considered the gold standard." "If the NIH's position is that rct evidence is your standard, then this must change." (In February 2021, the CDC said: "children and adolescents can also transmit SARS-CoV-2 infection to others.")[95]

Caputo acknowledged in September that Alexander and he had been seeking greater scrutiny of the MMWRs for 3.5 months.[96] "Our intention is to make sure that evidence, science-based data drives policy through this pandemic—not ulterior deep state motives in the bowels of CDC." Alexander's:

> position isn't popular with the career scientists sometimes. That's called science. Disagreement is science. Nobody has ever been ordered to do anything. Some changes have been accepted, most have been rejected. It's my understanding that that's how science is played.

Alexander was more combative. From June 30 to September 4, he had delayed the MMWR, concluding that "the potential benefits of [HCQ and CQ] do not appear to outweigh their risks," as well as a report about the spread of COVID at a Georgia sleepaway camp, which said children of all ages were susceptible and could communicate the disease. He complained to the CDC that the MMWRs "send the wrong message . . . NOT to re-open." He had written Redfield on August 8, demanding an "immediate stop" to reports until he could make line edits.

> The reports must be read by someone outside of CDC like myself, and we cannot allow the reporting to go on as it has been, for it is outrageous. Its [sic] lunacy. . . . Nothing to go out unless i [sic] read and agree with the findings how the CDC wrote it and i [sic] tweak it to ensure it is fair and balanced and "complete."

He wrote Caputo and Azar:

> *I request that CDC go back to that report and insert this* [or] *else Michael, pull it down and stop all reports immediately* [highlighted in red in the original.] CDC to me appears to be writing hit pieces on the administration. CDC tried to report as if once kids get together, there will be spread and this will impact school reopening. . . . that was the aim and that's how it read and its [sic] disingenuous. Very misleading by CDC and shame on them. Their aim is clear. This hurts any president or administration. This is designed to hurt this Presidenet [sic] for their reasons which I am not interested in. I am interested in this or any President being served fairly and their tax payers [sic] money not be used for political reasons. They, CDC, work for him. The public wants honesty and fair reporting so that they can be informed, not to be deceived.

Caputo explained: "most often, the MMWRs are [issued] for purely scientific reasons. But in an election year, and in the time of Covid-19, it's no longer unanimously scientific. There's political content." "Whenever they come out with that list"—one paragraph summaries of MMWRs—"there's concern across [DHHS] that some of the scholarship has been tainted by politics." "It must be difficult for [CDC] to be criticized by an Oxford-educated scientist who has been published in peer-reviewed journals 67 times." (Alexander had a master's from Oxford; there was no indication of the content of the articles, where they were published and whether they were co-authored.) Trump complained that the CDC was "asking schools to do very impractical things. I will be meeting with them!!!" Pence said that because "we just don't want the guidance to be too tough . . . the CDC is going to be issuing a new set of tools." Trump had earlier told Senate Republicans that because the CDC "blew it" on covid tests, he had installed a team of "geniuses" led by Kushner (who had no scientific training).

On August 30, Alexander wrote acting CDC Chief of Staff Witkofsky:

> the last 2 MMWR reports have been more positive than usual and I find [that] encouraging. Have we been able to at last to [sic] impress upon them that it is easy to see how they report? And now they are forced to balance? . . . Maybe you are having a huge impact and this is tremendous. Well done![97]

He wrote Caputo on September 9, claiming success in two "examples of CDC adjusting writing based on my inquiry," a "small victory but a victory nonetheless and yippee!!!" Two days later, he asked Atlas: "can you help me craft an op-ed on possible damage to children [sic] immune systems with lock downs and masks?" "I do think locking down our kids (and healthy adults) and masking them can dampen their functional immune systems." (There was no evidence for this.) The two men wanted to rebut a CDC report on COVID deaths among young people, which Atlas claimed had been "timed for the election" in order to keep schools closed. Alexander said: "We need to blunt the edge as it is misleading"; instead, CDC should "help people push back to school." Alexander edited the September 15 op ed, in which Atlas declared: "Science tells us that young adults are at extremely low risk for serious illness or death from COVID-19." Atlas quoted epidemiologist John Ionnidis (his colleague at Stanford) that the risk of dying was "almost zero" and concluded: "The president's approach is based on the demands of science and common sense." (Ionnidis had pronounced on cable news the previous spring that no more than 10,000 Americans would die and condemned social distancing.) Alexander wrote Caputo on September 13:

> in my view the parents got it [COVID] more likely when they picked up the kids and came into contact with the school personnel or teachers as happens with my wife and I when we pick up our kids form [sic] school.

(He offered no evidence for this.) Caputo had written Alexander on May 16: "I know the president wants us to enumerate the cost of not reopening. We need solid estimates to be able to say something like: 50,000 more cancer deaths! 40,000 more heart attacks! 25,000 more suicides!" "You need to take ownership of these numbers. This is singularly important to what you and I want to achieve." (There was no evidence for these numbers.)

Caputo launched a public relations campaign "to defeat despair and inspire hope," with a budget of nearly $300 million, which Congress had intended for coronavirus relief.[98] He claimed this was "demanded of me by the President of the United States. Personally," and Democrats were "dead set against it" because "they cannot afford for us to have any good news before November because they're already losing." He hired cronies without competitive bids; one company, owned by a business associate, had no public record. The campaign slogans were "Helping the President will Help the Country" and "Keep America Well." (The first sounded embarrassingly like "What's good for General Motors is good for the country," smugly pronounced by GM's former CEO who had become Eisenhower's Secretary of Defense; the second was an ungrammatical knockoff of "Make America Great Again.") Caputo created PSA Celebrity Tracker to determine whether potential endorsers favored or opposed Trump, rejecting 264 of the 274 who were considered—Jennifer Lopez for criticizing Trump's immigration policies; three of the ten chosen withdrew. Caputo abandoned the campaign in less than two months, after spending $1.5 million to film just two and a half public service announcements, none of which aired.

A day after learning that his recent scan had found cancer, Caputo wrote on Facebook on September 13:[99]

> There are scientists working for the government who do not want America to get better. . . . It must be all bad news from now until the election. Frankly, ladies and gentlemen, that's sedition. They are sacrificing lives in order to defeat DT . . . this is war. Joe Biden is *not going to concede*. . . . They're going to have to kill me, and unfortunately I think that's where this is going . . .. my health is failing. My mental health is definitely failing. I don't like being alone in Washington. The shadows on the ceiling in my apartment, there alone, those shadows are so long.

He and his family "have been continually threatened and in and out of criminal court dealing with harassment prosecutions." "I don't like being alone in Washington" because "I can't carry a gun." He extolled Alexander as "a genius" and accused the CDC of harboring a "resistance unit" that sought to undermine Trump. Scientists "deep in the bowels of CDC" walked "around like they are monks" and "holy men." They engaged in "rotten science" and had become "political animals." They "haven't gotten out of their sweatpants except for meetings at coffee shops" to plot "how they're going to attack Donald Trump next." "To allow people to die so that you can replace the president" was a "grievous sin." "And these people are all going to hell." He predicted Trump would win the election, but Biden would refuse to accept the result.

> And when Donald Trump refuses to stand down at the inauguration, the shooting will begin. The drills that you've seen [BLM demonstrations in Portland] are nothing. If you carry guns, buy ammunition, ladies and gentlemen, because it's going to be hard to get.

"There are hit squads being trained all over this country." "You understand that they're going to have to kill me, and unfortunately, I think that's where this is going." (This was a bizarrely prophetic account of what Trump and his supporters did on January 6.)

After making these statements, Caputo deactivated his personal Twitter and Facebook accounts and apologized to HHS staff for accusing scientists of "sedition." But DHHS continued to defend him as "a critical, integral part of the president's coronavirus response, leading on public messaging as Americans need public health information to defeat the covid-19 pandemic." Caputo had defiantly vowed on his Facebook page: "They will not move me. I'm not going anywhere. You know why? Because the President of the United States supports me." But on September 16, he took a 60-day leave to "focus on his health and the well-being of his family" and never returned. The same day (and soon after, *Politico* revealed Alexander's efforts to influence the MMWRs), DHHS said Alexander also would be leaving "permanently," and McMaster University said he was neither teaching nor speaking for it. But he was unrepentant: CDC had written "pseudoscientific reports." "None of those people have my skills. I make the judgment whether this is crap."

7. Scott Atlas

In April, Trump introduced Scott W. Atlas to the coronavirus task force. This senior fellow at Stanford's conservative Hoover Institution optimistically predicted: "Coronavirus is going to be gone by September. By the end of September, it will be a memory." Fauci replied, "I don't think that's correct."[100] (He was right: at the end of September 2020, there had been just over 7 million confirmed cases; 30 months later, the total had exceeded 103 million.)[101] Atlas confidently promised 100 million vaccine doses by the end of the year, later lowering this to 30 million. (In fact, just 4 million were available by early January.)

Because White House Communications Director Hope Hicks and Presidential Personnel Office Director Johnny McEntee had admired Atlas on Fox News, McEntee invited him to the White House in mid-July to meet Pence, Meadows, Stephen Miller, Kayleigh McEnany and others. That month, Kushner secretly hired Atlas to "help advise the president" (although he was a radiologist with no expertise in virology or epidemiology), directing him not to identify himself on conference calls. Atlas attended at least half a dozen meetings to brief Trump before press conferences and was authorized to publish at least two op eds. He had already published one in *The Hill* on April 22 entitled "The Data Is In—Stop the Panic and End the Total Isolation," declaring:

> We know from decades of medical science that infection itself allows people to generate an immune response—antibodies—so that the infection is controlled throughout the population by "herd immunity." Indeed, that is the main purpose of widespread immunization in other viral diseases—to assist with population immunity. . . . the overwhelming majority of people do not have any significant risk of dying from COVID-19 . . . vital population immunity is prevented by total isolation policies, prolonging the problem.

He said on Fox News Radio in July:

> These people getting the infection is not really a problem, and in fact, as we said months ago, when you isolate everyone, including the healthy

> people, you're prolonging the problem because you're preventing population immunity. Low-risk groups getting the infection is not a problem. In fact, it's a positive. . . . younger, healthier people . . . don't have a problem with the disease.

(By the end of July, there had been 91 covid deaths of those 0–17, increasing from 7 in March to 29 in July, and 752 covid deaths of those 18–29, increasing from 47 to 232. For all ages, there had been 150,000.)[102] He believed herd immunity required that just 20 percent be infected.

On August 12, Trump appointed Atlas to the Task Force, praising him:

> a very famous man who's also very highly respected. He's working with us and will be working with us on the coronavirus. And he has many great ideas. And he thinks what we've done is really good, and now we'll take it to a new level.

Atlas produced an undated "Strategy for Moving Forward: Covid-19," reiterating:

> The current strategy is misguided, because it is focused too broadly on "stopping all cases" and widespread testing. Stopping all cases is not necessary, nor is it possible. It instills irrational fear into [sic] the public.

Widespread testing "sets up an unattainable goal that is harming the president." Atlas touted unidentified "emerging research . . . suggesting that herd immunity may arise with a far lower population infection rate than originally thought." He helped write a Trump speech announcing that "our targeted strategy" would focus on "the high-risk group" and eliminate other measures so that the response no longer "interferes with the fastest route to eradicating the virus, population immunity."

Atlas had said in June that the goal was "a population [that] has enough people who have had the infection, and since these people don't have a problem with the infection, that's not a problem."[103] It was "literally irrational" to close schools: "there is a minimal, if any, risk of children transmitting the disease, even to their parents." He wrote an August 3 memo, "Specific Notes on Prioritized Testing," deploring that "people have been convinced that 'testing, testing, testing' is urgent for everyone—that is false." It was "harmful to do massive testing, especially since actions on many positive tests are not always necessary." It "would be both hugely disruptive to society, and interfere with the critical population immunity needed to eradicate the threat (not to mention contrary to American values of personal freedom)." "Lockdowns" would "hurt Americans more than the virus." That day, he asserted that children "have no risk for serious illness" and "they're not significant spreaders." "There should never be and there is no goal to stop college students from getting an infection they have no problem with." "[P]eople are kidding themselves" if they think testing is valuable. He called data about masks "very controversial" and railed against "the massive amount of fear bordering on hysteria." Kevin Hassett (a former chair of Trump's Council of Economic Advisers, who had advised the White House in the spring) called Atlas "a legendary physician, and one of the smartest guys I know." Rush Limbaugh said he was "a brilliant guy," who was "countering Fauci" and thinks that "by early October we could well be burned out of covid." Atlas himself boasted of being "contrarian" and "anti-Fauci" and said *The Lancet* and *NEJM* "feel compelled to be politically visible" and had "contaminated the discussion" with peer-reviewed articles that were "garbage science."

When Birx urged testing, masking and social distancing at an August 8 Task Force meeting, Atlas declared:

> I couldn't disagree more strongly. . . . No matter what we do, the outcome is going to be the same. *The same*! You don't need to mitigate. You don't need to test. All we need to do . . . is to protect the most vulnerable.[104]

Birx objected that "we can't protect the vulnerable if the virus is already in the community." Atlas (characteristically) interrupted her, maintaining that children did not get COVID, were not at risk if they did and could not transmit it; long COVID was exaggerated; heart damage findings were incidental; comorbidities were irrelevant; and testing falsely increased case counts. He concluded by playing his trump card: "You're going against the president's policies." (Subsequent studies strongly confirmed Birx's position that non-pharmaceutical interventions were effective.)[105]

On August 11, Birx emailed Fauci, Redfield and Hahn about that "very dangerous" Oval Office meeting, in which Atlas had declared "testing is very over rating [sic]" and "case identification is bad for the president's reelection—testing should only be of the sick."[106] He had claimed that the Task Force "got us into this ditch by promoting testing and falsely increasing case counts compared to other countries." On August 13, Birx saw a March 21 email from Atlas (forwarded by CMS Administrator Seema Verna):

> The total lockdown is a *massive overreaction* and super harmful to our entire society, destroying the economy, inciting irrational fear, and even diverting medical care away from sick people. . . . *Fear of exposure, or people who are without symptoms who are outside priority groups, do not need urgent testing, and should not seek it.* (emphasis in original)

That day, Birx emailed senior health officials, complaining that Atlas insisted COVID was comparable to the flu and "children are immune."

The Task Force approved a testing guidance; though weaker, it still recommended that those in close contact with someone infected isolate for 14 days.[107] But Atlas "aggressively spoke to [Redfield] in loud terms," declaring he lacked the authority to do that. And when the guidance was published on August 24, that recommendation had been deleted, over the objections of Giroir, Schuchat and Redfield. Giroir maintained "there was no weight on the scales by the President or the Vice President or Secretary Azar" and insisted that "all the doctors [on the Task Force] signed off on this . . . before it got to a place where the political leadership would have ever seen it." But Fauci observed: "I was under general anesthesia in the operating room last Thursday [August 22] and was not part of any discussion or deliberation regarding these new testing recommendations." He was "worried it will give people the incorrect assumption that asymptomatic spread is not of great concern. In fact, it is." The previous CDC Incident Manager of COVID-19 Response said the guidance "did not . . . align[] with the science." The current manager, Walke, feared it sent "the message that testing wasn't important anymore." Birx warned that "this marks the third week with significant declines in testing," with the result that "we cannot see the community spread that maybe [sic] happening." Atlas replied that Birx's "interpretation of the information is seriously incorrect and leads to wrong, harmful policy decisions." "The 'alarm' of fewer tests makes no sense" and "pushing more testing is destructive to opening." He wanted to make the tests less sensitive because he asserted (without evidence) that "the overwhelming majority of PCR tests are misleadingly positive." That month, Birx wrote Fauci, Hahn and Redfield, warning that the "Atlas Dogma" was "a true threat to a comprehensive and critical response to this pandemic" and would "reverse months of incredibly hard won gains" if "allowed to gain traction."

Dr. Thomas Frieden (Obama's CDC Director) said: "H.H.S. and the White House writing scientifically inaccurate statements such as 'don't test all contacts' on C.D.C.'s website is like someone vandalizing a national monument with graffiti." The Infectious Diseases Society of America was equally critical. AMA President Susan R. Bailey called the guidance "a recipe for community spread and more spikes in coronavirus." Harold Varmus (a former NIH Director) and Dr. Rajiv Shah (Rockefeller Foundation president, physician and health economist) accused the CDC of "promoting policies that prolong" the pandemic. California Gov. Newsom tweeted: "this will not be the policy of the State of California." Washington Gov. Inslee said the guidance would make his state "miss thousands of new cases and allow the virus to spread in our communities." New York Gov. Cuomo called the change "indefensible" and "political propaganda." "The only plausible rationale is that they want fewer people taking tests, because as the president has said, if we don't take tests, you won't know the number of people who are covid-positive." The National Association of County and City Health Officials and the Big Cities

Health Coalition urged Giroir and Redfield to reverse the guidance, and at least 33 states continued testing exposed asymptomatic people. When DoJ said it was considering investigating New York, New Jersey, Pennsylvania and Michigan COVID deaths in nursing homes, Cuomo and Michigan Gov. Whitmer called it a "nakedly partisan deflection" of their criticisms of testing cutbacks. On September 18, CDC reversed the guidance, recommending that all those who had been in close contact with someone with COVID should test and then isolate for 14 days, regardless of the test outcome.

Atlas said at an August Task Force meeting that herd immunity would be achieved with just 30 percent infected.[108] "You see why we're not seeing an increase in infections in these cities that were infected in February, March, April, and May? It's herd immunity." Redfield replied that 85–95 percent of the population had to be infected for herd immunity. (He later told the Select Subcommittee: "I thought for COVID-19, that there is no herd immunity.") Fauci challenged Atlas after the meeting: "you had places that went way up [in case numbers] and came down and then went back up again so how is that herd immunity?" (Indeed, although daily new cases nationwide declined to 25,000 in September, they increased tenfold to 250,000 in January 2021.)[109] At a meeting in late August, Atlas attacked Birx: "You just want to shut down the country! I speak for the president, and we are not shutting down the country!" Birx retorted: "just know that you are killing people."

Trump confirmed Atlas's influence by parroting him on Laura Ingraham's Fox program on August 31: "Well, once you get to a certain number—we use the word 'herd,' right—once you get to a certain number it's going to go away."[110] Atlas seemed embarrassed, falsely asserting the next day: "There's never been any advocacy of a herd immunity strategy coming from me to the president, to anyone in the administration, to the task force, to anyone I've spoken to." Undaunted, Trump said at a public event two weeks later: "you'll develop herd—like a herd mentality." (The real herd mentality was displayed by Trump and his epigones.) "It's going to be herd-developed, and that's going to happen." But Azar told the Select Subcommittee on October 2: "Herd immunity is not the strategy of the U.S. government with regard to coronavirus."

On August 25, Atlas organized a White House roundtable with Bhattacharya, Kulldorff and Meissner, authors of the Great Barrington Declaration, and Joseph Ladapo (all discussed later). Birx declared:

> I can't be part of this with these people who believe in herd immunity and believe we are fine with only protecting the 1.5M Americans in LTCF [long-term care facilities] and not the 80M+ with comorbidities included [sic] the unacceptable death toll among Native Americans, Hispanics and Blacks.[111]

(Compared with those for white people, death rates were twice as high for American Indian or Alaska Native and 1.7 and 1.6 times as high for Hispanic and Black people.[112] Birx later wrote that more than 130,000 lives could have been saved by "optimal mitigation across the country." More died of covid between November 1, 2020, and March 1, 2021, than any other four-month period.) Birx complained that the four doctors "believe that all the curves are predetermined and mitigation is irrelevant—they are a fringe group without grounding in epidemics, public health or on the ground common sense experience." When Kushner proposed canceling the meeting, Atlas protested that he would be "very upset," it would be unacceptable and Trump should meet the doctors. The meeting took place and lasted far longer than planned. Redfield said Atlas organized the event "to convince people that herd immunity was going to save us, and this thing [COVID-19] was going to go bye-bye."

Atlas constantly interrupted Birx at Task Force meetings, disputing her (accurate) assertion of asymptomatic transmission. Fauci objected that "instead of looking at the data and making a conclusion, [Atlas] makes a conclusion and picks up the data to fill in." Fauci told Birx that Atlas's claims were "so ridiculous" but added: "maybe we should sit down with him." Birx replied: "This guy is fucking crazy. We can't deal with him. He's a nutcase." When a reporter wrote that he had overheard Redfield stating on the phone that "everything [Atlas] says is false," Atlas responded: "everything I have ever said is directly from the data and the science. It echoes what is said by many of the top medical scientists in the world, including those at Stanford, Harvard, and Oxford" (the affiliations of the Great Barrington Declaration authors named earlier). But even Fox News host Chris Wallace told viewers to "wear the damn mask." "Dr. Scott Atlas is not an epidemiologist, is not an infectious disease expert—he has no training in this area at all." "Listen to people like Anthony Fauci . . . Deborah Birx." On September 11, when YouTube took down a Hoover Institution interview in which Atlas said younger people could not transmit the virus, he complained that this was the kind of censorship found in "Third World countries—the countries we used to be proudly distinguished from." In October, Fauci expressed concern that Atlas and his cronies "created a false equivalency." People say: " 'Well, one smart doctor says this and another smart doctor says that, and so who knows whose [sic—"who's"] right?' " "That is really dangerous . . . because in reality you may have one smart doctor or a group of smart doctors who are right and the other smart doctor who is actually dead wrong."

In late August, Birx told Pence: "what I have been saying and what I will continue to say in every state contradicts what the president is saying publicly," which was Atlas's line. Pence appeared to side with her: "You need to do what you need to do."[113] But Marc Short prohibited her from designating counties in her reports as red and yellow (because their case numbers were high), threatening that if she did so, "the reports won't go out." She responded by burying those data in the state-specific recommendations to governors (which Short did not bother to read). When she and Redfield rewrote a CDC guidance and put it on the Centers website without seeking approval, Meadows called and asked angrily: "What the hell do you think you're doing. . . . There's no 'buts' here. You went over my head. . . . You went around the whole approval process. You do not make unilateral decisions. It's that simple." She replied: "I did what I needed to do." He repeated: "don't do that again without talking to me first" but did not remove the guidelines.

In mid-September, Olivia Troye quit her job as Pence's coronavirus task force representative, accusing Trump of promulgating "false narratives and incorrect information of the virus" and endorsing Biden.[114] Pence dismissed her as "a disgruntled employee that has decided to play politics during an election year." Trump claimed he had "no idea who she is." Lt. Gen. Keith Kellogg (Pence's National Security Adviser) maintained he had fired her for poor performance and escorted her out of the White House. McEnany attacked both her, and Miles Taylor (who earlier had resigned as DHS chief of staff in protest against politicization) as "profile[s] in cowardice" (inverting the title of JFK's well-known book "Profiles in Courage"). The same month, Max Kennedy Jr. (Robert's grandson) disclosed that, as a member of the COVID-19 Supply Chain Task Force the previous spring, he had been instructed by Brad Smith (CMS deputy administrator, a political appointee) to create a model of the pandemic because the experts' models were "too catastrophic." "They think 250,000 people could die," Smith said, "and I want this model to show that fewer than 100,000 people will die in the worst-case scenario." Smith told Kennedy:

> Just put a growth rate on it and make sure it ends up at the right numbers. It just needs to be a model that shows a worst case of one hundred thousand people dying and a low case of twenty thousand.

"Look around. Does it look like 250,000 people are going to die? I don't think so." Kennedy and another volunteer refused, and he soon quit, but Kevin Hassett, former CEA chair, produced the desired model. (There had been 16,000 deaths by April 2020; three years later, there were more than a million—four times the figure Smith wanted to counter.)[115]

After Birx told Pence's office she wanted Atlas off the Task Force, the Vice President directed the two of them to work out their disagreements.[116] Atlas was unrepentant: "any policy discussion where data isn't being challenged isn't a policy discussion." He "emphatically" denied that anyone had advocated "a wide-open strategy of achieving herd immunity." But he endorsed the Great Barrington Declaration (later) and tweeted: "Masks work? NO."

(Twitter removed the tweet for misinformation but only after it had been retweeted 1,800 times and received 73,000 likes and replies and appeared on Facebook pages.) He told the Task Force: "Young people have very low risk of this. In fact, for people under 70, the case mortality of this is less than 0.5 percent." (That was little comfort to the 185,208 people 50–64 who had died from COVID as of April 13, 2022, representing 1.4 percent of the 12,903,508 people in that age group who contracted the disease.)[117]

On September 9, 78 researchers and doctors at Stanford Medical School accused Atlas of advocating "falsehoods and misrepresentations of science."[118] A week later, 98 faculty members repeated this to *The Stanford Daily*. Atlas stopped attending Task Force meetings at the end of the month. In November, 85 percent of the Stanford University Faculty Senate voted to condemn Atlas's "disdain for established medical knowledge," which "violates medical ethics."

> We support using masks, social distancing, and conducting surveillance and diagnostic testing. We also believe in the importance of strictly following the guidance of local and state health authorities. Dr. Atlas has expressed views that are inconsistent with the university's approach in response to the pandemic.

Condoleezza Rice (who had been Bush's Secretary of State and now headed the Hoover Institution, where Atlas was a fellow) said his views were inconsistent with Hoover's policies on masks, social distancing and testing. But he retained his position there, even though he was no longer a member of the medical school faculty.

Just before the election, Atlas gave an interview that was aired on the Russian propaganda outlet RT, accusing the media of "gross distortion" and a "frenzy of focusing on the number of cases" and declaring that "the disease is deadly only to the elderly and the high-risk people."[119] He tweeted about "lockdowns, facts, frauds," sneering: "if you can't handle the truth, use a mask to cover your eyes and ears." He subsequently apologized for giving the interview, claiming he had not known RT was an official organ of the Russian government. (Michael Flynn made a similar mistake, see Abel 2024a.) A month after the election, he resigned as Trump's coronavirus adviser.

Several weeks later, Atlas wrote *The Washington Post*: "I firmly deny the false accusations that . . . I advocated for 'herd immunity' via letting the infection spread as a scientific approach to the pandemic."[120] But he had said on *Tucker Carlson Tonight* on Fox News on June 29:

> [W]e're going to see more cases. . . . the overwhelming majority of these cases are younger, healthier people. These people . . . do not have the serious complications. They do not die. And so it's fantastic news that we

> have a lot of cases but we don't see deaths going up. . . . We like the fact that there's a lot of cases in low-risk populations because that's exactly how we're going to get herd immunity, population immunity.

He had assured Fox News's Laura Ingraham on July 23: "the fatality rate is much lower." (Daily COVID deaths increased more than sixfold, from 523 on July 4, 2020, to 3,403 on January 13, 2021.)[121] Fauci said of Atlas:

> If you ever wanted to spread confusion and give license to the people in the cities and states who did not want to abide by any of the public health measures, you gave them license to do it. They could say, "look, this guy who's a well-respected Stanford person who the president seems to like is saying this thing; why should we listen to Fauci?" I think he was disruptive to what Birx and I were trying to do.

Atlas was not the only self-styled expert opposing the leading government scientists. On September 3, Steven Hatfill (Navarro's unpaid adviser) wrote: "I actually lost it and told Fauci he was full of crap a couple of weeks ago" for opposing HCQ.[122] "Two members of the COVID-19 Task Force (Drs. Fauci and Hahn) need to be urgently replaced with a *competent multidisciplinary team of doctors and public health experts actually experienced in operational medicine* [emphasis in original]." On September 19, Hatfill emailed a White House official: "States favorable to Trump have a lower COVID Case Fatality Rate than the [shit] states that do not." (That was true of densely populated cities in New York and California during the pandemic's early months but had reversed permanently by the end of June.) On September 22, Hatfill wrote Meadows: "the President has been grossly misadvised by the COVID Task Force on the proper pandemic response to COVID-19" and again recommended HCQ. (Hatfill, an American, had failed his M ChB degree at the University of Rhodesia before receiving it a year later, doing a one-year internship in a rural South African hospital and working for the apartheid government for two years. He began but never completed a Ph.D., though he falsely claimed that degree and three master's degrees. He also falsely claimed to have been a "captain in the U.S. Special Forces." Virginia revoked his license to practice medicine in 2004 for providing false information in his renewal application. Even his lawyer admitted that Hatfill had "puffed on his resume" and "forged a diploma.")

8. Pressure for a Vaccine

On September 4, Trump said a vaccine would "probably" be ready in October.[123] "The vaccine will be very safe and very effective, and it'll be delivered very soon. You could have a very big surprise coming up . . . even during the month of October." "We'll have the vaccine soon, maybe before a special date. You know what date I'm talking about." This provoked immediate resistance. The FDA's Peter Marks, who had told the NIH vaccine working group in August he would resign if there were political interference with his agency, reiterated this threat. Moncef Slaoui (Operation Warp Speed head and former GlaxoSmithKline CEO) said there was "no intent" to administer the vaccine before the independent safety monitoring board had affirmed its effectiveness and seconded Marks's threat. Azar said: "President Trump has made it clear, and I've made it clear, these decisions will be driven by the standards of science and evidence and FDA's gold standards." After the BioN-Tech founder warned that vaccines "could be politicized," Pfizer CEO Albert Bourla organized a full-page ad in *The New York Times* on September 8 by Pfizer, BioN-Tech, Moderna, AstraZeneca, GlaxoSmithKline, Sanofi, Johnson & Johnson, Merck and Novavax (all of which were developing vaccines), promising to "stand with science" to make the "safety and well-being" of those vaccinated their "top priority" and "adhere to high scientific and ethical standards" for clinical trials. NIH Director Collins advised Congress that predicting the date a drug would be approved "is well beyond anything that any scientist right now could tell you." After a test subject contracted an unexplained illness, AstraZeneca halted its trial, saying: "we cannot compromise on safety." On September 10, the Directors of the seven main FDA centers (all career officials) wrote a *USA Today* op ed:[124]

> We continue to make decisions on the safety and effectiveness of medical products based on the available science. . . . Maintaining the American public's trust in the FDA is vital. If the agency's credibility is lost because of real or perceived interference, people will not rely on the agency's safety warnings. Erosion of public trust will leave consumers and patients doubting our recommendations. . . . Protecting the FDA's independence is essential if we are to do the best possible job of protecting public health and saving lives.

FDA Commissioner Hahn said: "I wholeheartedly agree with them."

On September 15, Trump declared optimistically on *Fox & Friends*: "we're rounding the turn on the pandemic." "We're going to have a vaccine in a matter of weeks . . . will it be before the election? It could be."[125] At a news conference, he said optimistically that the vaccine "could be announced in October" and distributed "to the general public immediately—when we go, we go." After Biden questioned whether a vaccine approved by this administration would be safe, Trump condemned the comment as "anti-vaccine." But a day later, Redfield cautioned a Senate committee that only a "very limited supply" of vaccines might be available to health care workers and the most vulnerable in November or December; the "American public" would have to wait until late second or third quarter of 2021. Giroir told the Senate the same thing. Slaoui had earlier said on NPR there would be enough vaccines for 20–25 million by the end of the year and the rest of the population by mid-2021. Until then, Redfield added, masks are "the most important, powerful public health tool we have," indeed "more guaranteed to protect me against Covid than when I take a Covid vaccine."

Told by Azar's deputy not to contradict the president, Redfield replied: "I have a higher calling to tell the truth." But in a concession to Trump, he backed away from his emphasis on masks, adding: "I 100 percent believe in the importance of vaccines and the importance in particular of a Covid-19 vaccine." Trump retorted that Redfield had "made a mistake. . . . It's just incorrect information." The vaccine would be available "to the general public, immediately"; "under no circumstance will it be as late as the doctor said." "We think we can start sometime in October. So as soon as it's announced, we'll be ready to start." "We'll be able to distribute at least one hundred million vaccine doses by the end of 2020, and a large number much sooner than that." He added: "There are people that don't think masks are good." "I see that in restaurants there are people with masks and they're playing around with their mask and their fingers are in their mask and then they're serving with plates." "We did a great job" about COVID-19 "except, public relations-wise, my people got outplayed." He denied minimizing the pandemic: "I actually, in many ways, up-played it, in terms of action. . . . with a vaccine, I think it will go away very quickly." Meadows echoed his boss: "we can get the vast majority of those at risk with a distribution model that would be available at the end of October" and 300 million doses in January. "If I were a betting man, I would bet on President Trump." Redfield's timetable was "not based on those that are closest to the process." (Meadows would have lost his bet; only 2.9 million people were vaccinated in 2020, little more than a tenth of the eligible 21 million health care workers and just 170,000 of the 3 million nursing home residents.)[126] Trump had fumed to Azar in August: "These drug companies and Hahn and the FDA. They're going to keep us from having a vaccine before the election. They're going to delay this. You've got to stop them." But in September, Azar had warned Trump that "we are not going to get a vaccine before the election." The president responded: "Putin approved Sputnik and then got the data later." (The Russians launched Sputnik in 1959, when Putin was seven years old.) Azar warned: "If we do that, nobody will take the vaccine. . . . If career people at FDA don't sign off on this, we have something people will literally never take."

When *The Washington Post* reported on September 22 that FDA guidelines made it "unlikely [a vaccine] will be cleared by Election Day," Trump accused Hahn and the FDA of "colluding to prevent his re-election." Hahn replied: "I was adamant about the fact that we weren't going to change one word of that document . . . because I knew that the minute we changed one word in that guidance people would not trust our process." The White House complained that "this false narrative that Democrats and some in the media are advancing, suggesting that politics is influencing approvals, is unconscionable and dangerous."

Hahn had promised Congress the FDA would not be "pressured by anyone."[127] "I want to assure and emphasize [that] every one of the decisions we have reached has been made by career FDA scientists based on science and data, not politics." The agency wanted manufacturers to provide safety data on clinical trial participants for two months after the second shot. Hahn said Meadows urged the FDA to "try to shrink this as much as possible," and officials in Azar's office and the White House objected that two months was not "appropriate." Hahn resisted this pressure because the guidance "needed to stay in the scientific and clinical domain" and "any changes would be obviously reported and would further reduce vaccine confidence."

On September 23, Meadows told Hahn during a Task Force meeting that the White House would not sign off on the FDA guidance.[128] Trump complained that the agency's plan to require tougher standards for emergency use authorization of vaccines "sounds like a political move more than anything else" and "has to be approved by the White House," which "may or may not approve it." The same day, Marks sent FDA Principal Deputy Commissioner Amy Abernathy an early draft of the vaccine surveillance plan, noting that the agency had advised sponsors of the vaccine EUA request to submit Phase Three trial data "that include a median follow-up duration of at least two months after completion of the full vaccination regimen to help provide adequate information to assess a vaccine's benefit-risk profile." The plan had appeared in the media before the White House had a chance to comment. Trump protested: "Why would they be adding great length to the process?" "That's a lot of lives you're talking about." Attorney General Barr backed his boss (in a speech about the legal system): "all this nonsense about how something is dictated by science is nonsense." When Trump proposed firing Hahn, Azar warned: "if you fire an FDA commissioner in the middle of this, we'll get a vaccine that no one will take." Asked by Trump simply to approve it, Azar explained that "it has to work its way through the FDA process, but trust me to work with Peter Marks to get the job done."

When Johnson & Johnson announced progress on its vaccine, Trump welcomed the "Big news," adding: "@FDA must move quickly!" He had "tremendous trust in these massive companies" testing the vaccines. "I don't know that a government" as big as "the federal government could do as well." (He disregarded the radically different incentive structures, which had been the reason for creating the FDA more than a century earlier.) The FDA decision "has to be approved by the White House. We may or may not approve it." The same day, Meadows told Hahn the FDA had to provide a "very detailed justification" for the standards. "I found it very interesting that we would actually have a new guidance that came out just a few weeks before we're hopefully going to have some very good results on three clinical trials from some of these vaccines." But he denied pressuring the FDA: "Why would we do that?" "My challenge to the F.D.A. is just make sure it's based on science and real numbers. . . . We're trying to make sure that the guidance we give is not an inhibitor to getting things out fast."

On September 24, Marks attributed the delay to the fact that side effects tended to develop 42–60 days after the second dose.[129] Trump made clear his own very different priorities: "we need a vaccine before the election and this guidance is going to delay that." Azar advised him:

> There is no way there's going to be an FDA-approved vaccine before the election. There may be data, and you can own that. . . . That's your win, as is the fact that you'll have tens of millions of doses by the end of the year.

Scott Gottlieb (Trump's first FDA Commissioner) said:

> I don't know of any precedent where the White House asked to adjudicate scientific and clinical guidances, even in past public health emergencies. To build trust among patients and providers, you wanted to leave these matters to the FDA process, which has a lot of rigor and integrity.

A group of prominent scientists and academics urged Pfizer to delay applying for an EUA until late November. Azar sought to reassure the public: "there's no political interference. The F.D.A.'s going to call those balls and strikes at the career level there. . . . Everything's going to be by science, data and rule of law." The president and CEO of the BIO trade group (which included the major pharmaceutical companies and all COVID-19 vaccine manufacturers except AstraZeneca) wrote Azar: "Any sign that the White House . . . is interfering in the process will simply erode public confidence." After Pfizer said its vaccine would not be authorized before mid-November, 60 scientists urged it not to rush the approval, praising the disclosure as evidence that Pfizer was "not being part of any political machinations." New York Gov. Cuomo declared his state would conduct an independent review of vaccines. "Frankly, I'm not going to trust the federal government's opinion." The governors of California, Washington, Oregon and Nevada concurred. Cuomo joined Michigan Gov. Whitmer in calling for an investigation of the Trump administration's "politicization of the pandemic response."

Although the president lacked authority over the FDA, it sought White House approval for its guidance, which required at least five cases of severe infection in the placebo group as evidence of the vaccine's efficacy.[130] The companies developing the vaccine supported the FDA, some declaring they would follow its guidance whatever the administration did. After a senior administration official asserted there was "no clinical or medical reason" for the guidance, the White House refused to approve it. The FDA considered sharing the standards with an outside advisory committee of independent experts. But the White House capitulated. Nevertheless, Trump boasted: "No president's ever pushed [the FDA] like I've pushed them." "The FDA is approving things in a matter of weeks that used to take a matter of years." But on October 6, after the agency released Vaccines and Related Biological Products Advisory Committee briefing materials calling for two months of surveillance, Trump angrily tweeted: "new FDA Rules make it more difficult for them to speed up vaccines for approval before Election Day. Just another hit job!" "We're going to have a great vaccine very, very shortly. I think we should have it before the election, but frankly, the politics gets involved, and that's ok. They want to play their games."

As approval of the vaccine appeared imminent, other issues became more prominent. In a lawsuit by four Pennsylvania counties, WD Pa Judge William Stickman IV (Trump) found Gov. Tom Wolf's "open-ended" lockdown unconstitutional.[131] Trump promptly retweeted nearly two dozen tweets praising the decision, declared states would open everything on November 4 (the day after the election) and hoped other judges would strike down closures. Parroting Atlas and Alexander, he claimed at a campaign rally on September 21 that COVID-19 "affects virtually nobody" under 18: "by the by, open your schools." (As of April 26, 2023, there had been 16,733,845 cases among those under 18, nearly a quarter of all cases.)[132] The same day, Fauci warned that COVID "can be serious in young people" with an underlying condition (which is found among 25–30 percent of that population). Sen. Johnson said: "there's a level of unjustifiable hysteria about covid that I think is just unfortunate . . . the vast majority of Americans probably don't even know they ever had it." "We should have followed the Sweden model," allowing the disease to infect younger people. (Cases in Sweden rose dramatically right after Johnson's comment, and deaths followed with the usual lag time.[133] As of November 4, 2021, Sweden had suffered one death for every 677 people, 3–9 times the rate of the other Nordic countries: Denmark 2,136; Finland 4,682; and Norway 5,928.) Although Redfield recommended extending the order docking cruise ships, the White House coronavirus task force overruled him. The order had been opposed by the Republican mayor of Miami and both of Florida's Republican senators (in a state crucial for the election). Trump had included the chairs of three major cruise lines in the Task Force on ways to reopen the country.

On September 29, seven former FDA Commissioners wrote a *Washington Post* op ed, warning that "the White House has said it might try to influence the scientific standards for vaccine approval put forward by the FDA" and urging Trump to let the agency do its job.[134] But at the presidential debate that day, Trump boasted that "we're weeks away from a vaccine" and declared that the companies "can go faster." He hoped to have 100 million doses of vaccine by the end of the year. Pfizer CEO Bourla told fellow pharmaceutical executives: "Once more, I was disappointed that the prevention for [sic] a deadly disease was discussed in political terms rather than scientific facts." When Biden said in the presidential debate that masks and social distancing could save 100,000 lives, Trump retorted: "Dr. Fauci said the opposite"—"masks are not good"—and "then he changed his mind." Fauci explained he had not recommended masks "very early on in the pandemic" because the few available were needed for health care providers. "Anybody who has been listening to me over the last several months knows that a conversation does not go by where I do not strongly recommend that people wear masks."

While being treated for COVID-19 in Walter Reed Hospital in early October, Trump went for a drive to "pay a little surprise to some of the great patriots we have out on the street."[135] An anonymous Secret Service agent protecting the president complained that he was "not even pretending to care now" about the agents' safety. After Trump was discharged, he boasted: "I'm back because I'm a perfect physical specimen and I'm extremely young." (He was obese and 74.) "People are going to get immediately better like I did." He also tweeted: "I can't get it (immune), and I can't give it." (Twitter flagged both tweets as "misleading and potentially harmful misinformation.") "I think this was a blessing from God that I caught" covid. "They call [Regernon] therapeutic, but to me it wasn't therapeutic, it just made me better. I call that a cure." (Trump clearly did not know the meaning of "therapeutic.") When he told Fauci "this really made a big difference," the physician replied, "No, this is an N equals 1. You may have been starting to feel better anyway." Trump retorted, "Absolutely not." Regernon's president and chief scientific officer predictably drew the "logical conclusion" that the drug had reduced Trump's virus level. But Dr. Peter Chin-Hong, an infectious disease specialist at UCSF Hospital, said there was "one million percent" no chance that Regernon had cured Trump in 24 hours, attributing the alleviation of his symptoms to dexamethasone (a steroid) and remdesivir. Trump told the public: "I have emergency use authorization all set up and we got to get it signed now." "We've authorized it." Regernon shares immediately jumped nearly 3 percent. Trump and Meadows pressed Hahn to accelerate the EUA. Trump promised seniors: "You're going to get the same medicine, you're going to get it free, no charge, and we're going to get it to you soon." But a spokesman for the Democratic majority on the House Appropriations Committee disagreed: "without new legislation, the Trump administration cannot make COVID-19 treatment available for free." An analysis of 38 million articles about the pandemic in English found that Trump was mentioned in nearly 38 percent of all "misinformation conversations," the largest number.

After Dr. Rick Bright resigned from NIH in October, his lawyer explained that the BARDA Director "can no longer countenance working for an administration that puts politics over science to the great detriment of the American people."[136] Bright complained to the Office of Special Counsel that he had been punished for whistleblowing and wrote in a *Washington Post* op ed:

> Public heath guidance on the pandemic response drafted by career scientists at the CDCP, has been repeatedly overruled by political staff appointed by the Trump administration. Career scientists throughout the DHHS hesitate to push back when science runs counter to the administration's unrealistically optimistic pronouncements.

When Bright "strongly objected" to HCQ and CQ, he "was shunted to NIH and assigned a more limited role." "Since early September . . . I was given no work."

The Partnership for Public Service named Fauci "Federal Employee of the Year" and honored other scientists.[137] Former President Obama said the contributions of civil servants "are even more critical, as we face down this pandemic and the economic uncertainty it's brought with it." Fauci reported that the "degree of friction" in public health efforts "definitely supersedes" what he had ever experienced. William Foege (who had received the Presidential Medal of Freedom in 2012 after serving as CDC Director under Carter and Reagan) wrote Redfield, blaming the "colossal failure of the public health system" on "the incompetence and illogic" of the White House, which "rejected both science and good management." Foege wrote in a *USA Today* op ed that adopting the "losing strategy" of herd immunity "for coronavirus is to ask for more suffering, more deaths and more social disruption." Over a thousand physicians, nurses, scientists and other health professionals (all former or current CDC Epidemic Intelligence Service officers) wrote in the *Epidemiology Monitor* in support of the CDC.

9. Run-up to the Election

Although the Trump had repeatedly disparaged Fauci, a campaign ad quoted the physician seeming to say of the president: "I can't imagine that anybody could be doing more" about the pandemic.[138] In his nearly five decades of public service, however, Fauci had never publicly endorsed a candidate, and the quote was not about Trump at all. Instead, Fauci had said that "a whole group of us" were "devoting almost full time" to covid, working until "twelve, one, two in the morning . . . every single day. So I can't imagine that under any circumstances anybody could be doing more." The campaign just doubled down on the lie: "the words spoken are accurate, and directly from Dr. Fauci's mouth." Trump said at a campaign event on October 10 that covid was "disappearing." He repeated at a North Carolina rally on October 15: "it's going to peter out." He boasted at a Florida rally: "I'll walk in there, kiss everyone in that audience." (He didn't and was notoriously germophobic.)[139] Fauci warned that in-person rallies were just "asking for trouble." "A number of states, right now, are having an increase in positivity." Trump's juvenile riposte was "Tony's pitching arm is far more accurate than his prognostications." (Fauci flubbed the first pitch of the baseball season, a limelight occasion Trump may have coveted; but the doctor was right about the pandemic. The 33,332 daily new cases on September 10 had nearly doubled to 62,413 on October 5, just before Trump spoke, and then rapidly increased nearly fivefold to peak at 300,777 on January 8.)[140] At an October 15 town hall event, Trump cited a study claiming that 85 percent of those wearing masks could get COVID. (In fact, scientists found masks were effective.)[141] He declared that the only alternative to reopening fully was staying home; there was no "middle ground" between downplaying the threat and telling the country, "Everybody's going to die." At an October 24 rally, he complained: "Covid, Covid, Covid, Covid, Covid, Covid. A plane goes down five hundred people dead, they don't talk about it." (The deadliest plane crash in the U.S., killing 273 in 1979, was widely reported. The only person killed by a civilian plane in the U.S. in 2020 was a trespasser at a Texas airport, also reported.)[142] "We're rounding the turn, we're doing great. Our numbers are incredible." Three days later, he assailed the "fake news": "All they talk about is Covid, Covid, Covid, Covid, Covid, Covid. I'm here, right? . . . I had it." Two days after that, he boasted: "I got better very quickly," Melania "got better very quickly" and Barron got over it "like twelve minutes later."

On October 4, Martin Kulldorff (epidemiology, Harvard), Sunetra Gupta (epidemiology, Oxford) and J.A. Bhattacharya (health economics, Stanford) issued the Great Barrington Declaration (named for a libertarian think tank in that Massachusetts town), claiming that "current lockdown policies are producing devastating effects on short and long-term public health."[143] These included the following:

> lower childhood vaccination rates, worsening cardiovascular disease outcomes, fewer cancer screenings and deteriorating mental health—leading to greater excess mortality in years to come, with the working class and younger members of society carrying the heaviest burden. Keeping students out of school is a grave injustice.

"[F]or children, COVID-19 is less dangerous than many other harms, including influenza." (Those under 18 suffered 486 flu deaths in 2019–20 and 1299 covid deaths in the first two years of the pandemic.)[144] "The most compassionate approach . . . is to allow those who are at minimal risk of death to live their lives normally to build up immunity to the virus through natural infection" because "we know that all populations will eventually reach herd immunity." (Eventually can be a long time, and the cost is high: 18 months later was it estimated that just 60 percent of Americans had had COVID-19 but 700,000 had died.)[145]

> Schools and universities should be open for in-person teaching. Extracurricular activities, such as sports, should be resumed. . . . Restaurants and other businesses should open. Arts, music, sport and other cultural activities should resume.

The Declaration's organizers claimed that 9,900 "medical and public health scientists" and 26,000 "medical practitioners" had signed it, but Britain's Sky News found names like Dr. Johnny Bananas and Dr. Person Fakename. (In April 2022, the Declaration's website claimed 900,000 signatures but without identifying their alleged credentials.)[146]

Scott Atlas arranged for the three authors to meet Azar in early October.[147] But NIH Director Collins warned it was "not true" they represented "a major alternative view that's held by large numbers of experts in the science community." Rather, they were the following:

> a fringe component . . . not mainstream science. It's dangerous. It fits into the political views of certain parts of our confused political establishment. . . . I'm sure it will be an idea that someone can wrap themselves in as a justification for skipping wearing masks or social distancing and just doing whatever they damn well please.

Confirming this fear, Azar tweeted on October 5: "Today I met with Dr. Atlas and three distinguished infectious disease experts . . . as part of our commitment to ensure we hear broad and diverse scientific perspectives," identifying them by their degrees and prestigious institutions. "[W]e heard strong reinforcement of the Trump Administration's strategy of aggressively protecting the vulnerable while opening schools and the workplace." Atlas told *The Hill* that the Declaration's "targeted protection of the vulnerable and opening schools and society policy matches the policy of the President and what I have advised." The three scientists also held a virtual roundtable with Florida Gov. DeSantis, advocating "focused protection."

Fauci cautioned on NBC News's *Good Morning America* that it would be "ridiculous" to "just let things rip and let the infection go—no masks, crowd, it doesn't make any difference."[148] WHO Director General Dr. Tedros Adhanom Ghebreyseus called herd immunity "scientifically and ethically problematic." More than 6,900 scientists, researchers and health care professionals rebutted the Declaration by signing the John Snow Memorandum, published in *The Lancet* on October 14. "The infection fatality rate of COVID-19 is severalfold higher than that of seasonal influenza and infection can lead to persisting illness, including in young, previously healthy people." Herd immunity "is a dangerous fallacy unsupported by scientific evidence." "Uncontrolled transmission in younger people risks significant morbidity and mortality across the whole population." "Furthermore, there is no evidence for lasting protective immunity to SARS-Cov-2 following natural infection." "[I]f we consider the risk of severe illness the proportion of vulnerable people constitute as much as 30% in some regions." "The evidence is very clear: controlling community spread of COVID-19 is the best way to protect our societies and economies until safe and effective vaccines and therapeutics arrive within the coming months." John M. Barry, author of *The Great Influenza: The Story of the Deadliest Pandemic in History*, wrote in a *New York Times* op ed that the Great Barrington Declaration ignored "harm to infected people in low-risk groups, protecting the vulnerable, and the number of deaths anticipated."

That month, Nobel Prize–winning economist Paul Romer wrote Atlas, urging a sharp increase in testing.[149] He replied: "that's not appropriate health care policy." There was a "likelihood that only 25 to 20 percent of people need the infection" to achieve herd immunity (a percentage he later raised to 20–40). (Scientists remain skeptical about ever achieving herd immunity for covid, given the virus's ability to mutate.)[150] Atlas continued to contend that large-scale testing and isolation violated civil liberties. "The overwhelming majority of people who get this infection are not at high risk. And when you start seeking out and testing asymptomatic people, you are destroying the workforce." But Thomas Frieden wrote in a *Washington Post* op ed that "a half-million more people could die if America pursues a 'herd immunity' plan." (He was tragically prescient. On the day, he wrote there had been 210,852 COVID deaths; a year later, there had been 754,051.)[151]

Two weeks before the election, Trump told an Arizona rally:

> [People are] getting tired of the pandemic—aren't they? You turn on CNN. That's all they cover, covid, covid, pandemic. Covid, covid, covid. . . . They're trying to talk people out of voting. People aren't buying it, CNN, you dumb bastards.

Arizona "is doing great with the pandemic."[152] (Although it was the 14th most populous state, it had the eighth highest number of cases, 58 percent more than two weeks earlier. Daily new cases increased from less than 500 in early October to nearly 15,000 in January.)[153] Trump griped that Fauci "has been here for 500 years. Every time he goes on television, there's always a bomb." "Biden wants to lock it down. He wants to listen to Dr. Fauci." Fauci had complained that "we don't allow him to do television, and yet I saw him last night on @60 Minutes, and he seems to get more airtime than anybody since the late, great, Bob Hope." Trump told a rally on October 19: "if I listened totally to the scientists, we would right now have a country that would be in a massive depression." On *Fox & Friends*, he accused Fauci of being a Democrat and a "good friend" of Cuomo's family. "He's been wrong" and "is a little bit sometimes not a team player." Reporters favored him "because they think he's against me." Suggesting it was all a matter of opinion, Trump said Fauci had "a view" and Atlas had "a different view." "[E]verybody has a different view."

Trump proclaimed on October 21: "That pandemic is rounding the corner."[154] (There had been 221,627 deaths. Two years later, there were over a million. Daily deaths increased nearly fourfold before the end of Trump's term.)[155] He tweeted on October 26:

> We have made tremendous progress with the China Virus, but the Fake News refuses to talk about it this close to the Election. COVID, COVID, COVID is being used by them, in total coordination, in order to change our great early election numbers. Should be an election law violation!

(There was a problem: the First Amendment.) On October 30, Trump said at a rally:

> Under the Biden lockdown, which he talks about and cherishes, countless Americans will die from suicide, drug overdoses and deferred medical care at a level like you haven't seen before. There will be no school, no graduations, no weddings, no Thanksgiving, no Christmas, no 4th of July, no Easter, no nothing. There will be no future for America's youth. . . . our doctors are very smart people. So what they do is they say, "I'm sorry but everybody dies of covid." They do that to get more money.

When challenged, he retorted: "Now they'll say, 'oh, that's terrible what he said,' but that's true. It's like $2,000 more, so you get more money." AMA President Bailey called this a "malicious, outrageous, and completely misguided charge." *The Washington Post* said: "it is time to get on the team of science and medicine." (Immediately after the election, Biden appointed a coronavirus task force headed by two leading doctors and including other respected doctors and scientists.)[156]

A week before the election, a White House Office of Science and Technology report claimed "ending the COVID-19 pandemic" as one of Trump's achievements.[157] (At that time, there had been 8 million cases in the US; 18

months later, there were ten times as many.)[158] Four officials on the coronavirus task force viewed the statement as a rebuke. Trump said on October 31:

> It's ending anyway, but we have the greatest companies in the world and we're literally weeks away. We'll eradicate more quickly the virus, wipe out the China plague once and for all, and it's back to work, back to work, which is what we want. You know what we want? We want normal.[159]

On October 31, Fauci warned in *The Washington Post*: "All the stars are aligned in the wrong place as you go into the fall and winter season with people congregating at home indoors. You could not possibly be positioned more poorly."[160] The White House was ignoring its scientists. Biden "is taking [covid] seriously from a public health perspective," while Trump is "looking at it from a different perspective . . . the economy and reopening the country." Fauci had "real problems" with Atlas, "a smart guy who's talking about things that I believe he doesn't have any real insight or knowledge or experience in." A Trump spokesman retorted that Fauci "knows the risks [from covid] today are dramatically lower than they were only a few months ago." (Daily new cases more than tripled from 39,235 on September 3 to 140,612 on November 3.)[161] The White House said:

> It's unacceptable and breaking with all norms for Dr. Fauci, a senior member of the president's coronavirus task force and someone who has praised President Trump's actions throughout this pandemic, to choose three days before an election to play politics. . . . [Fauci was] choosing to criticize the president in the media and make his political leanings known by praising the president's opponent—exactly what the American people have come to expect from The Swamp.

Trump's senior campaign manager Jason Miller urged the president and Meadows to fire Fauci. That evening, after a Florida rally chanted, "Fire Fauci," Trump hinted: "don't tell anybody, but let me wait until a little bit after the election." "He's been wrong on a lot." Europe's "draconian" restrictions had not been effective the first time. "Now they have to do it all over again. . . . I think I'll go over and explain it to them." (On Election Day, the U.S. had 28,497 cases/million people, whereas France had 24,129, Britain 17,757 and Germany 6,879.)[162] In his online show, Stephen Bannon said of Fauci: "I'd actually like to go back to the old times of Tudor England. I'd put the heads on the pikes."

The day before the election, in an internal report to the coronavirus task force, which she shared with others, Birx called for "much more aggressive action."[163] "We are entering the most concerning and most deadly phase of this pandemic . . . leading to increasing mortality." (Like other scientists, she sadly was correct; there had been fewer than a thousand deaths a day since the end of August, but the number climbed rapidly after she spoke to over 4,000 in January.)[164] She denied Trump's claims that the country was "rounding the turn" or that the increase in cases was due to testing, which actually was "flat or declining." "Cases are rapidly rising in nearly 30 percent of all USA counties." She advocated "consistent messaging about uniform use of masks, physical distancing and hand washing with profound limitation on indoor gatherings especially with family and friends." Peter Staley, a close friend, reported that Birx "feels totally sidelined and basically thinks Scott Atlas is dangerous and crazy and is just horrified that she's been pushed aside for somebody like that."

Marc Short accused her of leaking to the press; when she denied it, he retorted: "people do surprising things all the time. They don't think things through. They let their emotions get to them." On November 5 (two days after Trump lost the election), Meadows blamed her for what "people think":

> You saw the exit polls. You've seen what's going on in the critical races. You think that your words didn't matter? They did. Big time. . . . your reputation is toast. What you did or didn't do isn't going to change that.

For the first time, she was excluded from the next OWS briefing; and at the one that followed, she was scheduled to speak last instead of first. At the December 7 meeting, she said: "we are still in the midst of a national catastrophe, maybe one of the worst this country has ever faced." Pence interrupted to ask irrelevantly if she thought the pandemic was "worse than all the horrors this nation has faced?" She stood her ground: "the depth and breadth of the loss of life in this short period of time, this *is* catastrophic. It is only going to get worse." Pence dismissed that as a mere "projection" and accused her of "dishonor[ing] the sacrifice of our vets going all the way back to the Civil War." Birx replied that the U.S. could lose 500,000 people. (Two years later, there had been more than twice that many deaths.) A week after the inauguration, however, Pence urged Birx to tell her account of the response to the pandemic.

The day the election was called for Biden (November 7), Pfizer announced there had been 95 percent immunity from the trial of its vaccine. Meadows expostulated: "Look at what they did! They held back these results. If they would have reported these, the president would have won the election." At a Task Force meeting that day, Azar accused the FDA of delaying the results.[165]

10. A Lame Duck President

After Pfizer's announcement, Trump ordered Azar to "get to the bottom" of the delay.[166] Although Hahn said the timing was solely the result of Pfizer's independent decisions, Azar blamed the FDA. Trump screamed at Hahn, later tweeting:

> As I have long said, @Pfizer and others would only announce a Vaccine after the Election, because they didn't have the courage to do it before. Likewise, the @US_FDA should have announced it earlier, not for political purposes, but for saving lives! The @US_FDA and the Democrats didn't want to have me get a Vaccine WIN, prior to the election, so instead it came out five days later—As I've said all along!

On December 10, Hahn told Meadows: "we made the decision to move forward with the EUA." On December 11, before the formal announcement, Trump tweeted:

> While my pushing the money drenched but heavily bureaucratic @US_FDA saved five years in the approval of NUMEROUS great new vaccines, it is still a big, old, slow turtle. Get the dam [sic] vaccines out NOW, Dr. Hahn @SteveFDA. Stop playing games and start saving lives!!!

Hahn recalled that Meadows phoned and said in a "very demonstrative manner" that he wanted the EUA immediately, making a "truncated statement" that "could be perhaps related to my position" as commissioner. Hahn asked for "clarification" of the threat, but Meadows hung up. Soon thereafter, Azar tweeted: "BREAKING: The @US_FDA has informed Pfizer that it will rapidly work toward finalization and issuance of an emergency use authorization." Meadows ordered Hahn to authorize the Pfizer vaccine that day or resign. Hahn claimed: "this is [an] untrue representation of the phone call with the chief of staff. The FDA was encouraged to continue working expeditiously." Nevertheless, the FDA did issue the EUA that day. After DHHS promulgated a regulation giving political appointees at the FDA, CDC and CMS more power to reassign civil servants, Hahn warned that a career official "might be willing to do the bidding of an administration knowing his job is on the line in five years."

On December 22, Trump was still tweeting boastfully:[167]

> Distribution of both vaccines is going very smoothly. Amazing how many people are being vaccinated, record numbers. Our Country, and indeed the World, will soon see the great miracle of what the Trump Administration has accomplished. They said it couldn't be done!!!

Now, however, conservatives began attacking the vaccine. Sidney Powell, who had aggressively challenged Trump's electoral defeat (see Abel 2024b), warned that people would be divided into vaccinated and unvaccinated so "big government" could surveil the latter. "NO WAY #America. This is more authoritarian communist control imported straight from #China." And Candace Owens, a Trump ally, tweeted on December 9: "The same people that are out here yelling 'my body my choice' will be telling you that the government has a right to force vaccinate you for a virus that has a 99% survival rate."

There also was surprising resistance among the earliest groups eligible.[168] In November, two-thirds of a non-random sample of Los Angeles health care workers said they would delay getting it, a third of the members of the American Nurses Association would not get it and another third were undecided. At Houston Methodist Hospital, 117 employees sued to block a vaccine mandate, claiming it violated the Nuremberg Code (although 99 percent of the hospital's 26,000 employees had been vaccinated). SD Texas Judge Lynn Hughes (Reagan) dismissed the case, finding "this is not coercion." Health care workers staged national walkouts against vaccine requirements, supported by Liberty Counsel (an evangelical Christian law firm).

Trump kept chafing at Fauci's visibility, tweeting on Jan. 3:[169]

> Something how Dr. Fauci is revered by the LameStream Media as such a great professional, having done, they say, such an incredible job, yet he works for me and the Trump Administration and I am in no way given any credit for my work. Gee, could this just be more Fake News? . . . The number of cases and deaths of the China Virus is far exaggerated in the United States because of @CDCgov's ridiculous method of determination compared to other countries, many of whom report, purposely, very inaccurately and low. "When in doubt call it Covid" Fake News!

(In May 2022, WHO said nearly 15 million had died during the first two years of the pandemic, 2.5 times previous estimates.) After Birx, Fauci, Hahn and Redfield warned of a winter surge, Meadows said he did not believe their data and accused them of identifying a problem without a solution.

Just before the end of the Trump administration, Secretary of State Pompeo declared that WIV, which conducted COVID-19 research on bats, had collaborated with secret Chinese military projects, suggesting the pandemic had been an act of biological warfare.[170] But Christopher Ford, assistant secretary of state for international security and proliferation, called the analysis "gravely flawed." There was nothing "inherently suspicious—and suggestive of biological warfare activity—about People's Liberation Army involvement at WIV on classified projects."

Notes

CDC	Centers for Disease Control
CNN	Cable News Network

G	*Guardian*
MMWR	Morbidity and Mortality Weekly Report
NEJM	*New England Journal of Medicine*
NYT	*New York Times*
PNAS	*Proceedings of the National Academy of Sciences*
WP	*Washington Post*
WSJ	*Wall Street Journal*

1 Holshue et al., "First Case of 2019 Novel Coronavirus in the United States," 382 NEJM 929–936 (2020); CDC, "Outbreak of Pneumonia of Unknown Etiology (PUE) in Wuhan, China" (1.8.20); Kuo, "China confirms human-to-human transmission of coronavirus," G (1.20.20); Mangan, "Trump dismissed coronavirus pandemic worry in January—now claims he long warned about it," CNBC (3.17.20); Wright (2021: 14, 40–41, 46); Kessler (2020: 250); Woodward (2020: 230); Abutaleb and Paletta (2021: 13, 95); Leonnig and Rucker (2021: 35–38); Swan and Talev, "Navarro memos warning of mass coronavirus death circulated in January," Axios (4.7.20); USSHSGAC (2022: 80–81, 89, 96, 188–189); HPSCI (2022: preface unpaged 1; report pp. 14, 19, 28, 33, 35, 38); CCG (2023: 87–91).

2 Biden, "FLASHBACK: Trump is worst possible leader to deal with coronavirus outbreak," USA Today (1.27.20); Wright (2021: 43); Abutaleb and Paletta (2021: 29, 36–37); Woodward (2020: 232).

3 Leonnig and Rucker (2021: 42, 48); Boseley, "WHO declares coronavirus a global health emergency," G (1.30.20); WHO, "Timeline: WHO's COVID-19 response" (9.11.20); "US declares public health emergency from coronavirus," Boston Globe (2.1.20); Lewis (2021: 179); Robertson, "Trump's snowballing China travel claim," FactCheck.org (4.15.20).

4 Moon, "A seemingly healthy woman's sudden death is now the first known US coronavirus-related fatality," CNN (4.24.20); Debolt, "29 people had flu-like symptoms when they died in Santa Clara County. Nine tested positive for coronavirus," Mercury News (4.25.20); Woodward (2020: xviii–xx, 243–245); Barr (2022: 450); Birx (2022: 57); Stelter (2020: 12–13, 288); Kessler (2020: 251); Leonnig and Rucker (2021: 126); Politi, "Trump keeps promoting unproven drug for the coronavirus: I'm not a doctor. But I have common sense," Slate (4.5.20).

5 Kessler (2020: 252, 255); Bender (2021: 95); Martin and Burns (2022: 36); Leonnig and Rucker (2021: 89–90); Vergano, "The government asked us not to release records from the CDC's first failed COVID test. Here they are," Buzzfeed News (12.8.21); Gadarian et al. (2022: 52, 58–61); Miao, "White House abandoned plan to send 650 million face masks across the U.S. in April, report says," CNBC (9.17.20).

6 CDC Estimates of 2009 H1N1 Influenza Cases, Hospitalizations and Deaths in the United States, April–December 12, 2009 www.cdc.gov/h1n1flu/estimates_2009_h1n1.htm; CDC, "Flu View" www.cdc.gov/flu/weekly/weeklyarchives2009-2010/weekly45.htm.

7 Stelter (2020: 13, 296, 300–305); Karl (2021: 26); Peters and Grynbaum, "How right-wing pundits are covering coronavirus," NYT (3.11.20); Heath, "Americans divided on party lines over risk from Coronavirus: Reuters/Ipsos Poll," Reuters (3.6.20); Jurowitz and Mitchell, "Cable TV and COVID-19: How Americans perceive the outbreak and view media coverage differ by main news source," Pew Research Center (4.1.20); Gadarian et al. (2022: 91–105, 119, 135–153).

8 Abutaleb and Harris, "Trump-era hunt for pandemic 'lab leak' went down many fruitless paths," WP (6.16.21); Wright (2021: 217, 224); "Donald Trump's 'Chinese virus': the politics of naming," The Conversation (4.21.20); "President Trump calls coronavirus 'kung flu,'" BBC News (6.24.20); Woodward (2020: 333); Meadows (2021: 13, 127); Mueller and Zimmer, "G.O.P. Senator's report on Covid origins suggests lab leak, but offers little new evidence," NYT (10.28.22); "Wuhan's early covid cases are a mystery. What is China hiding?" WP (11.17.22); USSCHELP (2022: 4); HPSCI (2022: 19); Strobel and Gordon, "Covid emerged as Chinese lab faced biosafety issues, Senate Republican study finds," WSJ (4.17.23).
9 Abutaleb and Paletta (2021: 95); Swan and Talev, "Navarro memos warning of mass coronavirus death circulated in January," Axios (4.7.20); Woodward (2020: 251); Abutaleb, Parker and Dawsey, "Inside Trump's frantic attempts to minimize the coronavirus crisis," WP (2.29.20); Stanley-Becker and Sun, "Senior CDC official who met Trump's wrath for raising alarm about coronavirus to resign," WP (5.7.21); Diamond, "Messonnier, Birx detail political interference in last year's coronavirus response," WP (11.13.21); Lewis (2021: 216); Haberman (2022: 413); Abutaleb and Paletta (2021: 97, 100, 102, 106); Bender (2021: 93); Leonnig and Rucker (2021: 62); CCG (2023: 119).
10 "Woodward book: Trump says he knew coronavirus was 'deadly' and worse than the flu while intentionally misleading Americans," WP (9.9.20).
11 Schuchat, "Public health response to the initiation and spread of pandemic COVID-19 in the United States, February 24-April 21, 2020," 69(18) MMWR 551–56 (May 2020); Wright (2021: 78).
12 HSSCC (2022c: 6–7); Karl (2021: 19–20).
13 Borrell (2021: 76–77); Diamond, "Trump officials muzzled CDC on church covid guidance, emails confirm," WP (4.29.22); Santucci, "What we know about the White House coronavirus task force now that Mike Pence is in charge," USA Today (2.27.20); USSHSGAC (2022: 122–123, 126, 135, 192–194).
14 Department of State, COVID-19 Interim Review: Lessons Learned from the Department of State's Response to the COVID-19 Pandemic (June 2021); GAO, Scientific Integrity: HHS Agencies Need to Develop Procedures and Train Staff on Reporting and Addressing Political Interference (GAO-22–104613) (4.20.22).
15 Leonnig and Rucker (2021: 63); Stelter (2020: 13, 294, 306); Woodward (2020: 252); https://coronavirus.jhu.edu/region/united-states.
16 Lewis (2021: 216); Birx (2022: 57); Woodward (2020: 254–255, 273); Stelter (2020: 4, 7, 26).
17 Diamond, "New book offers fresh details about chaos, conflicts inside Trump's pandemic response," WP (6.21.21); Abutaleb and Paletta (2021: 58–60; 118, 121–123); Wright (2021: 81–82); Diamond, "Trump advisers privately warned of 'critical mistakes' as pandemic loomed," WP (9.14.21); Birx (2022: 4, 84–85); Leonnig and Rucker (2021: 68–69); USSHSGAC (2022: 185–187); "Surgeon general says risk of coronavirus remains low, most people will not need hospitalization," Fox News (3.6.20).
18 Parmet (2023: 1–2).
19 Hirsch, "Trump says, 'Anybody who wants a test gets a test' after Pence says US can't meet coronavirus testing demand," CNBC (3.6.20); Diamond, "Feuds, fibs and finger pointing: Trump officials say coronavirus response was worse than known," WP (3.29.21); Diamond, "New book offers fresh details about chaos, conflicts inside Trump's pandemic response," WP (6.21.21); Abutaleb and Paletta (2021); Leonnig and Rucker (2021: 76, 85–87); www.statista.com/statistics/1076314/covid-19-case-fatality-rates-select-countries-worldwide/; Martin and Burns (2022: 88); Werner and Stein, "Trump administration pushing to

block new money for testing, tracing and CDC in upcoming coronavirus relief bill," WP (7.19.20); Burleigh (2021: 15).

20 Edwards (2021: 132–133) Woodward (2020: 275); Wright (2021: 76, 89); Esper (2022: 269); CCG (2023: 112).

21 Woodward (2020: 278–279, 281–282, 284, 296); Leonnig and Rucker (2021: 79–80); HSSCC (2022a: 1); Stelter (2020: 307–309, 311); "Remarks by President Trump in Address to the Nation" (3.11.20); Sides et al. (2022: 136).

22 Liptak, "White House advises public to avoid groups of more than 10, asks people to stay away from bars and restaurants," CNN (3.16.20); Wright (2021: 117–118).

23 Martin and Burns (2022: 31).

24 "Study touting hydroxychloroquine flawed, experts say," AP (6.17.21).

25 Abutaleb and Paletta (2021: 155, 166, 169); Woodward (2020: 312); Birx (2022: 111, 114–115).

26 HSSCC (2022b: 8, 11–29); Burleigh (2021: 27, 148); Wright (2021: 126–128); Abutaleb and Paletta (2021: 219–228, 235–239); McCarthy, "Hydroxychloroquine in Australia: a cautionary tale for journalists and scientists" (8.26.22) https://reutersinstitute.politics.ox.ac.uk/hydroxychloroquine-australia-cautionary-tale-journalists-and-scientists.

27 Baker, Rogers, Enrich and Haberman, "Trump's aggressive advocacy of malaria drug for treating coronavirus divides medical community," NYT (4.7.20); Blake, "FDA's hydroxychloroquine reversal raises even bigger questions about Trump's role in pushing for the drug," WP (6.16.20); McGinley and Dawsey, "Touting criticized study, White House presses FDA to authorize hydroxychloroquine—again," WP (7.10.20); CCG (2023: 226–227).

28 Leonnig and Rucker (2021: 87–88).

29 Woodward (2020: 300); HSSCC (2022b: 11–29).

30 www.history.com/this-day-in-history/mccarthy-says-communists-are-in-state-department

31 Shear and Haberman, "Health Dept. official says doubts on hydroxychloroquine led to his ouster," NYT (4.22.20); Borrell (2021: 121); Stolberg, "Federal watchdog says coronavirus whistle-blower should be reinstated as it investigates," NYT (5.9.20); Diamond, "Trump advisers privately warned of 'critical mistakes' as pandemic loomed," WP (9.14.21); Stolberg, "'Lives were lost' as warnings went unheeded, whistle-blower tells House," NYT (5.15.20).

32 Birx (2022: 172–174); Meadows (2021: 59); Leonnig and Rucker (2021: 110–111, 181).

33 "FDA cautions against use of hydroxychloroquine or chloroquine for COVID-19 outside of the hospital setting or a clinical trial due to risk of heart rhythm problems" (6.15.20); Rowland, Cenziper and Rein, "White House sidestepped FDA to distribute hydroxychloroquine to pharmacies, documents show. Trump touted the pills to treat Covid-19," WP (10.31.20); Sommer, "Trump's new favorite COVID doctor believes in alien DNA, demon sperm, and hydroxychloroquine," Daily Beast (7.28.21); Crowley, "'Nobody likes me,' Trump complains, renewing defense of dubious science," NYT (7.29.20); Rouege, "Texas Medical Board takes 'corrective action' against doctor over hydroxychloroquine prescription for COVID patient," KHOU-11 (11.3.21) Budryk, "Doctor that promoted false hydroxychloroquine claims arrested in connection with Capitol riot," The Hill (1.22.21); Andrews and Paquette, "Trump retweeted a video with false covid-19 claims. One doctor in it has said demons cause illnesses," WP (7.28.20); Frenkel and Alba, "Misleading virus video, pushed by the Trumps, spreads online," NYT (7.28.20); "Don't fall for this video, Hydroxychloroquine is not a COVID-19 cure," PolitiFact (7.28.20).

34 Olewe, "Stella Immanuel—the doctor behind unproven coronavirus cure claims," BBC News (7.29.20); Pitofsky, "Doctor retweeted by Trump has warned of alien DNA, sex with demons," The Hill (7.29.20).
35 Dearen and Burke, "Pence ordered borders closed after CDC experts refused," AP (10.3.20).
36 HSSCC (2022c: 28–29).
37 Stelter (2020: 304); Leonnig and Rucker (2021: 93–95).
38 Rupar, "Deborah Birx praised Trump as attentive to scientific literature and details. Nope," Vox (3.27.20); Bump, "The public data for smaller states don't support the Coronavirus Task Force's optimism," WP (3.27.20); Bump, "The Coronavirus Task Force keeps downplaying the virus's spread in less-populated states," WP (4.16.20); Shear, Weiland, Lipton, Haberman and Sanger, "Inside Trump's failure: the rush to abandon leadership role on the virus," NYT (7.18.20); Mascarenhas and Howard, "10 things the 'pandemic doctors' revealed to Dr Sanjay Gupta about their time fighting covid-19," CNN (3.29.21).
39 "Trump wants masks on all nursing home workers, temperature checks for all, and separate COVID-19 units," McKnight's Long-term Care News (4.3.20).
40 Victor, Serviss and Paybarah, "In his own words, Trump on the coronavirus and masks," NYT (10.2.20); Wright (2021: 149–150); Abutaleb and Paletta (2021: 195); Sides et al. (2022: 140).
41 Sides et al. (2022: 152, 156–159); Rabin, "Masks cut covid spread in schools, study finds," NYT (11.10.22).
42 Birx (2022: 89–90, 155–156, 164).
43 https://coronavirus.jhu.edu/region/united-states; CCG (2023: 128–129).
44 Liptak, Vazquez, Valencia and Acosta, "Trump says he wants the country 'opened up and just raring to go by Easter,' despite health experts' warnings," CNN (3.24.20); Birx (2022: 152); Shear, Weiland, Lipton, Haberman and Sanger, "Inside Trump's failure: the rush to abandon leadership role on the virus," NYT (7.18.20); Craig and Dennis, "Governors form groups to explore lifting virus restrictions; Trump says he alone will decide," WP (4.14.20); Flynn and Chiu, "Trump says his 'authority is total.' Constitutional experts have 'no idea' where he got that," WP (4.14.20); Kim, Dawsey and Dennis, "Trump's inaccurate assertion of 'total' authority sparks challenge from governors," WP (4.15.20); Savage, "Trump's claim of total authority in crisis is rejected across ideological lines," NYT (4.15.20); Abutaleb and Paletta (2021: 198, 203); Fritze and Jackson, "Trump calls to 'liberate' states where protesters have demanded easing coronavirus lockdowns," USA Today (4.17.20); Meade, "The movement against coronavirus lockdowns is still going—and still angry," WP (8.10.20).
45 CCG (2023: 154, 176–178).
46 Shepherd, "Trump coronavirus adviser tells Michigan to 'rise up' against new shutdown orders," WP (11.16.20); Wright (2021: 147); Gabbatt, "How the alleged plot to kidnap Michigan's Democratic governor unraveled," G (10.8.20); "Scott Atlas's rabble-rousing will lead to illness and death. He should be fired," WP (11.17.20).
47 Borrell (2021: 151); Sun, "CDC Director warns second wave of coronavirus is likely to be even more devastating," WP (4.21.20); Edwards (2021: 32, 119–120); Abutaleb and Paletta (2021: 334).
48 Clark, "Trump suggests 'injection' of disinfectant to beat coronavirus and 'clean' the lungs," NBC News (4.24.20); Burleigh (2021: 148); Abutaleb and Paletta (2021: 239–241); Gittleson, "Birx on Trump's disinfectant 'injection' moment: 'I still think about it every day,'" ABC News (3.15.21); Birx (2022: 190–191); O'Laughlin, "Health officials: Man drank toxic cleaning product after Trump's comments on disinfectants," 7News (4.28.20); Folley, "Two men in Georgia

drank disinfectants in efforts to prevent COVID-19, officials say," The Hill (4.28.20).

49 Woodward (2020: 321, 325, 330); Leonnig and Rucker (2021: 142); Abutaleb and Paletta (2021: 292); Birx (2022: 197, 206, 208, 212–213).

50 LaFraniere, Weiland and Shear, "Trump pressed for plasma therapy. Officials worry, is an unvetted vaccine next?" NYT (9.13.20); Kaplan, LaFraniere, Weiland and Haberman, "How the F.D.A. stood up to the President," NYT (10.21.20); Abutaleb and Paletta (2021: 297–301); Meadows (2021: 169–171); HSSCC (2022b: 31–35) McGinley and Abutaleb, "Trump administration bars FDA from regulating some laboratory tests, including for coronavirus," WP (8.21.20); Hawkins and Iati "Coronavirus update: infections are trending upward in the midwest," WP (8.23.20); Dawsey, McGiney, Ohnson and Kim," Trump to announce emergency authorization of convalescent plasma as 'breakthrough' covid-19 treatment," WP (8.23.20); LaFraniere, Fink, Thomas and Haberman, "F.D.A. allows expanded use of plasma to treat coronavirus patients," NYT (8.24.20); Thomas and Fink, "F.D.A. grossly misrepresented' blood plasma data, scientists say," NYT (8.25.20); "Politicizing medical science will cost American lives," NYT (8.25.20); Mason, "FDA commissioner disputes Trump, says no 'deep state' thwarting vaccine," Reuters (8.24.20); Hamburg and Sharfstein, "The FDA must stand up for itself and for science, not politics," WP (8.26.20); "The F.D.A. commissioner's fuzzy math," NYT (8.26.20); "2 F.D.A. public relations experts are fired after plasma fiasco," NYT (8.28.20); Rowland, Cenziper and Rein, "White House sidestepped FDA to distribute hydroxychloroquine to pharmacies, documents show. Trump touted the pills to treat covid-19," WP (10.31.20); Borrell (2021: 194–195); Diamond, "Feuds, fibs and finger pointing: Trump officials say coronavirus response was worse than known," WP (3.29.21).

51 Leonnig and Rucker (2021: 246–249).

52 Diamond, "Trump officials celebrated efforts to change CDC reports on coronavirus, emails show," WP (4.9.21); Mendez, "Trump officials bragged about pressuring CDC to alter covid reports, emails reveal," CNBC (4.9.21); Barnes, "Supreme Court, in rare late-night ruling, says California may enforce certain restrictions on religious gatherings," WP (5.30.20); South Bay United Pentecostal Church v. Newsom (SC 5.29.20); Barnes, "Supreme Court denies plea from Nevada church that it is hurt while casinos reopen," WP (7.24.20); Calvary Chapel Dayton Valley v. Sisolak (SC 7.24.20) Noori et al., "Trump calls on governors to allow places of worship to open this weekend," WP (5.22.20); Liptak, "Justice upholds limits on religious services during health crisis," NYT (5.31.20); Barr (2022: 462–463); Diamond, "Trump officials muzzled CDC on church covid guidance, emails confirm," WP (4.29.22).

53 Abutaleb, Dawsey and Sun, "Top Trump health appointee taking medical leave after incendiary remarks," WP (9.16.20).

54 Tan, "The radical adventures of conservative radio host Mike Caputo," Buffalo News (3.5.16); Longman, "Who is Michael Caputo and what can he tell us?—The Russian connections keep piling up," Washington Monthly (5.21.17).

55 Mazzetti, Weiland and Stolberg, "Under Pence, politics regularly seeped into Coronavirus Task Force," NYT (10.8.20); Meadows (2021: 75).

56 HSSCC (2022c: 13–26, 31–34); Borrell (2021: 171).

57 https://data.cdc.gov/widgets/nr4s-juj3?mobile_redirect=true.

58 www.cdc.gov/flu/about/burden/index.html; www.cdc.gov/flu/about/burden/preliminary-in-season-estimates.htm.

59 HSSCC (2022c: 12–13).

60 https://coronavirus.jhu.edu/region/united-states.

61 Pence, "There isn't a coronavirus 'second wave,'" WSJ (6.16.20); Wright (2021: 178–180); Abutaleb and Paletta (2021: 327); Sides et al. (2022: 142).
62 https://data.cdc.gov/NCHS/Provisional-COVID-19-Deaths-Focus-on-Ages-0-18-Yea/nr4s-juj3.
63 Weiland, "Emails detail effort to silence C.D.C. and question its science," NYT (9.19.20); Meadows (2021: 57); HSSCC (2022c: 13).
64 Wilson, Diaz and Klein, "Former Trump appointee encouraged her immunity strategy for covid-19, internal emails reveal," CNN (12.17.20); Diamond, "'We want them infected': Trump appointee demanded 'herd immunity' strategy, emails reveal," Politico (12.16.20); Abutaleb, Parker, Dawsey and Rucker, "The inside story of how Trump's denial, mismanagement and magical thinking led to the pandemic's dark winter," WP (12.20.20); HSSCC (2022a: 7); Diamond, "Trump official pressured CDC to change report on covid and kids," Politico (10.5.20); Meadows (2021: 148).
65 https://data.cdc.gov/widgets/nr4s-juj3?mobile_redirect=true.
66 Abutaleb and Paletta (2021: 331); Meckler, "With pressure and threats, Trump pushes to fully reopen schools. Schools say: 'not so fast,'" WP (7.9.20); Goodnough, "C.D.C. calls on schools to reopen, downplaying health risks," NYT (7.25.20); Meckler and Weiner, "CDC director concedes schools in 'hot spots' face tougher call on reopening" WP (7.25.20).
67 Mazzetti, Weiland and LaFraniere, "Behind the White House effort to pressure the C.D.C. on school openings," NYT (9.29.20).
68 www.cdc.gov/flu/spotlights/2019-2020/2019-20-pediatric-flu-deaths.htm; www.statista.com/statistics/1191568/reported-deaths-from-covid-by-age-us/.
69 Sun and Dawsey, "CDC feels pressure from Trump as rift grows over coronavirus response," WP (7.10.20).
70 Hartocollis and Jordan, "As universities seek to block visa rules, Trump threatens tax status," NYT (7.11.20); Hartocollis, "17 states sue to block student visa rules," NYT (7.14.20); "Trump administration walks back rule that would have stripped some foreign student visas," NYT (7.14.20).
71 Claiborne, "IRS ignored bid to audit 'enemies' list," WP (12.21.73); Charlton, "Congressional unit says Dean gave I.R.S. 2d 'enemies' list," NYT (12.21.73).
72 Haberman, "Trump aides undercut Fauci as he speaks up on virus concerns," NYT (7.13.20); McGinley and Abutaleb, "White House effort to undermine Fauci is criticized by public health experts, scientists and Democrats," WP (7.13.20); Crowley, "'Nobody likes me,' Trump complains, renewing defense of dubious science," NYT (7.29.20); Wagner, Kornfield and Olorunnipa, "White House backs away from Fauci attacks days after promoting them," WP (7.15.20); Navarro, "Anthony Fauci has been wrong about everything I have interacted with him on," USA Today (7.14.20); Wright (2021: 191); Leonnig and Rucker (2021: 217–220); Barr (2022: 450–451, 459); Abutaleb and Paletta (2021: 341–343); McGinley and Abutaleb, "White House effort to undermine Fauci is criticized by public health experts, scientists and Democrats," WP (7.13.20); Frieden, Koplan, Satcher and Besser, "We ran the CDC. No president ever politicized its science the way Trump has," WP (7.14.20); "Anthony Fauci has been wrong about everything I have interacted with him on: Peter Navarro," USA Today (7.14.20); Russonello, "Fauci calls White House criticism 'bizarre,'" NYT (7.16.20); Barr, "USA Today, facing backlash, says Navarro opinion piece attacking Fauci does not meet its standards," WP (7.17.20); Acosta, "White House blocks CDC from testifying on reopening schools next week," CNN (7.17.20); "Trump adds to White House criticism of Fauci," NYT (7.19.20).
73 www.nytimes.com/interactive/2021/us/covid-cases.html.

74 Coleman, "US testing official: 'Dr. Fauci is not 100 percent right,'" The Hill (7.12.20); Kranish, "Brett Giroir, Trump's testing czar, was forced out of a job developing vaccine projects. Now he's on the hot seat," WP (4.20.20).
75 Nazaryan, "Former 'Wheel of Fortune' host Chuck Woolery has been accused of anti-Semitism after controversial tweets," Newsweek (5.30.17).
76 Diamond, "Trump officials celebrated efforts to change CDC reports on coronavirus, emails show," WP (4.9.21); Mendez, "Trump officials bragged about pressuring CDC to alter covid reports, emails reveal," CNBC (4.9.21).
77 Blake, "Fauci finally loses his patience with Rand Paul," WP (9.24.20); Gebellhof, "Anthony Fauci owes no one an apology," WP (12.2.20).
78 Werner and DeBonis, "White House blocks Fauci from testifying before House panel next week," WP (5.2.20); Brufke, "White House prohibits Coronavirus Task Force members from testifying before Congress in May," The Hill (5.4.20); Hohmann, "White House moves to shield Trump from oversight of his coronavirus response," WP (5.4.20).
79 Stracqualursi, "Birx warns US is 'in a new phase' of coronavirus pandemic with more widespread cases," CNN (8.2.20); Klein, "Trump criticizes Birx for the first time after she issues coronavirus warnings," CNN (8.3.20); Kornfield, "Criticized by science community and Trump, Birx said she 'always' considered quitting," WP (1.22.21); Bump, "Birx both exemplifies and blames the cherry-picking that spared the Trump presidency," WP (1.25.21); Wang, "Birx tells CNN most U.S. covid deaths 'could have been mitigated' after first 100,000," WP (3.28.21); Birx (2022: 266–268, 276); Diamond, "Feuds, fibs and finger pointing: Trump officials say coronavirus response was worse than known," WP (3.29.21); Mascarenhas and Howard, "10 things the 'pandemic doctors' revealed to Dr Sanjay Gupta about their time fighting covid-19," CNN (3.29.21).
80 https://coronavirus.jhu.edu/region/united-states
81 Woodward (2020: 377, 384); Woodward and Costa (2021: 113);
82 Abutaleb and Paletta (2021: 349); Birx (2022: 280–281).
83 www.who.int/docs/default-source/coronaviruse/20200630-covid-19-sitrep-162.pdf.
84 Bump, "The most dangerous false positive: Trump's ongoing insistence that the pandemic is under control," WP (8.3.20).
85 www.nytimes.com/interactive/2021/world/covid-cases.html
86 Mascarenhas and Howard, "10 things the 'pandemic doctors' revealed to Dr Sanjay Gupta about their time fighting covid-19," CNN (3.29.21); Abutaleb and Paletta (2021: 351, 355–356); USSHSGAC (2022: 200).
87 Booth, "Lancet editor Richard Horton has harsh words for Trump, hope for science," WP (7.29.20); Horton (2021); "Scientific American Endorses Joe Biden," Scientific American (10.2.20); "Scientific American, "backing Biden, makes its first ever presidential endorsement," NYT (9.15.20); "Dying in a leadership vacuum," 383 NEJM 1479 (10.8.20); "Why *Nature* supports Joe Biden for US president," 586 Nature 335 (10.14.20); Reardon, "Leading scientists urge voters to dump Trump," Scientific American (10.16.20); Macia McNutt and Victor J. Dzau, "NAS and NAM Presidents Alarmed By Political Interference in Science Amid Pandemic" (9.24.20) www.nationalacademies.org/news/2020/09/nas-and-nam-presidents-alarmed-by-political-interference-in-science-amid-pandemic; https://nlcampaigns.org/Joe_Biden_endorsement.pdf.
88 Woolhandler et al. (2021).
89 Mandavilli, "'We were helpless': despair at the C.D.C. as the pandemic erupted," NYT (3.21.23).
90 Hanage et al. (2020).

91 "The administration orders hospitals to bypass the C.D.C. with key virus data, alarming health experts," NYT (7.14.20); Sumner, "White House instructing governors to send National Guard to hospitals to oversee data on Covid-19," Daily Kos (7.15.20); Budryk, "Governors urge Trump to delay changes to hospital Covid-19 reporting," The Hill (7.16.20); Whelan, "Covid-19 data will once again be collected by CDC, in policy reversal," WSJ (8.20.20); Stolberg, "Trump administration orders hospitals to report data or risk losing funding," NYT (8.26.20); Stolberg, "Health experts warn about perils of new virus data collection system," NYT (8.13.20).
92 HSSCC (2022c: 13, 40–45); Weiland, "'Like a hand grasping': Trump appointees describe the crushing of the C.D.C.," NYT (12.16.20).
93 Bernstein and Sun, "CDC director allegedly ordered deletion of email seeking to interfere with coronavirus guidance, House panel chair says," WP (12.10.20); Diamond, "Feuds, fibs and finger pointing: Trump officials say coronavirus response was worse than known," WP (3.29.21); Weiland, Stolberg and Goodenough, "Political appointees meddled in C.D.C.'s 'holiest of the holy' heath reports," NYT (9.13.20).
94 Owermohle, "Emails show HHS official trying to muzzle Fauci," Politico (9.9.20).
95 CDC, "Science Brief: Transmission of SARS-CoV-2 in K-12 Schools and Early Care and Education Programs—Updated" (2.12.21; updated 12.17.21) www.cdc.gov/coronavirus/2019-ncov/science/science-briefs/transmission_k_12_schools.html#:~:text=Similar%20to%20adults%20with%20SARS,or%20die%20from%20COVID%2D19.
96 Sun, "Trump officials seek greater control over CDC reports on coronavirus," WP (9.12.20); Diamond, "Trump officials interfered with CDC reports on Covid-19," Politico (9.11.20); Owermohle, "Emails show HHS official trying to muzzle Fauci," Politico (9.9.20); Sun and Dawsey, "CDC feels pressure from Trump as rift grows over coronavirus response," WP (9.9.20); "Trump loyalists tried to influence C.D.C. virus reports," NYT (9.13.20); Weiland, Stolberg and Goodenough, "Political appointees meddled in C.D.C.'s 'holiest of the holy' health reports," NYT (9.13.20); HSSCC (2022c: 37–38).
97 Diamond, "Trump officials celebrated efforts to change CDC reports on coronavirus, emails show," WP (4.9.21); Mendez, "Trump officials bragged about pressuring CDC to alter covid reports, emails reveal" CNBC (4.9.21); Atlas, "Science says: Colleges should all reopen (with precautions)," NY Post (9.15.20); Lewis (2021: 295).
98 HSSCC (2022c: 46–51).
99 Abutaleb, Sun, Dawsey and Helderman, "Top Trump health appointee Michael Caputo warns of armed insurrection after election," WP (9.15.20); LaFraniere, "A Trump aide's bizarre warning of conspiracies and 'hit squads,'" NYT (9.15.20); Iati et al., "Trump health appointee apologizes to HHS staff after accusing scientists of 'sedition,'" WP (9.15.20); Abutaleb and Dawsey, "Top Trump health appointee taking medical leave after incendiary remarks," WP (9.16.20); Weiland and LaFraniere, "Health official to take leave of absence after he attacked federal scientists," NYT (9.17.20); Abutaleb, "Trump's $250 million coronavirus ad campaign had 'partisan' edge, down to the celebrities chosen to participate," WP (10.29.20); Wright (2021: 203–204); Borrell (2021: 214).
100 Bender (2021: 241); Borrell (2021: 229); Perez, "Who is Dr. Scott Atlas? Trump's new covid health adviser seen as counter to Fauci and Birx," Forbes (8.12.20); Weiland, Stolberg, Shear and Tankersley, "A new coronavirus adviser roils the White House with unorthodox ideas," NYT (9.2.20); Abutaleb and Dawsey, "New Trump pandemic adviser pushed controversial 'herd immunity' strategy,

worrying public health officials," WP (9.2.20); "Dr. Scott Atlas: there is no risk to children from Covid-19, I don't know why people deny this," Sunday Morning Futures with Maria Bartiromo, Fox News (7.9.20); HSSCC (2022a: 2–10, 17–18); Leonnig and Rucker (2021: 227); Abutaleb and Paletta (2021: 414).

101 https://covid19.who.int/region/amro/country/us.

102 www.cdc.gov/nchs/nvss/vsrr/covid_weekly/index.htm; https://ourworldindata.org/covid-deaths#what-is-the-cumulative-number-of-confirmed-deaths.

103 Abutaleb and Paletta (2021: 354, 357, 361, 363–366).

104 Birx (2022: 283–285, 291).

105 Andrew G. Atkeson, "Behavior and the Dynamic of Epidemics," Brookings Papers on Economic Activity (3.24.21); Benjamin Rader et al., "Mask-Wearing and Control of SARS-CoV-2 Transmission in the USA: A Cross Sectional Study," The Lancet (1.19.21); Kathryn R. Fair et al., "Estimating COVID-19 Cases and Deaths Prevented by Non-Pharmaceutical Interventions, and the Impact of Individual Actions: A Retrospective Model-Based Analysis," Epidemics (June 2022); Michael J. Ahlers et al., "Non-Pharmaceutical Interventions and COVID-19 Burden in the United States," medRxiv (9.28.21); Catalina Amuedo-Dorantes et al., "Timing of Social Distancing Policies and COVID-19 Mortality: County-Level Evidence from the U.S.," 34 Journal of Population Economics 1444–1472 (4.8.21); Xiaoshuang Liu et al., "Differential Impact of Non-Pharmaceutical Public Health Interventions on COVID-19 Epidemics in the United States," 21 BMC Public Health (5.21.21).

106 Weiland and Stolberg, "Birx, Trump's covid coordinator, told congressional investigators that the White House asked her to water down guidance to states," NYT (6.23.22); HSSCC (2022c: 26).

107 Goldstein and Sun, "Controversial change in guidelines about coronavirus testing directed by White House Coronavirus Task Force," WP (8.27.20); Stolberg, "Top U.S. officials told C.D.C. to soften coronavirus testing guidelines," NYT (8.27.20); O'Donnell, Chandler and Maddipatla, "Most U.S. states reject Trump administration's new covid-19 testing guidance," Reuters (8.28.20); Varmus and Shah, "It has come to this: ignore the C.D.C.," NYT (9.1.20); Young, "DoJ may investigate blue states over covid deaths at nursing homes," Politico (8.26.20); Mandavilli, "C.D.C. testing guidance was published against scientists' objections," NYT (9.18.20); Farzan, Hassan, Noack, Taylor, Villegas, Hawkins, Firozi and Denham, "CDC reverses controversial guidance, saying tests are for anyone who contacts someone with covid-19," WP (9.18.20); Birx (2022: 295–296); Diamond, "Messonnier, Birx detail political interference in last year's coronavirus response," WP (11.13.21).

108 Leonnig and Rucker (2021: 231); Bender (2021: 242); HSSCC (2022a: Redfield Interview p. 4).

109 www.nytimes.com/interactive/2021/us/covid-cases.html

110 HSSCC (2022a: 21).

111 "Every shout-out for shots is valuable. Even the one from Trump," WP (12.24.21); Alba, "Redfield voices alarm over influence of Trump's new coronavirus adviser," NBC News (9.28.20); Grynbaum, "Chris Wallace, awaiting virus test, tells Fox News viewers: 'wear the damn mask,'" NYT (10.3.20); HSSCC (2022a: 5, 11–12, 14).

112 www.kff.org/coronavirus-covid-19/issue-brief/covid-19-cases-deaths-and-vaccinations-by-race-ethnicity-as-of-winter-2022/#:~:text=As%20of%20December%202022%2C%20age,3.2%20per%20100%2C000%20for%20Asian.

113 Birx (2022: 302, 348–352).

114 Dawsey, "Former Pence aide says she will vote for Biden because of Trump's 'flat-out disregard for human life' during pandemic," WP (9.17.20); "Olivia

Troye: former Pence aide says General Keith Kellogg is lying about firing her," heavy.com (Sept. 2020); Leonnig and Rucker (2021: 97–98).

115 https://covid.cdc.gov/covid-data-tracker/#datatracker-home.

116 Abutaleb, Rucker, Dawsey and Cost, "Trump's den of dissent: inside the White House Task Force as coronavirus surges," WP (10.19.20); Wu, "Trump aide belittles masks, stirring furor and debunking," NYT (10.20.20); Stolberg, Haberman and Weiland, "Trump calls Fauci 'a disaster' and shrugs off virus as infections soar," NYT (10.20.20).

117 www.statista.com/statistics/1254271/us-total-number-of-covid-cases-by-age-group/

118 Bruggeman and Cathey, "Former Stanford colleagues warn Dr. Scott Atlas fosters 'falsehoods' and 'misrepresentations of science,'" ABC News (9.10.20); McCaskill, "Scott Atlas apologizes for interview with Kremlin-backed RT," Politico (11.1.20); https://int.nyt.com/data/documenttools/read-the-open-letter-from-stanford-doctors-on-scott-atlas/813b50f72b6543b4/full.pdf.

119 Dawsey and Abutaleb, "Scott Atlas resigns as Trump's coronavirus adviser after months of feuding with administration health officials," WP (12.1.20); Birx (2022: 382–383).

120 Abutaleb, Parker, Dawsey and Rucker, "The inside story of how Trump's denial, mismanagement and magical thinking led to the pandemic's dark winter," WP (12.20.20); https://archive.org/details/FOXNEWSW_20200630_040000_Tucker_Carlson_Tonight/start/1320/end/1380; Bump, "Scott Atlas will forever be the face of surrender to the coronavirus," WP (12.1.20).

121 https://ourworldindata.org/coronavirus/country/united-states#what-is-the-daily-number-of-confirmed-deaths.

122 Diamond, "Trump's election challenges distracted from covid response, White House adviser told colleagues," WP (9.24.21); Chase and Owens, "The pandemic has been deadlier in red states," Axios (3.25.22); Schorn, "Tables turned in anthrax probe," CBS News (3.9.07).

123 "President Trump's vaccine chief sees a "very, very low chance' of a vaccine by Election Day," NYT (9.4.20); Bellware et al., "Coronavirus vaccine project chief says he would quit if there was political interference," WP (9.4.20); Yan, Holcome and Erdman, "Doctors warn against rushing a covid-19 vaccine as Fauci says it's critical to have a safe Labor Day," CNN (9.3.20); Thomas, Weiland and LaFraniere, "Pharma companies plan joint pledge on vaccine safety," NYT (9.5.20); Parker, "Trump says he's open to investigation of DeJoy's campaign fundraising," WP (9.8.20); "Nine drugmakers pledge to thoroughly vet any coronavirus vaccine," NYT (9.8.20); Drug Manufacturers' ad, NYT (9.9.20); Stolberg, "Health official tries to reassure public that science will set vaccine approval," NYT (9.10.20); Cavazzoni et al., "We're following the science to protect public health in pandemic," USA Today (9.10.20); Weiland, "F.D.A. regulators publish rare self-defense amid rising vaccine pressure," NYT (9.11.20); Baker and Glasser (2022: 527–528); Kormann, "Countdown to immunity," New Yorker (12.1.20).

124 Abutaleb and Paletta (2021: 383); Cavazzoni et al., "We're following the science to protect public health in pandemic," USA Today (9.10.20).

125 "Trump dismisses Woodward reporting, pushes possibility of coronavirus vaccine before election," WP (9.15.20); Miller and Freking, "Trump denies downplaying virus, casts doubt on mask usage," AP (9.16.20); Russonello, "Trump hits out at C.D.C. director," NYT (9.17.20); Baker, "Trump scorns his own scientists over virus data," NYT (9.17.20); Gearan and Sun, "Trump contradicts health advisers on coronavirus vaccine timetable as death toll mounts," WP (9.18.20); "Health officials sidestep questions about Trump's timeline for

'enough vaccines for every American by April,'" NYT (9.21.20); Leonnig and Rucker (2021: 274, 281–282).

126 Spalding and O'Donnell, "U.S. vaccinations in 2020 fall far short of target of 20 million people," Reuters (12.31.20).

127 HSSCC (2022b: 37–41).

128 Barrett and Zapotosky, "Barr accuses Justice Department of headhunting and meddling with politics," WP (9.17.20); Firozi et al., "Trump attacks FDA plan for tougher standards on emergency vaccine approval as a 'political move,'" WP (9.24.20); Stolberg, "Trump may reject tougher F.D.A. vaccine standards, calling them 'political,'" NYT (9.24.20); Zimmer and Thomas, "Johnson & Johnson's vaccine advances, sparking optimism in race," NYT (9.24.20); Barron, "Coronavirus update," NYT (9.25.20); McGinley, Abutaleb and Dawsey, "Trump, White House demand FDA justify tough standards for vaccine, raising concerns of political interference," WP (9.26.20); "Top White House official denies pressuring F.D.A. on vaccine guidelines," NYT (9.28.20): Borrell (2021: 215); Abutaleb and Paletta (2021: 387–388).

129 Leonnig and Rucker (2021: 283–284); Stolberg, "Biotech industry pushes Trump administration to release new vaccine guidelines," NYT (10.2.20); Thomas and Weiland, "Pfizer says it won't see vaccine authorization before mid-November," NYT (10.16.20); Gold and McKinley, "New York will review virus vaccines, citing politicization of process," NYT (9.25.20); Murphy and Siemaszko, "U.S. hits 7 million covid cases, 2 governors call response worst in world," NBC News (9.24.20); "Office of the California Governor, Newsom says California will also independently review vaccine," NYT (10.20.20); Cowan, "'We believe in science.' Washington, Oregon and Nevada join California's vaccine-review plan," NYT (10.28.20).

130 Burton, "White House takes issue with FDA's plans for authorizing a covid-19 vaccine," WSJ (10.2.20); Armus et al., "White House blocks FDA's ramped up coronavirus vaccine guidelines," WP (10.6.20); Zeller and Perrone, "White House nixes updated FDA guidelines on vaccine approval," AP (10.6.20); LaFraniere and Weiland, "White House blocks new coronavirus vaccine guidelines," NYT (10.6.20); Armus et al., "White House clears FDA coronavirus vaccine standards it tried to derail," WP (10.6.20); Wagner, Iati and Sonmez, "Trump tweets that he's leaving hospital today," WP (10.5.20); Feuer, "Trump says 'no president's ever pushed' the FDA like him, vaccine coming 'very shortly,'" CNBC (10.7.20).

131 Kornfield, "Trump seizes on judge's ruling that Pennsylvania lockdown Is 'unconstitutional,'" WP (9.15.20); Farzan et al., "Trump incorrectly claims that coronavirus affects 'virtually' no young people," WP (9.22.20); Thrush, "Trump falsely says the coronavirus pandemic 'affects virtually nobody,' as U.S. death toll nears 200,000," NYT (9.22.20); Sonmez, "Sen. Ron Johnson, who has covid-19, says he'll 'go in in a moon suit' if necessary to vote on Barrett's confirmation," WP (10.5.20); Kaplan, "White House blocked C.D.C. order to keep cruise ships docked," NYT (10.1.20); Pflum, Strickler, Bennet and Fitzpatrick, "'Toxic': CDC staffers say morale inside the public health agency has plummeted during the pandemic," NBC News (10.25.20).

132 https://covid.cdc.gov/covid-data-tracker/#demographics.

133 www.worldometers.info/coronavirus/country/sweden/; www.statista.com/statistics/1113834/cumulative-coronavirus-deaths-in-the-nordics/.

134 Borrell (2021: 218); Barron, "Coronavirus Update," NYT (10.1.20); Woodward and Costa (2021: 123).

135 Dawsey, Leonnig and Knowles, "Secret Service agents, doctors aghast at Trump's drive outside hospital," WP (10.5.20); Petro, "I'm a former Secret Service executive. The willingness to put agents in danger is inexcusable," WP (10.6.20); Wagner, Iati and Sonmez, "Trump tweets that he's leaving hospital today," WP

(10.5.20); Mandavilli and Tully, "Contact tracing efforts are restricted to the two days before Trump's diagnosis," NYT (10.6.20); Haberman and Thomas, "Trump calls his illness 'a blessing from God,'" NYT (10.8.20); Bellware, "'I don't think I'm contagious,' Trump claims one week after positive coronavirus diagnosis is announced," WP (10.8.20); Johnson, McGinley and Dawsey, "Trump pushes FDA to quickly clear coronavirus antibody treatments, erroneously calling them a 'cure,'" WP (10.9.20); Baker and Haberman, "Trump lashes out at his Cabinet with calls to indict political rivals," NYT (10.9.20); Olorunnipa, Dawsey and Parker, "Trump will speak at a public event at the White House" WP (10.10.20); Brulliard and Sonmez, "Trump says he's not contagious. Health experts say that's not certain," WP (10.12.20); McNeil, "Fauci on what working for Trump was really like," NYT (1.25.21); Stolberg and Weiland, "Study finds 'single largest driver' of coronavirus misinformation: Trump," NYT (10.1.20); Evanega, Lynas, Adams and Smolenyak, "Coronavirus misinformation: quantifying sources and themes in the COVID-19 'Infodemic,'" https://int.nyt.com/data/documenttools/evanega-et-al-coronavirus-misinformation-submitted-07-23-20-1/080839ac0c22bca8/full.pdf.

136 Stolberg, "A senior vaccine scientist who blew the whistle on political interference resigns," NYT (10.7.20); Rick Bright, "I couldn't sit idly and watch people die from Trump's chaotic, politicized pandemic response, so I resigned," WP (10.8.20); Burleigh (2021: 29).

137 Davidson, "In subtle rejoinder to Trump, science carries the night at the Sammies awards for federal workers," WP (10.7.20); "A public health giant gives a scathing indictment of Trump's pandemic response," WP (10.8.20); Stolberg, "'Battered by Trump, the C.D.C.'s director faces pressure to speak out," NYT (10.10.20); William Foege, "Former CDC director: For COVID-19, attempt to build 'herd immunity' is a losing strategy," USA Today (10.29.20); www.epimonitr.net/EIS-Officers-Letter-In-Support-Of-CDC.htm.

138 Kessler, "Trump campaign twists Fauci comment to suggest praise of president," WP (10.12.20); Franck, "Fauci says comments in Trump ad taken 'out of context' and used 'without my permission,'" CNBC (10.11.20); Olorunnipa, "Trump returns to public campaigning, falsely claiming that the virus that infected him is 'disappearing,'" WP (10.11.20); Bender (2021: 299); Farzan et al., "Trump says he feels 'powerful' and will 'kiss' supporters as infections surge in 17 states," WP (10.13.20); "Dr. Fauci warns that a Trump ad 'may turn off a lot of people' by taking him out of context," NYT (10.13.20); Nakamura, Dawsey and Abutaleb, "Trump again attacks Fauci's guidance as coronavirus infections tick upward," WP (10.14.20); Blake and Scott, "5 takeaways from the dueling Trump and Biden town halls," WP (10.16.20); Wright (2021: 244).

139 "Trump's history of germaphobia," WP (6.17.19).

140 www.google.com/search?q=us+covid+rates+over+time&oq=us+covid+rates+over+time&aqs=chrome..69i57j0i22i30l2j0i390l3.5002j0j4&sourceid=chrome&ie=UTF-8.

141 Howard et al., "An evidence review of face masks against COVID-19," 118(4) PNAS e2014564118 (1.11.21) https://doi.org/10.1073/pnas.2014564118.

142 Benzkofer, "Worst plane crash in U.S. history," Chicago Tribune (5.25.14); "Jetliner hits, kills man on Austin airport runway," NBC 5 (5.8.20).

143 Achenbach, "Proposal to hasten herd immunity to the coronavirus grabs White House attention but appalls top scientists," WP (10.14.20).

144 www.cdc.gov/flu/about/burden/2019-2020.html; https://data.cdc.gov/widgets/9bhg-hcku?mobile_redirect=true.

145 Mandavilli, "The coronavirus has infected more than half of Americans, the C.D.C. reports," NYT (4.26.22).

146 https://gbdeclaration.org/.
147 Mandavilli and Stolberg, "A viral theory cited by health officials draws fire from scientists," NYT (10.20.20).
148 Barron, "Coronavirus update," NYT (10.16.20); www.johnsnowmemo.com/john-snow-memo.html; http://dx.doi.org/10.1016/S0140-6736(20)32153-X; Barry, "Herd immunity? Or 'mass murder'?" NYT (10.19.20).
149 Tankersley, Weiland and Cochrane, "White House opposes expanded virus testing, complicating stimulus talks," NYT (10.17.20); Frieden, "The path to 'herd immunity' would be linked with half a million dead Americans," WP (10.18.20).
150 Mayo Clinic, "Herd immunity and COVID-19: What you need to know" www.mayoclinic.org/diseases-conditions/coronavirus/in-depth/herd-immunity-and-coronavirus/art-20486808; D'Souza and Dowdy, "Rethinking Herd Immunity and the Covid-19 Response End Game" (9.13.21) https://publichealth.jhu.edu/2021/what-is-herd-immunity-and-how-can-we-achieve-it-with-covid-19; Association for Professionals in Infection Control and Epidemiology, "Herd Immunity" https://apic.org/monthly_alerts/herd-immunity/; Murray, "COVID-19: The Myth of Herd Immunity," Institute for Health Metrics and Evaluation (10.1.20) www.healthdata.org/video/covid-19-myth-herd-immunity.
151 www.ama-assn.org/system/files/2020-10/covid-health-equity-data-101820.pdf; www.nytimes.com/interactive/2021/us/covid-cases.html.
152 Scherer and Dawsey, "Trump attacks 'Fauci and all these idiots,' says public is tired of pandemic, public health restrictions as infection rates rise," WP (10.20.20); Crowley, "In Arizona, Trump dismisses the virus and again claims Democrats will 'destroy' the suburbs," NYT (10.20.20); Stolberg, Haberman and Weiland, "Trump calls Fauci 'a disaster' and shrugs off virus as infections soar," NYT (10.20.20); Haberman and Crowley, "Trump calls on Barr to 'act' against Biden before election," NYT (10.21.20); Barron, "Coronavirus update," NYT (10.21.20).
153 https://usafacts.org/visualizations/coronavirus-covid-19-spread-map/state/arizona.
154 Leonnig and Rucker (2021: 326); Abutaleb and Paletta (2021: 415–419); Dawsey and Abutaleb, "'A whole lot of hurt': Fauci warns of covid-19 surge, offers blunt assessment of Trump response," WP (11.1.20); "Days of deception are over. It is time for truth on the pandemic," WP (11.4.20).
155 https://coronavirus.jhu.edu/region/united-states.
156 Abutaleb, "President-elect Biden announces coronavirus task force made up of physicians and health experts," WP (11.9.20).
157 Banco, "Trump's Covid Task Force is livid over the Trump White House's 'we ended covid' report," Daily Beast (10.28.20); Shear and Stolberg, "With winter coming and Trump still in charge, virus experts fear the worst," NYT (11.4.20); www.rev.com/blog/transcripts/donald-trump-rally-speech-transcript-butler-pa-october-31.
158 "Coronavirus in the U.S.: Latest map and case count," NYT (4.28.22).
159 www.rev.com/blog/transcripts/donald-trump-rally-speech-transcript-butler-pa-october-31.
160 Dawsey and Abutaleb, "'A whole lot of hurt': Fauci warns of covid-19 surge, offers blunt assessment of Trump response," WP (11.1.20); Farzan and Noack, "Trump suggests he will fire Fauci after election," WP (11.2.20); Peiser, "Twitter bans Steve Bannon for video suggesting violence against Fauci, FBI Director Wray," WP (11.6.20).
161 www.statista.com/statistics/1102816/coronavirus-covid19-cases-number-us-americans-by-day/.
162 https://ourworldindata.org/grapher/total-and-daily-covid-cases-per-million?time=2020-11-03&country=~GBR.

163 Sun and Dawsey, "Top Trump adviser bluntly contradicts president on covid-19 threat, urging all-out response," WP (11.3.20); Stolberg and Haberman, "'We are entering the most concerning and most deadly phase of this pandemic,' Birx wrote in a White House memo," NYT (11.3.20); Kornfield, "Criticized by science community and Trump, Birx said she 'always' considered quitting," WP (1.22.21); Birx (2022: 385–386, 391–393, 414–415, 433).
164 https://coronavirus.jhu.edu/region/united-states.
165 Abutaleb and Paletta (2021: 422–423).
166 McGinley, Dawsey, Abutaleb and Johnson, "Trump rails against 'medical deep state' after Pfizer vaccine news comes post-Election Day," WP (11.12.20); HSSCC (2022b: 40–41); LaFraniere, "Trump slams the F.D.A. ahead of expected vaccine authorization," NYT (12.11.20); "White House orders FDA Chief to authorize Pfizer-BioNTech vaccine Friday or submit his resignation," WP (12.11.20); Thomas, LaFraniere, Weiland, Goodenough and Haberman, "F.D.A. clears Pfizer vaccine, and millions of doses will be shipped right away," NYT (12.12.20); Borrell (2021: 248); Weiland and Sanger-Katz, "Last-minute rule seeks term limits on top career officials," NYT (1.16.21).
167 Alba and Frenkel, "From voter fraud to vaccine lies: misinformation peddlers shift gears," NYT (12.16.20); Dwoskin and Dawsey, "The Trump administration wants to take credit for a covid vaccine. Trump supporters are undermining it," WP (12.25.20).
168 Rowland, "Doctors and nurses want more data before championing vaccines to end the pandemic," WP (11.21.20); Hawkins, "117 staffers sue over Houston hospital's vaccine mandate, saying they don't want to be 'guinea pigs,'" WP (5.30.21); Diamond, "153 people resigned or were fired from a Texas hospital system after refusing to get vaccinated," WP (6.23.21); Gigante, Downie and Fishbein, "Federal court upholds employer's covid-19 vaccine mandate" (1.15.21) www.lawandtheworkplace.com/2021/06/federal-court-upholds-employers-covid-19-vaccine-mandate/; Diamond, Mueller, Baumhardt and Myers, "'I feel defeated': Mask and vaccine mandates cause new divides as officials try to head off virus surge," WP (8.15.21).
169 Kornfield and Jacobs, "As coronavirus death toll surpasses 350,000, Trump calls U.S. count 'far exaggerated,'" WP (1.3.21); Mueller and Nolen, "Death toll during pandemic far exceeds totals reported by countries, W.H.O. says," NYT (5.5.22); Abutaleb, Parker, Dawsey and Rucker, "The inside story of how Trump's denial, mismanagement and magical thinking led to the pandemic's dark winter," WP (12.20.20).
170 Atwood, "Pompeo-led effort to hunt down Covid lab theory shut down by Biden administration over concerns about quality of evidence," CNN (5.25.21).

3

THE COVID-19 PANDEMIC AFTER THE 2020 ELECTION

Once Biden took office and kept repeating the mantra that his administration would "follow the science,"[1] the politics of the pandemic mutated (like the coronavirus itself). Instead of Trump touting magic bullets and promising quick bogus cures while compromising scientific integrity, Republicans used the pandemic to undermine the new administration, and dissident doctors sought fame (and fortune) by offering quack remedies.[2]

1. Rogue Medical "Experts"

Sen. Johnson (outgoing chair of the Homeland Security and Governmental Affairs Committee) reprised Trump's unfounded accusations against medical professionals, suggesting that they opposed HCQ because Trump endorsed it and favored remdesivir because it cost 150 times as much.[3] Johnson even imitated Trump's false innuendos: "Maybe there's a little bias, maybe there's a little conflict, maybe there's a little agenda." He had three doctors testify, including a Yale professor criticized by more than two dozen colleagues and a Brawley, California, family doctor who relied on anecdote. Johnson sought testimony by AAPS Executive Director Jane M. Orient, who advocated for HCQ, questioned vaccinations for young people "because the effect on fertility has not been determined" and asked why Fauci was "dictating care for 340 million Americans." Johnson also sought testimony from a cardiologist who opposed masking and social distancing and two doctors promoting ivermectin. He complained that "there's a blackout on good information in social media and media. So people are being denied information to make intelligent choices for themselves." He refused to get the vaccine because he had had covid, which "provides me the best immunity possible." (The CDCP

DOI: 10.4324/9781032629124-3

disagreed.)[4] At a Senate hearing, Sen. Paul asked Fauci: if people had had the vaccine or covid and were "not spreading the infection, isn't [wearing a mask] just theater?" Fauci replied that the studies Paul quoted "look at in vitro examination of memory immunity," which "does not necessarily pertain to the actual protection."

Johnson said: "we are over 3,000 deaths of, after, within 30 days of taking the vaccine," according to the Vaccine Adverse Event Reporting Scheme (VAERS), and "about 40 percent of those occur on day zero, one or two."[5] But CDC replied: "a review of available clinical information, including death certificates, autopsy, and medical records has not established a causal link to COVID-19 vaccines." Johnson had earlier asserted that governments should not shut down the economy if just 3.45 percent of the population were to die of covid (which would be more than 11 million people). In April, he said he was "highly suspicious" of pressures to vaccinate.

Other physicians abused the trust of their patients.[6] Dr. Steven LaTulippe and his staff in Salem, Oregon, refused to mask and directed patients to "take off the mask of shame." He sought to expose "corona mania." COVID had "been with us forever." "The problem with the mask itself is . . . pustulosis of the nose, impetigo of the face . . . migraine headaches, fatigue, confusion."

> I'm challenging the system a little bit because what everybody is calling [Oregon Gov.] Kate Brown's legal mandate is really an illegal mandate. She has no jurisdiction to be imposing shutdowns and to be telling any doctor how to practice medicine. I don't think she knows as much as I do about microbiology, virology, epidemiology and infection [sic] disease.

The Oregon Medical Board issued an emergency suspension of his license for "actively promot[ing] transmission of the virus within the extended community" by his poor example and regularly misinforming patients that mask wearing was "very dangerous." It subsequently revoked his license and fined him $10,000 for engaging in "dishonorable or unprofessional conduct" by misinforming patients that masks were ineffective and endangered their health by forcing them to re-inhale carbon dioxide.

Simone Gold (a Beverly Hills doctor who had graduated from Rosalind Franklin University in Chicago in 1989) and John Strand (the nonscientist head and Communications Director of America's Frontline Doctors, or AFLDS) promoted HCQ and warned of the vaccine's risks.[7] AFLDS published a white paper in January 2021 denouncing vaccines. Gold pleaded guilty to illegally entering the Capitol on January 6 and having Strand film her denouncing vaccines and served 60 days in prison, but she was still licensed to practice in California. AFLDS later sued her for misappropriating the group's funds. Judy Mikovits (who had a Ph.D. in biochemistry) claimed covid was a flu virus, which masks "activated," causing it to recur.

YouTube, Vimeo and Facebook removed her video "Plandemic" asserting this but only after it was shared or commented on 8 million times, and *Science* withdrew her 2009 paper attributing chronic fatigue to viral infection after two co-authors repudiated the results. Far-right extremists were maintaining that "covid-19 vaccines are weapons of mass destruction—and could wipe out the human race"—and those administering them "will be tried as war criminals."

AFLDS was accused of charging for consultations that never occurred and medications that never arrived and should not have been prescribed.[8] One member, Dr. Lee Merritt, who claimed the virus was a genetically engineered bioweapon and vaccination increased the risk of death from COVID, was able to renew her license in Nebraska. *The Intercept* found that AFLDS had prescribed HCQ and ivermectin to hundreds of thousands of patients, and online health care companies associated with it had charged patients millions of dollars. AFLDS had more than 200,000 followers on Telegram; Gold had more than 380,000 on Twitter. NPR found no action against 16 doctors who spread disinformation. The president of the Federation of State Medical Boards said a recent survey of its members discovered that over half had seen an increase in complaints against doctors disseminating COVID misinformation, and 21 percent had taken some disciplinary action.

Fox News (Steve Doocy and Maria Bartiromo), Sen. Johnson and Trump continued to promote HCQ, which Trump called one of the things "they are now admitting I was right about."[9] Their evidence was a study of 255 patients at Saint Barnabas Medical Center in Livingston, NJ, by Dr. Stephen M. Smith, who often appeared on Fox News and claimed that HCQ and azithromycin produced "a survival rate 2.9 times the other patients." (Given a U.S. case fatality rate of 1 percent, the study population was far too small to permit statistical analysis.) Smith had graduated from Yale Medical School in 1989, did graduate work in infectious disease at NIH in 1995, had a subcertification in infectious disease and had founded the Smith Center for Infectious Diseases and Urban Health. He said on Laura Ingraham's program in April 2021: "I think this is the beginning of the end of the pandemic. I'm very serious." (Case numbers more than doubled over the following year.) He boasted that none of the 72 patients he treated with the drug had to be intubated. "The chance of that occurring by chance, according to my sons Leon and Hunter who did some stats for me, are .000-something." "It's ridiculously low." (There was no control group, and the population was too small for statistical analysis because only 10 percent of hospitalized COVID patients were being intubated at that time.)[10] He cited a French study with similar results, claiming: "you actually have an intra-cohort comparison saying that this regimen works." (That study had similar flaws, see Chapter 2.)

Sherri Tenpenny, a Cleveland-area doctor, testified to the Republican-dominated Ohio House of Representatives that vaccines left people "magnetized" and could "interface" with 5G cellular towers.[11] "I'm sure you've seen the pictures all over the Internet of people who have had these shots and now they're magnetized. They can put a key on their forehead. It sticks." The lawmakers thanked her for that "enlightening" testimony. She falsely claimed on *Coach Dave Live* (an Ohio podcast) that vaccines interfered with fertility. Tenpenny received her Doctor of Osteopathic Medicine from Kirksville College of Osteopathic Medicine in 1984; after more than a decade as ER Director at Blanchard Valley Hospital in Findlay, Ohio, she opened her own practice. She and a partner charged $623 for a six-week "Mastering Vaccine Info Boot Camp" intended to "sow seeds of doubt" about public health information. In December 2020, Facebook deactivated her page for spreading misinformation; nevertheless, a March 2021 analysis of Twitter and Facebook found that she was one of the 12 individuals and organizations, which together produced up to two-thirds of all anti-vax data. She also opposed masks. In a February 2021 video, she said: "Some people are going to die from the vaccine directly, but a large number of people are going to start getting horribly sick and get all kinds of autoimmune diseases. 42 days to maybe a year out." An April video reiterated those claims. Twitter permanently suspended her in early July, as did YouTube in September. Nevertheless, the Ohio State Medical Board renewed her license in October.

Joseph Mercola, another osteopathic doctor, said COVID vaccines were "a medical fraud" and "alter your genetic coding, turning you into a viral protein factory that has no off-switch."[12] His online article making that claim was translated into Spanish and Polish, reaching 400,000 people on Facebook, where he had published over 600 disinformation articles. *Freedom's Phoenix* (a local news site) and the *Atlanta Business Journal* published an article by him in March 2021, falsely calling vaccines "gene therapy" and questioning their usefulness, and another in April, claiming that Bill Gates exercised "shadow control" over WHO and was responsible for the pandemic. Mercola said avian flu was a conspiracy of government, big business and the media. His website, the most popular alternative-health source on the Internet, claimed that homeopathy could treat autism and vaccines were detrimental to health. He had stopped practicing medicine in 2009 to devote himself to the far more profitable business of promoting health products and vitamins, boasting he was worth $10 million and had sold more than $100 million in merchandise in 2017. His National Vaccine Information Center and Organic Consumers Association websites received more than 800,000 visits a year. His website promoting alternative COVID remedies was taken down in April 2021 after the FDA issued a warning letter. In September 2021 YouTube removed his accounts.

Andrew Wakefield, a British doctor who lost his UK license for falsely claiming a link between the MMR vaccine and regressive autism, moved to Texas to continue advocating against vaccinations, directing the 2016 film "Vaxxed: From Cover-Up to Catastrophe," which was pulled from the Tribeca Film Festival and removed from Amazon Prime.[13] Wakefield attended Trump's inaugural ball and called for a "shake-up" of the CDC. During his 2016 campaign, Trump also had claimed that vaccines caused autism. Robert F. Kennedy Jr. had published an article in *Rolling Stone* and *Salon* in 2005 claiming that vaccines with thimerosal damaged children's brains, causing autism.[14] After it was debunked, *Salon* removed it. Monthly visits to Kennedy's Children's Health Defense website rose from under 84,000 in January 2020 to 1.4 million in March 2022, and revenue increased from $1.1 million in 2018 to $6.8 million in 2020.

Dr. Vladimir Zelenko (who practiced in Kiryas Joel, New York, until the Hassidic community forced him to leave) posted a video on YouTube and Facebook claiming a 100 percent success rate for HCQ.[15] He spoke on Bannon and Giuliani podcasts, was promoted by Hannity, and talked to Meadows. He also claimed that more children died from COVID vaccines than from the disease.

Dr. Christiane Northrup (an ObGyn) said on the Lillian McDermott radio show in Florida that vaccines "change human DNA." Ty Bollinger (who called himself a "medical researcher" but had no scientific training) argued against vaccinations on News4 WSMV Nashville, an NBC-affiliated station. Dr. Daniel Stock told the Mt. Vernon, Indiana, school board that vaccines were ineffective, masks did not slow the spread of infection, vaccinated people could shed the virus, and drugs and supplements prevented hospitalization.[16] His videos had gotten nearly 100 million likes and shares on Facebook and 6.2 million views on Twitter, 2.8 million on YouTube, and over 940,000 on Instagram. Although the Federation of State Medical Boards (FSMB) recommended action against such doctors, and the AMA said they violated ethical codes, the Indiana Medical Board could only act on complaints from the state Attorney General, whose office would not disclose whether it was investigating Stock. In January 2021, a San Francisco doctor who claimed that 5G technology caused the pandemic surrendered his medical license.

Five doctors wrote in a *Washington Post* op ed: "State medical boards should punish doctors who spread false information about covid and vaccines."[17] In July, the FSMB (representing 71 regulatory agencies in 50 states, DC, and U.S. territories) denounced physicians who spread disinformation. Physicians for Human Rights was seeking to discipline doctors who disseminated covid misinformation. No License for Disinformation published "Disinformation Doctors: Licensed to Mislead" in December 2021. In response to a FSMB report warning that "physicians' status and titles lend credence to their claims," and with support from the California Medical Association and the AMA, California enacted the first bill in the nation to make giving patients false or misleading medical information "unprofessional conduct" subject to discipline by the Medical Board of California. But in a challenge backed by the ACLU, ED California Judge Shubb (GHWB) found the law unconstitutionally vague.[18]

On *Fox & Friends*, Dr. Mehmet Oz cited an "important randomized study still unpublished from Wuhan, China" with 62 patients, claiming that among the half who got HCQ, "their fevers broke instead of three days, which is the norm over there on this treatment, they got two days."[19] The study had not been peer-reviewed and had no control group; the comparison was between those who received more or less of the drug. Dr. Neil Schluger, chair of the New York Medical College Department of Medicine, commented: "it's likely that patients who died rapidly received less total [drug] because they were dead" or "received lower doses on a daily basis . . . because they were sicker to begin with." A week earlier a Canadian study found "no evidence that hydroxychloroquine reduced symptom duration or prevented severe outcomes."

Oz had a BA from Harvard and an MD and MBA from University of Pennsylvania. He became a professor at Columbia University Vagelos College of Physicians and Surgeons in 2001; but 10 colleagues sought his dismissal in 2015 because he had "repeatedly shown disdain for science and for evidence-based medicine." After more than 1,300 doctors signed a critical letter, Columbia severed its ties with him. Oz also had been criticized by a Senate committee for promoting weight-loss pills. He had promoted homeopathy, said apple juice contained unsafe levels of arsenic (the FDA disagreed), and warned that women carrying cellphones in their bras could get breast cancer (the Breast Cancer Foundation NZ found "no evidence" for this). A 2014 *British Medical Journal* article concluded that fewer than half of the 80 health recommendations on his tv show were supported by evidence. Two of the show's researchers said producers initiated most of the medical claims, which they took from the Internet, and rejected the researchers' counterevidence.

In December 2021, Oz announced he would seek the Republican nomination for the Senate in Pennsylvania.[20] He said the pandemic had been mishandled by "elites," who suppressed dissent, "mandated" policies, "closed our parks, shuttered our schools, shut down our businesses and took away our freedom." "Elites with yards told those without yards to stay inside, where the virus was more likely to spread." In April 2020, citing a medical journal, he declared that opening schools "may only cost us 2 to 3 percent in terms of total mortality." (That would be 6.64–9.96 million dead.) He later said he "misspoke." In February and March 2021, Oz promoted HCQ and CQ more than 25 times on Fox News, calling the small discredited French evaluation of the drugs "a game changer." But he stopped when a Veterans Affairs study showed that patients treated with HCQ were more likely to die than untreated patients, conceding that "we are better off waiting for the randomized trials." Trump had appointed him to the Council on Sports, Fitness and Nutrition and supported Oz's Senate run, but he lost to John Fetterman.

After Republicans won control of the Central District Health Board of Ada County, Idaho (which includes Boise), it replaced Ted Epperly (a former president of the American Academy of Family Physicians), who supported mask mandates, with Ryan Cole (a pathologist), who attacked the "fake vaccine . . . the clot shot, needle rape."[21] Cole claimed that other mRNA vaccines caused cancer and autoimmune diseases, citing a paper whose author said it rejected those claims. Cole asserted that COVID vaccines had killed 1,200 people in a single month, based on a misreading of VAERS data. He said the vaccines were "something for which the side effect would be death and/or permanent disability" and recommended against them for children and those who had had COVID. Cole's videos attracted a million views. He spoke in more than 15 states and four foreign countries. Idaho passed a law in March giving county leaders veto power over health board orders. Ada County Commissioner Rod Beck said: "with this whole vaccine thing, we haven't taken other alternative viewpoints." Lt. Gov. Janice McGeachin asserted there was "clear" evidence that people "may be significantly worse off health-wise if they get vaccinated." Only 40 percent of Idahoans were fully vaccinated, compared with 54 percent of the nation. Leaders of the Idaho Medical Association complained to the Idaho Board of Medicine, seeking an investigation of Cole for prescribing ivermectin to COVID patients, but the Board declined to investigate. The Washington Medical Commission (where he was also licensed) investigated him after the American Board of Pathology complained that he improperly prescribed drugs over a telehealth platform and spread false information about COVID. The WMC has said that physicians "who generate and spread COVID-19 misinformation, or disinformation, erode the public trust in the medical profession and endanger patients."

Some chiropractors also opposed vaccinations.[22] Steven Baker, practicing in Idaho, produced a podcast claiming that vaccines turned people into "modern-day zombies," who spewed spike proteins with every breath and discharge of body fluid and could disrupt the menstrual cycles of nearby women. James Bogash, a member of the Arizona Association of Chiropractic, said "natural immunity is stronger and longer lasting than acquired immunity." (CDC disagreed.) Greg Werner, a New York practitioner, declared that the germ theory "doesn't exist" because "if it did EVERYONE would be sick ALL the time." J. Zimmerman, who practiced in New Jersey, said VAERS showed that the vaccine caused COVID. (All these invocations of VAERS data confused correlation with cause; there were many possible causes of death other than the vaccine.) Only two of 11 state organizations contacted advised chiropractors to refer patients to medical doctors for medical questions. The American Chiropractic Association took no stance on vaccines.

By contrast, 57 medical groups, including the AMA and American Nurses Association, representing millions of health care workers, called for mandatory vaccinations of all health personnel.

Social media aggravated the harm from such misinformation by disseminating it widely.[23] A Facebook post questioning the vaccine was the single most popular item in January–March 2021. Another site with covid misinformation, among the 20 most popular, contained an article from the South Florida *Sun Sentinel* reporting that the CDC was investigating a doctor who died two weeks after being vaccinated. Months later, the medical examiner's office said it could not determine the cause of death, but Facebook released this report only after *The New York Times* said it had been withheld by senior officials.

Dr. Mercola warned on Substack that the government might put the unvaccinated in concentration camps and claimed that more children died from the vaccine than from COVID.[24] The Substack CEO and two co-founders asserted that hosting "writers with whom we strongly disagree" was a "necessary precondition for creating more trust in the information ecosystem as a whole." (The opposite seems more likely.) More than 270 doctors and scientists wrote an open letter asking Spotify to drop Joe Rogan, one of the most popular podcasters, for disseminating vaccine conspiracy theories; and many prominent performing artists withdrew from the streaming service in protest. Nevertheless, it declined to remove anyone, though it linked misinformation to its fact-based COVID-19 hub. YouTube banned Dan Bongino for COVID misinformation about mask efficacy. But these minimal steps did not stop the 153 most influential anti-vax social media accounts and groups from recruiting 2.9 million new followers between January 2020 and January 2022.

After Fox News promoted studies encouraging COVID patients to use ivermectin (a drug approved only for deworming horses), prescriptions jumped from a pre-pandemic weekly average of 3,600 to more than 88,000 in August 2021.[25] NIH had found the studies flawed, and the FDA warned against the drug, tweeting: "You are not a horse." Calls to poison control centers increased fivefold from July to August. When West Chester Hospital (Ohio) refused to administer ivermectin to a COVID patient on a ventilator in a medically induced coma and his wife sued, Butler County Common Pleas Judge Gregory Howard ordered the hospital to do so. Dr. Fred Wagshul (who had studied medicine in the Dominican Republic in the 1970s) wrote the prescription, declaring that the science behind the use of ivermectin for COVID was "irrefutable" and accusing the CDC and FDA of a "conspiracy" to block it. "If we were a country looking at another country allowing those [COVID-19] deaths daily . . . we would have been screaming, 'Genocide!'" Though he later retracted the word, he insisted ivermectin was more effective than vaccines. Wagshul was founder of the Front Line Covid-19 Critical Care Alliance, which promoted ivermectin and explained how to obtain it.

Dr. Leanne Chrisman-Khawam, a professor at Ohio University Heritage College of Osteopathic Medicine, called FLCCCA "snake oil salesmen." Butler County Court of Common Pleas Appeals Court Judge Michael A. Oster Jr. reversed Howard's order. "There can be no doubt that the medical and scientific communities do not support the use of ivermectin as a treatment for Covid-19." A West Chester Hospital spokesman said: "we do not believe that hospitals or clinicians should be ordered to administer medications and/or therapies, especially unproven medications and/or therapies, against medical advice." Social media then disseminated the following statement:

> My name is William Campbell, in 2015 I won the Nobel prize in medicine for the discovery of Ivermectin. It cures many diseases including COVID-19. The fake news and big pharma want you to live in fear. Fauci won't promote Ivermectin because he is the little parasite it destroys.

The quote was fabricated. Drew University, where Campbell teaches, reported it to Twitter. Although Facebook removed some groups promoting ivermectin, others remained, and Healthcare Heroes for Personal Choice offered guidance on how to evade such takedowns by removing or misspelling buzzwords.

Erin Jones sued to compel Texas Health Huguley Hospital in Fort Worth to let Dr. Mary Talley Bowden administer ivermectin to Jones's husband.[26] After a trial judge granted Bowden temporary hospital privileges, Second Court of Appeals Chief Justice Bonnie Sudderth (appointed by two Texas Republican governors, Perry and Abbott) dismissed the lawsuit: "Judges are not doctors. We are not empowered to decide whether a particular medication should be administered." Houston Methodist Hospital, where Bowden also had privileges, suspended her for spreading "dangerous" misinformation, telling patients that data "suggests that the vaccine is not working." Palm Beach County's 15th Judicial Circuit Judge James Nutt dismissed a similar lawsuit by Ryan Drock. So did Jefferson County (Kentucky) Circuit Court Judge Charles Cunningham, saying the court "cannot require a hospital to literally take orders from someone who does not routinely issue such orders."

Luc Montagnier, who won a Nobel prize as codiscoverer of the HIV virus but later made dubious claims that DNA emitted electromagnetic radiation (in articles published in his own journal) and that long-term antibiotics could treat autism, also opposed COVID-19 vaccines for allegedly causing viral variants.[27] He published a *Wall Street Journal* op ed with Jed Rubenfeld (a Yale law professor with no scientific background) calling the vaccine mandates legally indefensible and "contrary to the public interest . . . absent any evidence that the vaccines are effective in stopping the spread of the pathogen."

2. Mea Culpas and Recriminations by Trump Administration Officials

The change of administration elicited further information about Trump's politicization of science. Resigning as CDC head, Redfield deplored "the inconsistency of civic leaders [i.e. politicians] to reinforce the public health message."[28] He claimed he had never "caved," complaining "there are some people that will only be satisfied if you personally criticize the president. I'm a chain-of-command kind of guy."

A day after Biden's inauguration, Fauci recollected that he "got into trouble" for challenging Trump.[29] "There were things that were said" about "hydroxychloroquine and other things like that, that . . . were not based on scientific fact." "You didn't feel that you could actually say something and there wouldn't be any repercussions about it." It was "liberating" now to feel "you can get up here and talk about what you know, what the evidence—what the science is." Previously, when he "would try to express the gravity of the situation," Trump always replied: "Well it's not that bad, right?"

> It was clear that he was getting input from . . . people he knew from business, saying, "Hey, I heard about this drug, isn't it great?" . . . And I would try to . . . calmly explain that you find out if something works by doing an appropriate clinical trial; you get the information, you give it a peer review. And he says, "oh, no, no, no, no, no, no, no, this stuff really works." . . . It wasn't just hydroxychloroquine, it was a variety of alternative-medicine-type approaches. We would say things like . . . "Infectious diseases run their own course unless one does something to intervene." And then he would . . . start talking about, "it's going to go away, it's magical, it's going to disappear." . . . I'm not going to proactively go out and volunteer my contradiction. . . . But he would say something that was clearly not correct, and then a reporter would say, "Well, let's hear from Dr. Fauci." I would have to get up and say, "no, I'm sorry, I do not think that is the case." . . . his inner circle were quite upset that I would dare publicly contradict the president. That's when we started getting into things I felt were unfortunate and somewhat nefarious—namely allowing Peter Navarro to write an editorial in USA Today saying I'm wrong on most of the things I say. Or to have the White House Press Office send out a detailed list of things I said that turned out not to be true—all of which were nonsense. . . . Mark Meadows would call me up expressing concern that I was going out of my way to contradict the president. . . . [Navarro] had a whole list of reprints that were completely nonsense. . . . After that, I said I didn't want to be bothered with him. . . . there were a couple of times where I would make a statement that was a pessimistic viewpoint about what direction we were going, and the president would call me up and say, "Hey, why aren't you more positive?"

Fauci never considered quitting:

> I felt that if I stepped down, that would leave a void . . . the skunk at the picnic would no longer be at the picnic. Even if I wasn't very effective in changing everybody's minds, the idea that they knew that nonsense could not be spouted without me pushing back on it, I felt was important.

Rachel Walensky, who succeeded Redfield as CDC Director, said agency personnel "have been muzzled" and "the science has not always been followed." Retiring from that post at the end of June 2023, Walensky declared that "scientific expertise should not take a back seat to partisan will."[30] Acknowledging that "public health and scientific recommendations inevitably intersect with social values and policy . . . is not to suggest that elected leaders—regardless of party—should disregard science or undermine its integrity."

Birx claimed she had "always" contemplated quitting.[31] "Colleagues of mine I had known for decades . . . decided that I had become this political person." At a low point, she visited George W. Bush, with whom she had worked on global AIDS prevention, and confided: "I am not having the impact on the White House with the current pandemic that I would like . . .. I think I should return full time to my PEPFAR position at the State Department." But she remained because Bush was adamantly opposed, saying, "You need to finish. You can never quit." However:

> when it became a point where I wasn't getting anywhere—and that was like right before the election—I wrote a very detailed communication plan of what needed to happen the day after the election and how that needed to be executed.

Four days after Biden's inauguration, she reported that during the Trump administration, someone had been "creating a parallel set of data and graphics that were shown to the president." "I saw the president presenting graphs that I never made." Atlas tweeted a chart that deliberately underestimated the death toll and declared that listening to "additional scientists outside the administration" was "the way to arrive at the best policies." Birx now wished she had been "more outspoken publicly" on testing. She told the House Select Subcommittee on the Coronavirus Pandemic that "the White House had gotten somewhat complacent through the campaign season." "I believe if we had fully implemented the mask mandates, the reduction in indoor dining, the getting friends and family to understand the risk of gathering in private homes, and we had increased testing, that we probably could have decreased fatalities" by 130,000.

Atlas, by contrast, was unrepentant.[32] On January 4, 2021, he issued a statement about masks, maintaining that "The President has been right all along." "Joe Biden's policy is mask mandates and lockdowns. That is also the CNN and MSNBC attack narrative." "[T]he research studies, the best data, indicates [sic] that general masks are not effective." "[T]here is vanishingly little hard evidence that masks actually work to block transmission of the virus. They may even be harmful in certain settings." He tweeted again two weeks later: "Masks work? NO."

On March 29, 2021, after CNN screened a documentary on the pandemic, Trump reprised his attack on Fauci and Birx, calling them:[33]

> two self-promoters trying to reinvent history to cover for their bad instincts and faulty recommendations, which I fortunately almost always overturned. They had bad policy decisions that would have left our country open to China and others, closed to reopening our economy, and years away from an approved vaccine—putting millions at risk. . . . Dr. Fauci and Dr. Birx moved far too slowly, and if it were up to them we'd currently be locked in our basements as our country suffered through a financial depression. . . . Dr. Fauci was incapable of pressing the FDA to move [the vaccine] through faster. I was the one to get it done. . . . Dr. Fauci is also king of "flip-flops" and moving the goalposts to make himself look as good as possible. . . . he wanted to keep our country open to countries like China. I closed it against his strong recommendation, which saved many lives. Dr. Fauci also said we didn't need to wear masks, then a few months later he said we needed to wear masks, and now two or three of them. Fauci spent U.S. money on the Wuhan lab in China—and we know how that worked out.
>
> Dr. Birx is a proven liar with very little credibility left. Many of her recommendations were viewed as "pseudo-science" and Dr. Fauci would always talk negative [sic] about her and, in fact, would ask not to be in the same room with her. The states who followed her lead, like California, had worse outcomes on Covid, and ruined the lives of countless children because they couldn't go to school, ruined many businesses, and an untold number of Americans who were killed by the lockdowns themselves. [As of November 18, 2021, California had fewer cases/population than 36 states.[34]] . . . I only kept Dr. Fauci and Dr. Birx because they worked for the U.S. Government for so long—they are like a bad habit! [They had civil service protection.]

Trump told the Republican National Committee in April that Fauci wanted people to wear five masks: "Have you ever seen anybody that is so full of crap?" A supporter suggested that the vaccine should be called "Trumpcine" (which would make Trump a cow because of the etymology of "vaccine"—perhaps appropriate given his body image).

Navarro denounced Fauci as "a sociopath and a liar" who "had nothing to do with the vaccine."[35] "Fauci is the father of the actual virus." Meadows complained that "there was no policy, medical or otherwise, that Dr. Fauci wouldn't weigh in on when President Trump was in the White House." Sen. Rubio said Fauci's job was "not to mislead or screw" Americans into doing "the right things," such as wearing face masks. Sen. Graham told Fauci to visit the border to witness the "biggest super spreader event." Migrants were "standing on top of each other" and were "dumped off in Texas." Meadows also found it "curious we haven't heard the same Dr. Fauci on Joe Biden releasing thousands of COVID untested migrants into the U.S." But DHS said all those intercepted were tested and quarantined if positive, and Fauci objected: "I have nothing to do with the border."

Conservatives revived the calumny that WIV had deliberately created COVID-19 and Fauci was responsible for funding the research. Fox's Tucker Carlson called him "Lord Fauci, Patron Saint of Wuhan" and blamed the pandemic on "the experiments [in Wuhan] that clearly went so wrong."[36]

> This wouldn't have happened if Tony Fauci didn't allow it to happen . . . in a functional country, there would be a criminal investigation into Tony Fauci's role in the covid pandemic that has killed millions and halted our country, changing it forever.

Accused by Sen. Paul of funding "gain-of-function" research in Wuhan, Fauci retorted: "you are entirely and completely incorrect . . . the NIH has not ever and does not now fund gain-of-function research in the Wuhan Institute." A month later, however, Trump repeated that canard: "Now everybody is agreeing that I was right when I very early called Wuhan as the source of COVID-19, sometimes referred to as the China Virus." (It was he who coined and popularized the derogatory term, deliberately conflating the city where the virus originated with the laboratory without offering any evidence.) China should be charged $10 trillion for the coronavirus. Fauci was a "radical masker," who might want people to wear 3–4 masks and goggles for years. "He's not a great doctor, but a hell of a promoter. He likes television more than any politician in this room." Trump repeated Navarro's claim that Fauci had "been wrong on almost every issue." Sens. Hawley and Paul demanded his resignation, and Hawley sought a "full congressional investigation." Gov. DeSantis said: "in Florida, we choose freedom over Fauci-ism, and we're much better off for doing that." (It was no accident that the epithet sounded like "fascism," given that Fauci was Italian American. Florida, which had the seventh highest ratio of cases/population in November 2022, was hardly "better off" than other states.)[37] Because NIH had given $3.7 million to EcoHealth Alliance, which sub-granted $600,000 to WIV over five years, Rep. Scalise and Sen. Paul said Fauci was involved in a cover-up, and NIH had funded the creation of the virus. Fauci replied: "are you really saying that we are implicated because we gave a multi-billion dollar institution

$120,000 a year for bat surveillance?" In June 2021, Pompeo was still blaming WIV: "it's the cumulative evidence. It's the absence of evidence for other theories as well." Although NIH Director Collins was "not at all convinced that a natural origin is the only explanation," he explained that "an expert trying to design an even more effective coronavirus would never have come up with this design." Jon Stewart declared on Stephen Colbert's late-night show at CBS that the pandemic "was more likely caused by science," though his only "evidence" was the fact that "the disease is the same name as the lab."[38] (That was so only because Fauci's detractors deliberately misnamed the disease.)

Fauci said, "I haven't seen" evidence "that proves the lab leak theory . . . because I'm not sure it exists."[39] "I feel, as do the overwhelming majority of scientists who have knowledge of virology and knowledge of evolutionary biology, that the most likely explanation for this is a natural leap from an animal reservoir to a human." A month later, Sen. Paul again attacked Fauci: "knowing that it is a crime to lie to Congress, do you wish to retract your statement of May 11 where you claimed that the NIH never funded gain-of-function research in Wuhan?"[40] Fauci replied: "I have never lied before Congress, and I do not retract that statement." The research had been "judged by qualified staff up and down the chain as not being gain-of-function." Paul accused Fauci of "trying to obscure responsibility for four million people dying around the world from a pandemic." Fauci answered: "I totally resent the lie that you are now propagating, senator. . . . if anybody's lying here, senator, it is you." When Paul said "you've had the vaccine, and you're wearing two masks. Is that just theater?" Fauci lost his patience: "here we go again." The next day, Fauci added: "[Y]ou do not know what you're talking about, quite frankly, and I want to say that officially."

Others piled on. Marc Bernier, host of a show on WNDB in Daytona Beach, Florida, called himself "Mr. Anti-Vax" and accused the Biden administration of "acting like Nazis" in urging vaccinations—until he died of COVID.[41] Dick Farrel, who worked for radio stations in Miami and Palm Beach as well as Newsmax TV, called COVID mitigation efforts "a scam-demic" and Fauci "a power-tripping, lying freak." Jimmy DeYoung, a nationally syndicated Christian preacher in Tennessee and host of *Prophecy Today*, asked rhetorically whether the vaccine could be "another form of government control of people." The White Coat Waste Project launched a campaign against Fauci, claiming that NIAID had funded an experiment in Tunisia in which beagles were trapped in mesh cages filled with diseased sand flies. It turned out that Tunisian scientists had mistakenly listed NIAID (which Fauci directed) as a funder in a journal article. Nevertheless, WCWP drafted a letter signed by 24 members of Congress from both parties asking NIAID to disclose its funding of research on dogs. Social media linking Fauci and puppies was posted or shared 375,000 times in five days, eliciting two billion views. Donald Trump

Jr. was selling "Fauci Kills Puppies" t-shirts and hoodies, while FauciLied-DogsDied trended on Twitter. Although the journal quickly corrected the article, WCWP refused to believe the denial. Fauci said: "this attack on me, which clearly has political overtones to a nonpolitical scientist, I feel, is dangerous to the entire field of science and [shows] how people try to intimidate scientists." NIH Director Collins said:

> What's happening to Dr. Fauci is a very bright, blazing warning sign that we are, as a culture, in a dangerous place, that we have decided that those figures who are highly visible, who are saying things we don't like, have to be taken down.

At a January 2022 hearing of the Senate Committee on Health, Education, Labor and Pensions, Sen. Burr accused Fauci and others of spreading "skepticism and mass confusion" through mixed messaging.[42] Sen. Paul called Fauci "the lead architect for the response from the government, and now 800,000 people have died." Fauci replied:

> In usual fashion, senator, you are distorting everything about me. You keep coming back to personal attacks on me that have absolutely no relevance. . . . why would a Senator want to do this? Go to Rand Paul's website and you see fire Dr Fauci with a little box that says contribute here. . . . So you are making [use of] a catastrophic epidemic for your political gain.

Such an "irresponsible" statement "kindles the crazies." "I have threats upon my life, harassments of my family." A man with a high-powered rifle and ammunition had been arrested in Iowa after threatening to murder him. He had a security guard and CCTV watching his house. Sen. Marshall displayed a giant paycheck with Fauci's $400,000+ salary and accused him of hiding his financial investments, creating an "appearance that maybe some shenanigans are going on." "You've lost your reputation. The American people don't trust the words coming out of your mouth." At the end of the hearing, Fauci called Marshall a "moron."

In July 2021, Trump doubled down on his unsubstantiated accusation that the virus had been created in a laboratory, claiming Facebook prohibited posts asserting this.[43]

> I said, Wuhan and it was like a bomb went up. Wuhan. Came from the Wuhan lab. Of course there were body bags all outside the lab. . . . They said it came from a thousand miles away from a bat or it came from another country. . . . But then it was finally revealed that this was most likely the truth. That it came from the lab. . . . Google and YouTube have deleted countless videos that dared to question the judgment of the World

> Health Organization, which has been wrong so often. It's been a really pipe organ for China. . . . Doctors and medical groups have been barred from these platforms for posting about therapeutics, such as hydroxychloroquine . . . which now, most recent studies, say is effective in combatting the virus. . . . The drug companies don't like three cents a pill.

The next month, Rep. McCaul released a report by Republican staff of the House Foreign Affairs Committee (of which he was the ranking member) claiming that "a preponderance of the evidence" showed that covid-19 had leaked from WIV before September 12, 2019, and there was "ample evidence" the laboratory had been working to modify coronaviruses to infect humans.[44] Redfield, who said he had felt "sidelined" and "threatened" for telling CNN in March 2020 he believed the virus originated in a Chinese lab, now claimed "growing evidence" for his theory. But an ODNI report required by Biden found that China did not develop the coronavirus as a bioweapon, though the Office could not determine its origins because of obstacles created by China. Four intelligence agencies and the National Intelligence Council (NIC) assessed with "low confidence" that the virus was "most likely caused by natural exposure" to an animal or a close progenitor virus, while one agency expressed "moderate confidence" that it "most likely was the result of a lab-associated incident" in WIV. Michael Worobey, a University of Arizona evolutionary virologist who had entertained the laboratory theory, now believed the virus originated in the Wuhan market because more than half of the earliest documented illnesses involved people directly connected to it, and the person known to be ill was a seafood vendor. In June 2022, the Scientific Advisory Group for the Origins of Novel Pathogens (created by WHO) said the possibility that the virus escaped from a lab needs "further investigation," but it offered no new data. (A year earlier, it had found that theory "extremely unlikely.") The group also said the data suggested that COVID-19 had a zoonotic origin, but it could not identify the animal or where the leap to a human occurred.

Republicans continued to politicize the issue. In February 2023, Acting NIH Director Lawrence A. Tabak told a House hearing that the virus studied in WIV "bears no relationship to SARS-CoV-2; they are genetically distinct."[45] Nevertheless, Rep. Griffith (R-Va) was convinced beyond "a reasonable doubt" that the virus had originated in that lab because China withheld information. Then the Department of Energy embraced the lab-leak theory with "low confidence"; the FBI had previously done so with "moderate confidence. Four other intelligence agencies and NIC still had "low confidence" that the origin was zoonotic.[46] Two scientists repeated that "all the evidence available for scrutiny points to the pandemic originating from transmission from live animals to humans." At a hearing of the House subcommittee, Fauci (whom Rep. Greene called an "enemy to the world") refuted claims that he had once embraced the lab-leak theory. Soon after the Energy Department statement, polls found that the lab-leak theory was believed by 64 percent (Quinnipiac) and 66 percent (YouGov), up from 30 percent in March 2020. After an international team of virus experts analyzed gene sequences from the Wuhan wet market and concluded that raccoon dogs there had the COVID virus, China removed the data from its website. Worobey said it was "one more brick on this massive wall of evidence that all fits together." Sarah Cobey, a University of Chicago epidemiologist and evolutionary biologist who had signed a May 2021 letter urging serious consideration of the lab-leak theory, now rejected it, saying: "ecologically, this is a closed case." But others found the evidence inconclusive. After 18 months of study, Senate Republicans released a 300-page report concluding it could not determine the source of the pandemic.[47] Robert Kadlec, who had been HHS Assistant Secretary under Trump and who oversaw the study, was incoherent: "even though there seems to be precedence [sic] for these events to be zoonotic, the evidence just doesn't support it, and what evidence there is seems to be contrary." Sen. Marshall (a doctor), who released the report, also hedged: the report did not prove "beyond a shadow of doubt" that "this virus originated from an unintentional lab leak," but "there's enough evidence, if this was a civil case, that would convince a jury." (Of course, he could not know that and was not a lawyer.) ODNI released a 10-page report finding no evidence that WIV caused the pandemic: five agencies favored natural transmission, two favored a lab leak and the CIA and another reached no conclusion.[48]

3. The Politicization of Science by Red States

With Biden in the White House and Democrats controlling Congress, states and localities became the principal arenas for political conflict over science.[49] More than a thousand lawsuits challenged pandemic mitigation measures.[50] Trump praised Govs. Noem (South Dakota) and DeSantis (Florida) for reopening their states. DeSantis said: "It's completely unacceptable for either the government or the private sector to impose upon you the requirement that you show proof of vaccine to just simply be able to participate in normal society." He prohibited government agencies and businesses from requiring "vaccine passports," which "reduce individual freedom" and "harm patient privacy." Nebraska Gov. Rickets refused to participate in any vaccine passport program. Rep. Greene called vaccine certificates "Biden's Mark of the Beast" (the symbol of the Antichrist). In April, DeSantis sued to block the CDC ban on cruise ships (an industry that had contributed nearly $8 billion to the state economy in 2016). Florida prohibited cruise lines from requiring passengers to prove vaccination. DeSantis pronounced: "we can either have a free society, or we can have a biomedical security state." But SD Florida

Judge Kathleen Williams (Obama) enjoined Florida's ban. The DeSantis re-election campaign was selling "Don't Fauci My Florida" and "Keep Florida Free" gear. The governor said: "if we had followed Fauci," the state would have been in worse financial shape. "Instead we followed freedom."

In June 2020, the Florida Department of Health stopped sharing data with the University of Florida Emerging Pathogens Institute, which defied a department order that it destroy coronavirus data.[51] After Broward County voted to require masks in schools, DeSantis issued an executive order "protecting the rights of parents" to decide whether their children wore them and prohibiting school and local mandates.[52] The state had just reported its highest one-day total of new cases, and only 49 percent of the population was vaccinated. DeSantis stood by silently at a press conference as an attendee said: "the vaccine changes your RNA. So for me, that's a problem." The governor subsequently named Joseph Ladapo, aligned with AFLDS, as Surgeon General. At his appointment, Ladapo sounded distressingly like Trump.

> We're done with fear. It's over here. Expiration date. . . . [T]here's nothing special about [vaccinations] compared to any other preventive measure. . . . Nurses, pregnant women who are being forced to sort of put something in their bodies that we don't know all there is to know about yet. No matter what people on TV tell you, it's not true. . . . This idea that we are foolish for . . . believing people who are telling us things that we don't have data for right now is ridiculous. And people need to continue and stick with their intuition and their sensibilities.

States should promote "good health" rather than vaccines, which had "been treated almost like a religion. It's just senseless." When meeting a state senator who had been diagnosed with breast cancer and was about to start radiation therapy (compromising her immune system), Ladapo refused to wear a mask or disclose whether he had been vaccinated. He explained: "it is important to me to communicate clearly and effectively with people. I can't do that when half of my face is covered." He said doctors should not be limited in their use of HCQ and claimed the science about ivermectin was "unsettled."

Morteza Hosseini, a major DeSantis donor and chair of the University of Florida Board of Trustees, had pushed the university to hire Ladapo, who was granted tenure in just two weeks.[53] In a *USA Today* op ed on March 24, 2020, he claimed to have "spent the past week taking care of patients with COVID-19 at UCLA's flagship hospital" and repeated that in the *Wall Street Journal*. But UCLA and four of his colleagues denied that Ladapo had been assigned to treat COVID-19 patients that week. His UCLA faculty supervisor declined to recommend him, saying: "The people of Florida would be better served by a Surgeon General who grounds his policy decisions and recommendations in the best scientific evidence rather than his opinions."

In October 2022, Ladapo warned that the Moderna and Pfizer-BioNTech vaccines carried an "abnormally high risk" of heart-related deaths for young men.[54] But this advice was based on 20 often-inaccurate death certificates of men who died within four weeks of vaccination, reported in a paper that listed no authors, was not peer-reviewed and acknowledged that its findings were "preliminary" and "should be interpreted with caution." (Ladapo repeated the error of asserting "post hoc ergo propter hoc.") The head of the Institute of Vaccine Safety at Johns Hopkins University School of Public Health said the paper would be rejected by any peer-reviewed journal. Ladapo had hoped mentors like David Cutler at Harvard Medical School would support him, but Cutler called the study deeply flawed and said that, as a peer reviewer, he would recommend against publication. Dr. Peter Marks, FDA's top vaccine official, explained: "we already know that myocarditis and pericarditis are somewhat increased in younger males who get the vaccine, but we also know that [the risk is] far outweighed by the benefits." DHHS called Ladapo's recommendation "flawed and a far cry from science." He refused to disclose the paper's authors and said it did not need peer review: "the point of this analysis was to look at a question that was important to answer." (But he had not offered a scientifically acceptable answer.) Twitter briefly removed but then restored the study, which was shared by more than 50,000. In April 2023, it was disclosed that Ladapo had inserted his dubious conclusion for the first time in the sixth and final draft of the report, which he edited; that version also omitted the finding in an earlier draft that the risk cardiac-related death from COVID was ten times greater than the risk from the vaccine. *The Washington Post* said Ladapo's actions "underscore how anti-vax activists create fear and suspicion" by "traffick[ing] in half-truths and unsubstantiated declarations."

After DeSantis directed state education officials to withhold funds from schools with mask mandates, Broward (Miami), Leon (Talahasee), Duval (Jacksonville) and Alachua (Gainesville) Counties defied him.[55] The Florida Board of Education offered to pay private school tuition for students who viewed the mask mandate as "harassment." U.S. Education Secretary Miguel Cardona offered federal relief funds for school districts penalized by the state. When Biden supported a school superintendent challenging the ban, Florida Education Commissioner Richard Corcoran responded: "My recommendation is every school superintendent have [sic] to comply with the law." DeSantis threatened that "the state Board of Education could move to withhold the salary of the district superintendent or school board members" who required masks. But when four local educators died of COVID within 24 hours, the Broward County School Board chair insisted it would defy the ban. More than 800 Florida physicians told DeSantis and the legislature to repeal anti-mask laws. Condemning "medical authoritarianism," DeSantis said we might be seeing "the most significant threat to freedom in my lifetime, certainly since the fall of the Berlin Wall." The state Board of Education voted unanimously to consider imposing penalties on the Broward and Alachua County school districts for mandating masks.

Three other counties joined the resistance: Miami-Dade, Hillsborough (Tampa) and Palm Beach.[56] The seven counties contained nearly 40 percent of the state's students. But the Florida Board of Education Chairman threatened to remove school district leaders and board members from their positions. Florida demanded that defiant school districts disclose board members' compensation so the state could withhold their pay. The Board said it would interrogate superintendents of districts imposing mask mandates. After Orange, Indian River and Sarasota counties joined the resistance, which then enrolled more than half of Florida students, the state withheld school board salary funds from Alachua and Broward counties. DeSantis's press secretary said: "the data shows that forced masking of young children has a negligible impact on covid prevalence and spread." In a lawsuit by parents from six counties, Leon County Second Circuit Judge John Cooper ruled that DeSantis could not prohibit mask mandates, comparing unmasked schools to drunk driving. The First District Court of Appeal in Tallahassee reversed, eliciting praise from DeSantis. After Gainesville required city employees to be vaccinated (while allowing religious exemptions), DeSantis said he would fine local governments imposing vaccine mandates $5,000 for each worker. More than 200 employees sued to challenge the vaccine mandate, the lead plaintiff claiming that "the vaccine changes your RNA." *The Washington Post* accused DeSantis of "a new low of cynicism and recklessness." The Florida Board of Education voted unanimously to withhold money from the eight school districts requiring masks. The Florida Department of Health fined Leon County (including Tallahassee) $3.6 million for violating the ban on "vaccine passports."

DeSantis called a special legislative session to "Keep Florida Free" by blocking the federal government's employer vaccine mandate (later).[57] He signed the new law at a car dealership in Brandon, Florida, exclaiming "Let's go, Brandon," which had become the euphemism for "Fuck Joe Biden" (after Brandon Brown won a Talladega Superspeedway car race). The law banned vaccine mandates by public school districts and local governments, let parents decide whether students should be vaccinated or wear masks, required private employer mandates to allow more exemptions and imposed $50,000 fines on employers who failed to allow any exemptions. Disney World ended its vaccine mandate because of the new law. As virus rates declined, school districts that had defiantly passed mask mandates repealed them, and DeSantis's approval rates rose.

In early 2022, DeSantis declared: "Florida is a free state—we reject the biomedical security state that curtails liberty, ruins livelihoods, and divides societies."[58] "These unprecedented policies have been as ineffective as they have been destructive. They are grounded more in blind adherence to Faucian declarations than they are in the constitutional traditions that are the foundation of free nations." Refusing to wear a mask, he met with high school students and told them to remove theirs. "Honestly, it's not doing anything. We've got to stop with this covid theater . . . this is ridiculous." He hosted a forum entitled "The Curtain Closes on COVID Theater," at which Ladapo condemned school closures and mask and vaccine mandates as "terrible, harmful policies," declaring: "Florida is going to be the first state to officially recommend against the covid-19 vaccination for healthy children." DeSantis said there is "a gap between the Faucian pronouncement of what needed to be done and the actual data that supported or did not support those policies." He tweeted: "We had a great discussion with renowned scientists that debunked many false narratives about COVID. Watch it before YouTube takes it down." One panelist, Joseph Fraiman, a New Orleans ER doctor, said: "the majority of studies haven't been able to find a single healthy child who died from covid. If you have a healthy child, the chances of that child dying are incredibly low, essentially close to zero, if not zero." (At the time, the CDC reported that nearly 16,000 children under 17 had died of COVID-19, more than 40 of them in Florida.) DeSantis said: "We always sided with the data and rejected the narrative. And our state is kind of like the center of the world. Everyone wants to come here."

Florida, Iowa, Kansas, Tennessee and Arkansas extended unemployment benefits to workers who were fired or quit because of vaccine requirements.[59] The Kansas Senate President said: "Kansans have made it clear that they choose freedom over Faucism." But the Kansas Chamber of Commerce president warned this "could cause significant financial harm to the state's [unemployment insurance] trust fund . . . and lead to increased taxes on Kansas businesses." Kansas limited contact tracing, transferred authority for health decisions from professionals to elected leaders and authorized lawsuits by anyone "aggrieved" by a mask mandate, business closure or limit on public gatherings. At least 32 states curtailed the ability of health officials to impose mask and vaccine mandates, close churches, schools and businesses and conduct contact tracing. Arkansas Republican Gov. Hutchinson regretted signing a mask ban and called a special session of the legislature to repeal it, but Republican legislators refused to act. Nevertheless, Pulaski County Circuit Judge Tim Fox enjoined the ban as unconstitutional, and the Little Rock mayor announced a mask mandate. Other voices criticized resistance to pandemic measures. *The New York Times* editorialized: "We know that masks work. That vaccines work. That mandates work." The four presidents who preceded Trump campaigned for vaccinations, as did celebrities.

In April, Texas Gov. Abbott claimed that "simple math" showed his state was "very close" to herd immunity.[60] "I don't know what herd immunity is, but when you add that to the people who have acquired immunity, it looks like it could be very close to herd immunity." (Only 19 percent of Texans were fully vaccinated, and another 10 percent had had COVID.) Fauci said herd immunity required 80–85 percent vaccinated or recovered. (New cases/day in Texas declined until July, after which they quickly increased fortyfold, from less than a thousand to over 40,000 in September, before declining again.)[61] Abbott prohibited school mask mandates, but the Texas Education Agency declined to enforce his order. Seven counties, 48 school districts and several large cities (including Austin, Dallas, San Antonio and Houston) refused to comply. Judges in Dallas, Bexar (San Antonio), Harris (Houston) and Travis (Austin) counties enjoined it; the Texas Fourth Court of Appeals upheld the Bexar County decision; and the Texas Supreme Court rejected an appeal. WD Texas Judge Lee Yeakel III (GWB) also enjoined Abbott's ban on school mask mandates for violating the ADA. The Fifth Circuit reversed (Oldham and Willett [both Trump] with Davis [Reagan] dissenting). Texas prohibited colleges and universities from requiring vaccines. Abbott prohibited cities, other government entities and anyone receiving state funds from requiring masks or vaccines or imposing any other "covid-19-related operating limits for any business or other establishment." But the Texas Fifth Court of Appeals in Dallas affirmed a district court ruling invalidating the mask mandate ban on the ground that it impeded the ability of the county's top elected official to protect his constituents.[62]

Tennessee fired Dr. Michelle Fiscus, the Department of Health official overseeing efforts to encourage teenage vaccination, and then halted all adolescent vaccine outreach.[63] A week later, the state resumed outreach to children and adolescents while still eschewing social media (almost the only thing kids read). Gov. Lee issued an executive order giving any parent or guardian "the right to opt out of any order or requirement that a student wear a face covering." However, the Tennessee Medical Association "strongly recommend[ed]" vaccinations as well as masks for those who could not vaccinate, and Dr. Sara Cross (a Memphis physician on Lee's Covid task force) warned: "opting out of wearing masks is putting all of our children in harm's way." Metro Nashville Public Schools and Shelby County (Memphis) Schools (two of the largest districts) vowed to continue enforcing the mandate, the Nashville DA refused to prosecute those who did so and Williamson County also imposed a mandate. Nashville music venues required proof of vaccination or a negative COVID test. Three U.S. district judges enjoined Lee's order: ED Tn Judge J. Ronnie Greer (GWB) (Knox County, containing Knoxville), MD Tn Judge Waverly D. Crenshaw Jr. (Obama) (Williamson County) and WD Tn Judge Sheryl H. Lipman (Obama) (Shelby County, containing Memphis). Gov. Lee signed a law prohibiting private businesses from requiring proof of vaccination and schools and governments from requiring vaccines or masks unless there were at least 1,000 confirmed covid-19 cases for every 100,000 residents within 14 days. This was opposed by the Metro Nashville Public Schools.

When the ACLU sued South Carolina over its ban on school mask mandates, invoking the ADA and the Rehabilitation Act, D SC Judge Mary Geiger Lewis (Obama) enjoined the ban.[64] Although a special session of the Kentucky legislature repealed a statewide school mask mandate instituted by the Democratic governor, 165 of the state's 171 school districts retained their mandates.

After the Arizona legislature banned school mask mandates, Gov. Ducey threatened to withhold federal pandemic relief from defiant school districts.[65] "In Arizona we are pro-parent. I want parents to do what they think is the right thing to do." But education groups challenged the ban in court, and more than a dozen districts (including Scottsdale Unified School District) defied it. When the U.S. Treasury Department threatened to withhold money intended to combat the pandemic if it was used to undermine school mask mandates, Arizona sued to prevent this.

In December 2020, Kaiser Health News and the AP found that at least 181 state and local public health leaders in 38 states had resigned, retired or been fired since April 1, 2020. By July 2021, at least 15 states had passed or were considering laws to limit the authority of public health agencies.[66] North Dakota prohibited a mask mandate; Montana barred quarantines of those exposed to COVID. After Missouri sued St. Louis County for mandating masks, the county promptly reversed itself. Governors in Texas, Arizona, Georgia and Nebraska opposed mask mandates; and nine states had banned or limited them (Arizona, Arkansas, Florida, Iowa, Montana, North Dakota, South Carolina, Tennessee and Texas). Largely following party lines, masks were banned in Utah, Arizona, Oklahoma, Texas, Iowa, South Carolina and Florida and mandated in Washington, Oregon, California, Illinois, Kentucky, Louisiana, Virginia, DC, Delaware, New Jersey and Connecticut. NDNY Judge David Hurd (Clinton) issued a TRO and then a preliminary injunction against employer-granted religious exceptions to a vaccine mandate. "No one can reasonably argue that it is an undue burden to wear a mask to accommodate a child with disabilities."

There were a few Republican exceptions to this pattern. Alabama Gov. Ivey and Arkansas Gov. Hutchinson urged vaccinations.[67] So did Idaho Gov. Little, saying: "I wish everyone could have seen what I saw in the I.C.U. last night." Reading the names of those who had recently died from COVID. West Virginia Gov. Justice said: "We've got to get vaccinated for all, not just for you but for everybody." In general, however, public opinion correlated strongly with party preference: 88 percent of Democrats supported mask mandates for unvaccinated schoolchildren, while 69 percent of Republicans opposed them; 80 percent of Republicans but just 36 percent of Democrats said people should be absolutely free to refuse a vaccine.

And behavior paralleled opinion: in November 2021, almost 40 percent of Republican adults were still unvaccinated, compared with just 10 percent of Democrats.

States not only resisted federal mandates, 19 also preempted local mandates.[68] Ohio required that any local mandate offer exemptions for "reasons of personal conscience." When Gambier Village approved a mandate, the county sheriff refused to enforce it. Tennessee prohibited local health officials from closing schools. Georgia Gov. Kemp criticized Atlanta for reimposing a mask mandate. Localities fought back. Seven school boards sued to block Virginia Gov. Youngkin's mask-optional order: Fairfax County Public Schools (the largest) led Alexandria, Arlington, Falls Church, Hampton, Prince William County and Richmond. 69 of the 130 school districts, with 67 percent of all students, were defying the governor's order. The ACLU also sued to block it, invoking the ADA and the Rehabilitation Act. Arlington Circuit Court Judge Louise DiMatteo issued a TRO. Yet after the state's new Republican Attorney General held that public universities could not require the vaccine, George Mason University dropped its requirement.

Liberty Counsel, a right-wing group which received more than 20,000 inquiries about religious exemptions, sued New York officials who denied them.[69] Online, a group of independent faith healers offered to provide religious exemption letters. A Texas evangelist wrote them in exchange for donations. A California megachurch did so for anyone who claimed to be a "practicing Evangelical that adheres to the religious and moral principles outlined in the Holy Bible." The minister of the Faith Baptist Church in Hudson, Iowa, said he would write a letter that "a Christian has no responsibility to obey any government outside of the scope that has been designated by God."

4. Congressional Resistance to Pandemic Public Health Measures

Right-wing Republican Reps. Mast, Greene, Roy, Boebert, Massie, Cawthorn, van Duyne, Gohmert, Norman and Miller-Meeks (a doctor) defied the House mask requirement.[70] About two dozen House Republicans refused to wear masks during floor votes. Mast (who paid $500 for a second offense) declared that the rule "is not based on science." Greene posted a photo of herself defying the ban (thereby violating another rule, against photos on the House floor). House Minority Leader McCarthy and Republican House members who were doctors sought to end the mandate, but Dr. Brian P. Monahan (Congress's attending physician) opposed the bill, which lost on a party-line vote. McCarthy said this "is not a decision based on science, but on a decision conjured up by liberal government officials who want to continue to live in a perpetual pandemic state." House Speaker Pelosi called him a moron. McCarthy asked "where the science in the building changes between the

House and the Senate." (The latter had no mandate, but its larger chamber contained less than a quarter as many members, and no senator was openly defiant. By March 2022, 127 representatives and 25 senators reported having had COVID.)[71] *The Washington Post* responded that McCarthy "could not be more wrong—and foolish." Employer vaccine mandates "are defensible, and sensible for in-person activity." Some Republicans claimed the CDC based its guidance on an Indian study that failed peer review (but CDC had not released the data behind its decision). Rep. Rodney Davis worried that Monahan was "getting pressure from the speaker sometimes to issue guidance that is motivated less by science and more by politics." On Monahan's recommendation, the House renewed the mandate. Reps. Greene, Massie and Norman sued Pelosi, claiming that fines deducted from their paychecks violated the Twenty-Seventh Amendment prohibiting compensation changes for a sitting member. (They lost.) Greene was fined more than $80,000 for over 30 violations, provoking her to rail against "communist Democrats" and "tyrannical dictators." Rep. Clyde was fined at least $30,000 for at least 14 violations but evaded payroll deductions by changing his withholding so he was paid only $1/month. When a staff member handed Rep. Boebert a mask, she threw it away, tweeting: "We might as well start calling this a Perma-demic. Permanent masking. Permanent state of emergency. Permanent control. This will go on until the American people just say enough is enough. The tyrants aren't giving this up!" She declared at CPAC: "We're here to tell government: We don't want your benefits, we don't want your welfare, don't come knocking on my door with your Fauci ouchie. You leave us the hell alone." (Members of Congress belong to the Federal Employees Health Benefits Program, one of the most generous, receive a pension after serving five years and have a travel allowance and franking privileges.) Rep. Roy denounced this "serious nanny state stuff that will only breed resentment." "This institution is a sham. We should adjourn and shut the place down." Sen. Johnson asked whether masks "do more harm than good—particularly to children who have a low risk of serious disease or death from Covid? Time to reclaim liberty and end this state of fear."

Vaccines provoked even fiercer resistance.[72] Several Republican House members publicly refused them. Trump eventually got the message. During the 2020 election campaign, he had claimed the vaccine as one of his greatest achievements. Even after leaving office, he told CPAC in February 2021 "how unpainful that vaccine shot is, so everybody get your shot." A month later, he called it "a great vaccine . . . a safe vaccine . . . something that works." The next month, he was still "encourag[ing] people to take it." In April, he told two reporters he was considering the administration's request that he tape a public service announcement urging vaccinations. But by July, he was characteristically hedging: "people are refusing to take the Vaccine because they don't trust [Biden's] administration. They don't trust the Election results, and they certainly don't trust Fake News." And a month after that, when an audience booed his endorsement of the vaccine, he promptly folded: "that's all right. You got your freedoms." In December, while calling the development of the vaccine "historic" and announcing at one event that he had gotten a booster, he said at another: "Forget about the mandates, people have to have their freedoms [sic]." Alex Azar, who had loyally supported Trump as HHS Secretary, wrote in *The New York Times*: "any claims that the vaccines are unsafe or ineffective, or that corners were cut are not true." "It would have been better" if Trump had been vaccinated "on national television so his supporters could see how much trust and confidence he has in what is arguably one of his greatest accomplishments." "[T]he Biden administration is exhorting all unvaccinated adults in our country to get their shots, and I fully support it in this call."

Sen. Cassidy explained that Americans "don't trust government" about vaccines because of "partisan comments coming out of the White House regarding the next Jim Crow laws." Rep. Greene claimed that COVID-19 was "not dangerous for non-obese people and those under 65." (On May 11, 2022, there had been 255,683 covid deaths of those under 65; just 40 percent of those 20–64 are obese.)[73] She denounced her subsequent 12-hour suspension by Twitter as a "Communist-style attack on free speech," declaring: "People have a choice, they don't need your medical brown shirts showing up at their door ordering vaccinations. You can't force people to be part of the human experiment." Rep. Cawthorn warned that if the government went door-to-door to vaccinate, "they could then go door-to-door to take your guns. They could go door-to-door to take your Bibles." Tucker Carlson said Biden's plan to "force people to take medicine they don't want or need" was "the greatest scandal in my lifetime, by far." Rep. Jason Smith (running for the Senate) asserted that "the Biden administration wants to knock down your door KGB-style to force people to get vaccinated." Shreveport City Councilmember Candy Peavy warned that the Biden administration was sending people door-to-door to "document unvaccinated Americans," and the vaccine was an "experimental gene therapy," which had killed thousands. Charlie Kirk's Turning Point USA texted that Biden is "sending goons DOOR-TO-DOOR to make you take a covid-19 vaccine" and declaimed: "Fauci for Prison." "LOCK YOUR DOORS, KIDS!!" (All this was pure fantasy.) When *Sesame Street*'s Big Bird got a vaccination on television in November 2021, Sen. Cruz condemned it as "government propaganda"; some right-wing media called Big Bird a communist.

Republican propaganda had its intended effect.[74] As early as April 2020, Democrats were substantially more interested in a vaccine than Republicans; a year later, 60 percent of Democrats who had not yet gotten the vaccine said they were extremely likely to do so—twice the proportion of Republicans. A July 2021 poll found that 74 percent of Democrats felt that the dangers of

COVID were greater than those of the vaccine, while 54 percent of Republicans felt the opposite. Only 32 percent of Republicans (compared to 65 percent of Democrats) said it was "definitely false" that the vaccine implanted microchips, and a much higher proportion of Republicans believed the vaccine caused infertility and endangered pregnant women. Although similarly small percentages of Democrats and Republicans (11 and 9) had disbelieved that vaccines caused autism in a 2013 poll, by July 2021, the percentage of Republicans had tripled. It was not surprising, therefore, that in September 2021, 80 percent of Democrats but only 33 percent of Republicans supported an employer vaccine mandate; and in December, 90 percent of Democrats but only 62 percent of Republicans had gotten at least one shot. Residents of states and counties that had voted for Trump were significantly less likely to be vaccinated.

Anti-vaxxers invoked "natural immunity" from infection with COVID as an argument against vaccinations.[75] On Fox News's "Sunday Morning Features," Rep. Mace (R-SC) called the decline in Florida cases and deaths a victory for "natural immunity."

> In some studies that I have read, natural immunity gives you 27 times more protection against future covid infection than vaccination. And so we need to take all of the science into account and not selectively choosing [sic] what science to follow when we are making policy decisions.

(Florida's seven-day average of cases increased almost a hundredfold in just six weeks, from 681 on November 28, 2021, to 65,551 on January 12, 2022.)[76] Mace was relying on an Israeli study that had not been peer-reviewed. A later CDC meta-analysis of more than 90 studies concluded that "for people who have been infected . . . vaccination provides a boost in the immune response and further reduces the risk of a repeat infection." Another CDC study found that among those who had had COVID, the unvaccinated were five times more likely than the vaccinated to get it again. Mississippi Gov. Reeves echoed Mace's views on NBC's *Meet the Press*. Although only 54 percent of his state's residents had been vaccinated, he claimed that 80–85 percent "have some level of immunity, either natural immunity or immunity from having taken the shots." (Mississippi's seven-day average increased almost thirtyfold in six weeks, from 241 cases on November 29, 2021, to 6,939 on January 19, 2022.)[77] Reeves and Wyoming Sen. Barasso warned that Biden's mandate (later) "hardened" vaccine skeptics. CD Ca Judge James Selna (GWB) upheld the University of California's vaccination requirement against a challenge by a UC Irvine medical school professor who claimed immunity from a prior infection.[78] Several Republican members of Congress who were doctors urged the CDC to acknowledge natural immunity.

In January 2022, thousands of anti-vaxxers demonstrated in Washington, chanting "Let's go, Brandon" and "Fuck Joe Biden."[79] Banners proclaimed that "Vaccines are mass kill bio weapons" and "Trump won" and called for the "arrest or exile" of Fauci, Bill Gates and Jacob Rothschild (the last, who had nothing to do with vaccines, was targeted out of anti-Semitism, as George Soros and Mark Zuckerberg were in the campaigns to overturn the 2020 election, see Abel 2024b). One placard showed Fauci behind bars with the caption "the lockdown America needs" and his decapitated head in a noose with the words: "HANG EM HIGH"; another called him "the new Josef Mengele from World War II." Speakers included Robert F. Kennedy Jr., an anti-vaxxer who proclaimed that "even in Hitler's Germany, you could cross the Alps to Switzerland. You could hide in an attic like Anne Frank did." (He later apologized for the Nazi analogy.) Kennedy warned: "the minute they hand you that vaccine passport, every right that you have is transformed into a privilege contingent upon your obedience to arbitrary government dictates. It will make you a slave." "Covid was clearly a bioweapons problem." (Kennedy also denied that Sirhan B. Sirhan had killed his father and warned that 5G wireless will "harvest our data and control our behavior." He also said: "prior to the introduction of Prozac, we had almost none of these events in our country and we've never seen them in human history, where people walk into a schoolroom of children or strangers and start shotting people." Before his inauguration, Trump had asked Kennedy—who had no scientific training—to chair his vaccine safety panel.) Facebook and Instagram dropped Kennedy's Children's Health Defense Fund because of its anti-vaccination positions. Dr. Robert Malone pronounced that "the science is settled" that vaccines are "not working." (He also exaggerated his role in inventing mRNA vaccines at the Salk Institute.) In April 2023, Kennedy announced he was seeking the Democratic nomination for president, a quixotic run presumably intended to publicize his extreme views, which included allegations that Tony Fauci and Bill Gates had conspired with drug companies to profit from vaccines.[80]

Seeking the Republican nomination for Ohio's senator, Jane Timken entitled her first ad "Fire Fauci," featuring a parent trying to put a mask on a screaming toddler, with the caption "child abuse."[81] "Fauci claims to be the bastion of science, but I think he's playing God." Josh Mandel, another Republican aspirant, called Fauci a liar and "one of the biggest frauds in American history." JD Vance (who won the nomination and the seat) labelled Fauci "a ridiculous tyrant." Dr. Mehmet Oz, seeking the Republican Pennsylvania Senatorial nomination, called Fauci a "petty tyrant." (He won the nomination but lost the election.) Kevin Nicholson, a Republican running for Wisconsin governor, said Fauci "should be fired and referred to prosecutors." (He lost.) Florida Gov. DeSantis was selling "Freedom over Fauci Flip-Flops."

Yet there were divisions on the right.[82] Sen. Minority Leader McConnell (who had contracted polio as a child) said: "these shots need to get in everybody's arm as rapidly as possible." But Sens. Paul and Johnson refused to get vaccinated because they had had COVID. Sen. Paul said on Fox News on November 29, 2021:

> When you talk about the peer reviewed studies of masks, there was one done in Denmark showed it didn't work. When you look at all of Sweden—1.8 million children have not been wearing masks for the last two years, they've had zero covid deaths. And you say, "Well, have the teachers been infected?" Well, it turns out the teachers are infected at the same rate as the rest of the public. So, they've had no masks for a year, year and a half. And it has worked. And that's a whole country.

(Cumulative coronavirus cases in Sweden jumped dramatically from 1.3 million at the end of December 2021 to 2.4 million six weeks later.[83] In January 2023, 57 percent of people in Denmark had had COVID-19, more than twice the percentage of those in Sweden [25] Norway [27] and Finland [26].)[84] A study in *Annals of Internal Medicine* found a benefit to mask wearers; even though it was not statistically significant, the article concluded: "Face masks are a plausible means to reduce transmission of respiratory viruses by minimizing the risk that respiratory droplets will reach wearers' nasal or oral mucosa." JAMA said:

> Compelling data now demonstrate that community mask-wearing is an effective nonpharmacologic intervention to reduce the spread of this infection, especially as a source control to prevent spread from infected persons, but also as protection to reduce wearers' exposure to infection.

The BMJ and the *Proceedings of the National Academy of Sciences* agreed.

The GOP Doctors Caucus and Reps. Scalise and Stefanik (the #2 and #3 House Republicans) urged vaccinations. But Scalise blamed vaccine hesitancy on Biden's criticisms of Trump (using selective quotations). Rep. Andy Harris (a doctor) said: "it is every citizen's right to choose to get a vaccine, and then to choose not to reveal whether they've gotten a vaccine." And Rep. Greg Murphy (another doctor) said: "just like any other medicines, there are side effects and this is a personal decision." Sen. Marshall (a third doctor) warned that every time White House Press Secretary Jen Psaki and Fauci spoke, "10,000 more people say I'm never going to take the vaccine." He claimed the vaccine had "pluses and minuses" for anyone under 50.

On Fox News, Sean Hannity said, "I believe in the science of vaccination"; and Steve Doocy agreed, "It will save your life." But Brian Kilmeade told viewers to "make your own decision"; and Laura Ingraham accused

Democrats of seeking to "de-platform, cancel, defame or eliminate inconvenient opinions regarding their Covid response." Vaccine proponents were trying to "frighten or pressure children . . . who face virtually no risk of serious illness." Breitbart News continued to present "news" under the heading "Mask/Vax Cult," whereas Newsmax CEO Christopher Ruddy said he was vaccinated, and "countless lives would have been saved if the vaccine was available earlier" (reviving Trump's smears of the FDA). Utah Gov. Cox accused conservative talking heads of "literally killing their supporters" by opposing the vaccine, and Alabama Gov. Ivey said it was "time to start blaming the unvaccinated folks." (Both were Republicans.)

There also were divisions among workers subject to mandates.[85] The National Education Association (the nation's largest teachers union) supported mandatory vaccinations or tests for all teachers. But municipal unions resisted the requirement that New York City's more than 300,000 workers be vaccinated. The Police Benevolent Association of the City of New York (its largest police union) sued to block the mandate, but Richmond County Supreme Court Judge Lizette Colon denied a TRO. About 25 percent of the New York Police Department and 45 percent of the New York Fire Department were unvaccinated. Six NYFD firefighters—wearing uniforms and driving a ladder truck—visited NYS Sen. Zellnor Myrie's office to protest the vaccine mandate, asked where he lived and told staffers they would have "blood on their hands." The firefighters were suspended. A week earlier, more than 2,000 firefighters took sick days in protest. Staten Island residents resisted the mandate, one warning: "If they're going to push this on kids . . . I can guarantee you one thing: Town halls and schools will be fucking burned to the ground." As the city mandate took effect on November 1, 2021, 9,000 unvaccinated workers were placed on unpaid leave, while another 12,000 had applied for a religious or medical exemption. When the deadline for correctional officers to be vaccinated arrived, only 82 percent of uniformed staff had complied; hundreds were put on unpaid leave, forcing many vaccinated employees to work 12-hour shifts.

New York City also required that all 56,000 religious and private school workers be vaccinated.[86] Only 51 percent of residents of Brooklyn's Borough Park (an Orthodox Jewish neighborhood) were vaccinated, compared with 77 percent of New Yorkers. Rabbi David Swiebel and Dr. Thomas Chadzutko (superintendent of the Roman Catholic Diocese of Brooklyn's schools) warned Mayor de Blasio it would be "devastating to our schools and the children they serve" if teachers quit.

On December 5, 2021, de Blasio required all of the city's 184,000 private employers to mandate employee vaccines by December 27.[87] 94 percent of city employees were already vaccinated. Appealing to racial divisions, Staten Island City Councilman Joe Borelli (the incoming Republican minority leader) warned: "In the Bronx, with 15% unemployment, 28% of residents will no longer be able to work on Dec. 27, including 44% of Black young adults." NYS Attorney General Letitia James supported a "vaccine mandate with a testing option." NYPD officer Anthony Marciano sued to block the public sector mandate. About 94 percent of the 378,000 NYPD employees were vaccinated, up from 86 percent in late October. New York Gov. Hochul announced a mask mandate in all public spaces that did not require vaccination. But the Madison County (Syracuse) board of supervisors refused to enforce the rule. And Nassau County Supreme Court Justice Thomas Rademaker struck it down, finding that NYS Health Commissioner Mary T. Bassett lacked authority to issue it. (Rademaker had run for the judgeship on the Conservative Party ticket.) Rep. Stefanik (now the #3 House Republican) called the decision "a win for . . . the freedom of all New Yorkers." Appellate Division Justice Robert J. Miller stayed Rademaker's order.

Teachers' unions opposed a return to in-person classes. Chicago schools closed after union members refused to work (but then returned to class).[88] Milwaukee anticipated "a fight." The Newark, NJ, union president declared: "I'd see the entire city of Newark unemployed before I allowed one single teacher's aide to die needlessly." The Kentucky statewide union said a walkout was "absolutely possible."

The president of the Federal Law Enforcement Officers Association (including the Secret Service, Air Marshalls and Transportation Security Officers) said: "Forcing people to undertake a medical procedure is not the American way and is a clear civil rights violation no matter how proponents may seek to justify it."[89] The San Francisco Deputy Sheriffs' Association warned that if members "are forced to vaccinate, a percentage of them will retire early or seek employment elsewhere." The national Fraternal Order of Police (with more than 350,000 members) endorsed the vaccine but added: "whether or not to accept [it] is a personal decision." Chicago branch President John Catanzara assailed the mandate imposed by Mayor Lightfoot: "We're in America, god damn it. We don't want to be forced to do anything. Period. This ain't nazi fucking Germany, [where they say] step into the fucking showers. The pill won't hurt you." He apologized for his language but urged members to flood the city with exemption requests: "Submit those all on Thursday, give them everything at one time, and that's it. Do not fill out the portal information." He threatened that "Chicago will have a police force at 50 percent or less" over the weekend. The mayor's office responded that the unvaccinated would "be placed in a non-disciplinary, no pay status." More than a third of Chicago police refused to report their vaccine status. Cook County Circuit Judge Raymond W. Mitchell enjoined enforcement of the vaccine mandate for Chicago police until the dispute was resolved by arbitration.

Dr. Fauci urged police to get vaccinated: "more police officers die of covid than they do from other causes of death."[90] In 2021, the Officer Down

Memorial Page listed five times as many deaths from COVID as from gunfire. But only half the Los Angeles Fire Department and 60 percent of the Los Angeles Police Department were fully vaccinated. About 3,000 LAPD workers (a quarter of the workforce) were expected to seek exemptions; six sued to block the vaccine mandate. CD Ca Judge R. Gary Klausner (GWB) denied a TRO to LAPD employees on October 27 and subsequently dismissed their lawsuit: "The Supreme Court has long rejected a fundamental right to refuse vaccination." (It did so in 1905.)[91] LA County Sheriff Alex Villanueva (whose force had a 54 percent vaccination rate) defied the county's vaccination mandate: "I don't want to be in a position to lose 5, 10% of my workforce overnight on a vaccine mandate." When the county required masks indoors in July, he declared: "forcing the vaccinated and those who already contracted Covid-19 to wear masks indoors is not backed by science." The County Board of Supervisors voted (4–0–1) to transfer power from department heads who did not enforce the mandate to the LA County Director of personnel. (Villanueva lost his re-election bid in November 2022.) 870 LAFD employees filed a notice of intent to sue. Firefighters in Spokane joined state workers in a similar suit; those in Orange County, Florida, also sued. The leader of a Baltimore police union told members not to disclose their vaccination status. San Jose let unvaccinated officers work through the end of the year but required testing. The Constitutional Sheriffs and Peace Officers Association (which claimed to enroll 10 percent of the nation's 3,000 sheriffs) asserted an unreviewable power to decide the constitutionality of anything. Its founder, former Arizona sheriff Richard Mack (an Oath Keepers board member), said: "We are defying tyrants. People appreciate and sympathize with the mission. They don't want to be told they have to wear a diaper on their face."

The Department of Defense also encountered defiance of its order that all active-duty military personnel be vaccinated.[92] Thousands refused or failed to meet the deadline. The Air Force discharged 27. Republican Sens. Marshall, Cruz, Lankford and Tuberville and Rep. Greene introduced legislation to prohibit giving dishonorable discharges to those who refused. Republican Oklahoma Gov. Kevin Stitt asked DoD to suspend the mandate for the National Guard, claiming it "violates the personal freedoms of many Oklahomans, as it asks them to potentially sacrifice their personal beliefs in order to not lose their jobs." He replaced a pro-vaccine commander with one who opposed the mandate. DoD said the unvaccinated would not be allowed to serve. Oklahoma sued to challenge the mandate. WD Ok Judge Stephen P. Friot (GWB) denied an injunction.

> It is unmistakably clear that the intent of Congress . . . is that the Guard and its members will at all events be prepared, conformably to federal military standards to be ordered into federal service . . . on little or no notice.

The administration is "acting well within the authority granted by the Constitution and laws of the United States."

> Adding a tenth . . . vaccine to the list of nine that all service members are already required to take would hardly amount to "an enormous and transformative expansion [of the] regulatory authority" the Secretary of Defense already possesses.

The commander complied by ordering that unvaccinated airmen could not participate in drills; DoD planned to recover pay from them.

MD Ga Judge Tilman Self III (Trump) enjoined the Air Force from taking "any adverse action" against an officer who refused vaccination.[93] Given "the Nation's essential commitment to religious freedom[,] Plaintiff's harm—a constitutional injury involving her right to freely exercise her religion—is not a mere trivial grievance." "And, what real interest can our military leaders have in furthering a requirement that violates the very document they swore to support and defend?" "The Court is unquestionably confident that the Air Force will remain healthy enough to carry out its critical national defense mission even if Plaintiff remains unvaccinated and is not forced to retire." The Air Force had granted just nine of the thousands of exemption applications. In another case, the Supreme Court held that the Air Force could discipline Lt. Col. Jonathan Dunn pending his appeal (Thomas, Alito and Gorsuch dissenting). When ordered to be vaccinated, resign or refuse the vaccine in writing, Dunn wrote a two-star general: "NUTS!" His commander condemned this "highly disrespectful affront to the chain of command" and "shocking lack of military decorum." The Air Force refused to commission three cadets who rejected vaccinations and was considering whether to reimburse the cost of their education.

The National Guards of Georgia, North Dakota and Florida said they would comply.[94] But Texas declared the decision "a personal matter," and Republican Alaska Gov. Dunleavy said the mandate "threaten[ed] the sovereign authority of the State of Alaska." He and the Republican governors of Wyoming, Iowa, Mississippi and Nebraska requested exemptions. Abbott wrote the DoD:

> As governor of Texas, I am the commander in chief of this state's militia. If the federal government keeps threatening to defund the Texas National Guard, I will deploy every legal tool available to me as governor in defense of these American heroes.

He sued Biden and other officials, claiming the vaccination order infringed on his "authority as Commander in Chief and on Texas's sovereignty." Nationwide, more than 220 members of the Air National Guard and 40 percent of the Army National Guard had refused vaccinations. In response, Army commanders relieved six active-duty leaders of their commands and issued 2,767 general officer written reprimands. Defense Secretary Austin wrote seven Republican governors (Alaska, Oklahoma, Texas, Idaho, Mississippi, Nebraska and Wyoming), rejecting National Guard exemptions.

In February, the Army announced it would begin discharging unvaccinated soldiers.[95] The Chief of Naval Personnel said administrative separation proceedings would be expedited to "maximize speed and equity in achieving a fully vaccinated force." The Marine Corps separated 103. The Navy separated 20 and considered 3,009 active-duty religious accommodation requests. ND Texas Judge Reed O'Connor (GWB) granted a preliminary injunction against the DoD on behalf of 35 sailors who refused the vaccine, 29 of whom had been denied a religious accommodation. He held that the pandemic "provides the government with no license to abrogate" the freedoms of Americans, including religious freedom, and dismissed the Navy's religious exemption process as mere "theater."

> The facts overwhelmingly indicate that the Navy will deny the religious accommodations. The Navy has, to date, never granted a religious accommodation request for the COVID-19 vaccine. In fact, in the past seven years, the Navy has never granted a single religious exemption for any vaccine. . . . There is no Covid-19 exception to the First Amendment. There is no military exclusion from our Constitution.

The "loss of religious liberties outweighs any forthcoming harm to the Navy," and "even the direst circumstances cannot justify the loss of constitutional rights." The plaintiffs had cited the fact that the vaccine was developed from aborted fetal cells and claimed that any modification of their bodies was an "affront to their Creator." The Supreme Court stayed the decision pending appeal to the Fifth Circuit (Alito, Gorsuch and Thomas would have affirmed). MD Fla Judge Steven Merryday (GHWB) prohibited the Navy from reassigning or demoting a commander who refused the vaccine, finding him "triumphantly fit and slim and strong . . . robustly healthy . . . young." The Navy responded by refusing to deploy his ship.

Religious leaders also resisted mandates.[96] Agudath Israel (an organization of Haredi Orthodox Jews, which had sued NY over pandemic restrictions on religious services in 2020) opposed a vaccine mandate, although individual synagogues were considering one. The Roman Catholic Diocese of Brooklyn won a state Supreme Court case against Cuomo's restrictions in November 2020. Cardinal Raymond Leo Burke had told a conference in Rome in 2020 that the vaccine might have microchips that would let the government control people. Although the New York archdiocese said, "There is no basis for a priest to issue a religious exemption to the vaccine," its vicar general said it was up to the unvaccinated to decide whether to wear masks and socially distance. Leaflets in at least a dozen languages contained targeted warnings: to Orthodox Jews that vaccines could change their DNA and were only 0.5 percent effective, to Polish Americans that vaccines were intended to "annihilate Christianity and the Polish Nation" and to Haitian Americans that vaccines sought to reduce the Black population. Some misinformation came from Alex Berenson (a Yale graduate, former *New York Times* reporter and novelist) and Oren Barzilay (head of the NYFD emergency medical workers union); more were disseminated by the St. Petersburg (Russia) Internet Research Agency (which also sought to swing the 2016 election to Trump, see Abel 2024b). The conservative media also stridently opposed pandemic public health measures. Fox News attacked vaccinations at least once on all but 16 of Biden's first 254 days in office, with a frequency increasing from 80 percent every day during the first three months to 99 percent during the next six.

Because of threats to health workers, the National Association of County and City Health Officials asked Attorney General Garland to extend the federal protection DoJ had given school board members, teachers and other employees during the pandemic.[97] When an Oregon nurse quarantined two dozen football players for 10 days after one tested positive for COVID, parents told her she should lose her nursing license. Another district nurse received a similar threat when she quarantined the volleyball team. The assistant dean for public health practice at the Johns Hopkins Bloomberg School of Public Health told Congress in September 2021 she had documented at least 1,500 incidents of harassment and violence against public health workers between March 2020 and January 2021. On October 4, Garland directed the FBI and U.S. Attorney's offices to advise local law enforcement agencies how to deal with threats against school board members concerning masks and vaccines. Republicans denounced this at HJC and SJC hearings. Sen. Tillis said: "the full force of the F.B.I. is not something a parent has to think about before they go before a school board to express their concerns and they get frustrated." Sen. Cotton attacked Biden for compromising the Justice Department's independence by directing Garland to do this. Sen. Cruz defended a parent who had given a Nazi salute and chanted "Heil Hitler" at a school board meeting. As soon as Republicans gained control of the House in January 2023, they began investigating the DoJ and FBI. *Science* found that 38 percent of 510 researchers who had published about COVID reported harassment. *Nature* found that 81 percent of 321 scientists who discussed COVID in the media had been attacked, and 22 percent had been threatened with violence, 15 percent with death. Surveys by the Johns Hopkins Bloomberg School of Public Health and the National Association of County and City Health Officials had similar findings.

After the House Select Subcommittee on the Coronavirus Crisis subpoenaed Peter Navarro, Trump railed:[98]

> The Communist Democrats are engaging in yet another Witch Hunt, this time going after my Administration's unprecedented and incredible coronavirus response, despite the fact that, sadly, more Americans died this year from COVID than in all of 2020. [The numbers actually were similar: 419,406 in the first 11 months of 2021 (38,128/month) compared with 350,555 in the last ten months of 2020 (35,056/month).[99]] It's a Witch Hunt that's been going on for years. Why don't they investigate Crooked Hillary, when so much has now been proved about her and her campaign's lies and dealings with Russia to smear me and spy on my campaign? I'm telling Peter Navarro to protect executive privilege and not let these unhinged Democrats discredit our great accomplishments.

Navarro said:

> This is yet another Democrat witch hunt plain and shallow [sic—"simple"]. I will be delivering a case of my new book *In Trump Time* to the Committee in thanks for their invitation. . . . Suggest they ask Tony Fauci when he knew his dangerous gain of function experiments were the likely technology used by the Chinese to spawn the deadly virus President Trump and I had to fight.

He defied the subpoena, citing a "direct order" from Trump.

As the Omicron variant spread, *Fox & Friends Weekend* host Rachel Campos-Duffy accused Transportation Secretary Buttigieg of invoking the pandemic so he "doesn't have to do his job of fixing the supply chain" and warned of "more lockdowns, more fear."[100] Pete Hegseth, another Fox host, said: "count on a variant about every October, every two years," which Democrats would exploit to influence elections. (Viruses are notorious for their ability to mutate.) Rep. Ronny Jackson (whom the DoD OIG found had abused alcohol and drugs and created a "negative" work environment as Trump's White House physician) said: "Here comes the MEV—the Midterm Election Variant!" "They NEED a reason to push unsolicited nationwide mail-in ballots. Democrats will do anything to CHEAT during an election—but we're not going to let them!" Lara Logan complained on Fox News: "If they keep testing for different strains of coronavirus, we're going to be locked down for the rest of our existence." "They've created a problem that can never actually be solved, so they can justify whatever it is they want to do." Dr. Marc Siegel, Fox's "medical expert," expressed "complete agreement" with Logan about the cost of shutdowns. He had asserted in March 2020:

"this virus should be compared to the flu. Because at worst—worst-case scenario—it could be the flu." Jeanine Pirro, another Fox host, said in early 2020: "all the talk about coronavirus being so much more deadly [than the flu] doesn't reflect reality." (COVID-19 actually caused more than 30 times as many deaths as the flu in the years 2019–20 to 2021–22.)[101]

At a conservative political conference, Fox News host Jesse Watters urged the audience to "ambush" Fauci.[102]

> Now you go in for the kill shot. The kill shot? With an ambush? Deadly. Because he doesn't see it coming. This is when you say: Dr. Fauci, you funded risky research at a sloppy Chinese lab. The same lab that sprung this pandemic on the world. You know why people don't trust you, don't you.

Watters claimed he was talking about embarrassing Fauci. "Imagine Tucker Carlson teases that . . . 'Coming up: Brave college student confronts Lord Fauci at dinner. Exclusive footage.' . . . That's what we want. That changes the whole conversation of the country." "Boom! He is dead. He's done." Watters added that ambushers should be "respectful." The audience laughed and applauded. Fauci commented: "That just is such a reflection of the craziness that goes on in society." "The guy should be fired on the spot." Fox said that Watters's "words have been twisted completely out of context." "It's more than clear that Jesse Watters was using a metaphor for asking hard-hitting questions to Dr. Fauci about gain-of-function research." On a prime-time Fox News show weeks earlier, Lara Logan had compared Fauci to Josef Mengele. Gov. DeSantis called Fauci a "Covid authoritarian" in a fundraising email. "We cannot allow our communities to become Faucian dystopias in which people's freedoms are curtailed and their livelihoods destroyed." Sen. Cruz had recently named Fauci as "the most dangerous bureaucrat in the history of the country." The previous April, Rep. Greene had introduced the Fire Fauci Act to eliminate his salary. Trump had called him "a radical masker." Tucker Carlson claimed that Fauci "created Covid" and spread "authoritarian germ hysteria." On October 4, 2021, Carlson accused Fauci of deciding "to unilaterally end Christmas." Carlson also blamed the spread of COVID on "sneezing, unvaccinated illegal immigrants coming into this country."

But in an interview with Daily Wire host Candace Owens (a leading purveyor of anti-vax conspiracy theories), Trump grandiloquently extolled the vaccines as "one of the greatest achievements of mankind" (by which he meant himself).[103] "Look, the results of the vaccine are very good, and if you do get it [COVID], it's a very minor form. People aren't dying when they take the vaccine." When Fox News host Bill O'Reilly and Trump both disclosed at a Dallas political event that they had gotten the booster, the crowd booed.

Trump remonstrated: "don't, don't, don't, don't." Earlier in his remarks, he had claimed: "What we've done is historic. Don't let them take away, don't take it away from ourselves. You're playing right into their hands when you sort of like, 'oh, the vaccine.'" "You shouldn't be forced to take it, no mandates. But take credit." Conspiracy monger Alex Jones threatened to "declare war" on Trump for supporting vaccines. In summer 2021, DeSantis had said: "if you look at the people that are being admitted to hospitals . . . over 95 percent of them are either not fully vaccinated or not vaccinated at all. These vaccines are saving lives." But the following December, seeking ways to distinguish himself from Trump, who was far ahead in the polls for the 2024 nomination, DeSantis told Fox News he had not gotten the booster: "that at the end of the day is people's individual decisions about what they want to do." Oklahoma Gov. Stitt said a week earlier he would not get the booster because "I'm perfectly healthy." Republicans on the House Judiciary Committee used their official Twitter account to declare: "if the booster shots work, why don't they work?" They later deleted the tweet. Texas Gov. Abbott declined to say the word booster or reveal whether he had gotten it. In 2022, more than a month after the Omicron booster became available in Baltimore, only about 5 percent of those eligible had gotten it; nationwide, just 10 percent had done so.

5. Biden's Vaccine Mandates

In September 2021, as part of a "National COVID-19 Preparedness Plan," Biden issued an executive order requiring businesses with more than 100 employees to have them immunized or tested weekly and mandating vaccinations for all employees of the federal government, Head Start programs, federally operated schools for Native Americans and health care facilities that accepted Medicare or Medicaid.[104] "Pandemic politics" were "making people sick, causing unvaccinated people to die." "[R]ight now local school officials [in Florida] are trying to keep children safe in a pandemic, while their governor picks a fight with them and even threatens their salaries or their jobs. Talk about bullying in schools." Biden set a January 4, 2022, deadline while allowing exceptions for those with disabilities or religious objections. The order produced predictable responses. Fauci was "very much in favor," as was *The New York Times*. The Business Roundtable "welcome[d] the Biden administration's fight against covid." But Goldman Sachs estimated that the mandate would only manage to vaccinate less than half the 25 million it covered by March, and a recent poll of 543 companies found that just 57 percent required or planned to require vaccinations. The American Federation of Teachers offered "complete support," but the president of the American Federation of Government Employees wanted any mandate negotiated.

Democratic New Jersey Gov. Murphy called anti-vax protesters "knuckleheads" who had "lost their minds." But Republicans were strongly opposed. Georgia Gov. Kemp denounced the mandate as "blatantly unlawful overreach." The governors of Texas, Missouri, Georgia, Wyoming and South Dakota threatened to sue. South Carolina Gov. McMaster boasted he would fight Biden "to the gates of hell." Mississippi Gov. Reeves acknowledged that "the vaccine itself is lifesaving" but insisted that "this is still America, and we still believe in freedom from tyrants." Montana Gov. Gianforte called the mandates "unlawful and un-American." Alabama Gov. Ivey denounced them as "outrageous" and "overreaching." Ohio Gov. DeWine said they were a "mistake." Utah Gov. Cox had "serious concerns" about their legality. Running for Virginia governor, Glenn Youngkin declared: "we just have to respect people's ability to express their liberty to say, 'no, I'm not going to get this vaccine for whatever reason.'" (He won in November.) RNC chair McDaniel said the Committee "will sue the administration to protect Americans and their liberties." House Minority Leader McCarthy tweeted, "NO VACCINE MANDATES." Rep. Stefanik called the mandate "authoritarian," the work of "a power hungry government." Fox News said an "authoritarian" Biden had declared "war on millions of Americans." Breitbart accused Biden of going "full totalitarian." The Federalist assailed the "fascist move."

24 Republican governors issued a statement threatening to "seek every legal option" against the mandates, which they called "disastrous and counterproductive" and a "threat to individual liberty."[105] Alabama Gov. Ivey directed state agencies not to punish anyone who ignored federal mandates and to "take all practical steps to notify the affected" that Alabama opposed all vaccine mandates. Denouncing Biden as "a habitual violator of the U.S. Constitution" and calling his plan "bullying," "yet another instance of federal overreach," Texas Gov. Abbott banned all vaccine mandates. But some of his state's largest employers, such as Southwest Airlines, AT&T and Hewlett-Packard Enterprises, imposed mandates; and American Airlines and the Greater Houston Partnership (including Exxon Mobil, Chevron and JPMorgan Chase) opposed the ban. The DoD ordered contractors in Texas to mandate vaccines for employees despite Abbott's ban.

Legal challenges were prompt, widespread and chaotic.[106] Florida sued to block the federal contractor mandate, soon joined by Kentucky, Tennessee and Ohio. Missouri, Alaska, Arizona, Arkansas, Montana, Nebraska, New Hampshire, North Dakota, South Dakota, Wyoming and Louisiana sued in the Eighth Circuit to block the large private employer mandate, as did four other states in the Fifth Circuit and Kentucky and six others in the Sixth. The Fifth Circuit (Jones [Reagan] and Duncan and Engelhardt [both Trump]) enjoined the employer mandate, initially staying the order to give the government time to respond but then making it permanent. The mandate "grossly exceeds OSHA's statutory authority" and was "a one-size-fits-all sledgehammer that makes hardly any attempt to account for differences in workplaces (and workers) that have more than a little bearing on workers' varying degrees of susceptibility to the supposedly 'grave danger' the Mandate purports to address." It does the following:

> imposes a financial burden on [employers] by deputizing their participation in OSHA's regulatory scheme, exposes them to severe financial risk if they refuse or fail to comply, and threatens to decimate their workforces (and business prospects) by forcing unwilling employees to take their shots, take their tests, or hit the road.

The U.S. Judicial Panel on Multidistrict Litigation randomly selected the Sixth Circuit to consolidate the more than 34 lawsuits (removing the case from the Fifth Circuit). The U.S. Chamber of Commerce urged businesses to comply with the federal mandate and ignore "preliminary actions" by the Fifth Circuit. But the National Retail Federation was one of the groups suing to block the mandate. The AMA and more than 60 other health care associations backed the employer mandate.

The en banc Sixth Circuit (8–8) rejected a request for immediate en banc review, returning the case to a three-judge panel.[107] Judge Karen Nelson Moore (Clinton) said: "the massive docket and profusion of briefs . . . require focused consideration by a devoted panel," which had "already devoted significant time to this case." Chief Judge Jeffrey S. Sutton (GWB) dissented, calling the policy a "blunt national vaccine mandate" and an "unprecedented assertion of administrative power." Judge John K. Bush (Trump) agreed it was a "*de facto* national vaccine mandate." The panel (Stranch [Obama] and Gibbons [GWB], with Larsen [Trump] dissenting) reinstated the mandate. "The record establishes that COVID-19 has continued to spread, mutate, kill, and block the safe return of American workers to their jobs. To protect workers, OSHA can and must be able to respond to dangers as they evolve." The mandate:

> is an important step in curtailing the transmission of a deadly virus that has killed over 800,000 people in the United States, brought our healthcare system to its knees, forced businesses to shut down for months on end, and cost hundreds of thousands of workers their jobs.

(COVID hospitalization rates jumped the same day.) Larsen disagreed:

> The virus that causes COVID-19 is not of course uniquely a workplace condition. Its potency lies in the fact that it exists everywhere an infected person may be—home, school, or grocery store, to name a few. So how can OSHA regulate an employee's exposure to it?

(Almost all workplace risks also occur outside of work.) The U.S. Labor Department extended the deadline to February 9. ND Texas Judge Mark Pittman (Trump) dismissed a lawsuit by United Airlines employees challenging the mandate.

In the case brought by Missouri and nine other states, D Mo Judge Matthew T. Schelp (Trump) held that CMS lacked authority to implement the vaccine mandate for the approximately 1.7 million workers at 76,000 facilities receiving Medicare and Medicaid funding.[108] He questioned the government's data on transmissibility and vaccination status and found the order "arbitrary and capricious." "Congress did not clearly authorize CMS to enact this politically and economically vast, federalism-altering, and boundary-pushing mandate, which Supreme Court precedent requires." Missouri Attorney General Eric Schmitt exulted: "our systems of checks & balances, federalism, separation of powers was meant to protect individual liberties. . . . Our win today . . . is a win for workers & a win for liberty."

WD La Judge Terry Doughty (Trump) did the same, issuing an injunction that applied nationwide except in the 10 states covered by Schelp's injunction.[109] "There is no question that mandating a vaccine to 1.3 million healthcare workers is something that should be done by Congress, not a government agency." He cited Dr. Peter A. McCullough's assertion that "the virus has achieved an immune escape from COVID-19 vaccines." But Judge Doughty failed to note that a hospital that had once employed McCullough recently obtained a restraining order, preventing him from claiming any association with it because of his unorthodox medical opinions. Doughty also cited Dr. Jayanta Bhattacharya for the proposition that "natural immunity provides equivalent or greater protection against severe infection than immunity generated by COVID-19 vaccines" (a view the CDC rejected). Bhattacharya, a co-author of the Great Barrington Declaration (see Chapter 2), also called lockdowns the "biggest public health mistake we've ever made." The Fifth Circuit (two Obama appointees and one GWB) reversed, allowing the administration to enforce the mandate for health care workers in about half the states. But that did not disturb Schelp's injunction in the 10 states that brought it, which the Eighth Circuit had left in place. The same day, ND Texas Judge Matthew J. Kacsmaryk (Trump) enjoined the mandate in Texas.

ED Ky Judge Gregory Van Tatenhove (GWB) issued a TRO in the three plaintiff states (Kentucky, Ohio and Tennessee) against the order that new government contracts require employee vaccination.[110] The Sixth Circuit denied a stay (John K. Bush [Trump] and Richard F. Suhrheinrich [GHWB], with R. Guy Cole Jr. [Clinton] dissenting in part). There were at least 12 other challenges to that mandate. In a lawsuit by Georgia, Alabama, Idaho, Kansas, South Carolina, Utah and West Virginia, SD Ga Judge R. Stanley Baker (Trump) issued a nationwide preliminary injunction, finding that the mandate would "have a major impact on the economy at large." "[E]ven in times of crisis this Court must preserve the rule of law and ensure that all branches of government act within the bounds of their constitutionally granted authorities." Amtrak, General Electric and Boeing promptly dropped their vaccine requirement.

SD Texas Judge Jeffrey V. Brown (Trump) also enjoined the vaccine mandate for federal employees and contractors.[111]

> What is that limit? As the court has already noted, Congress appears . . . to have limited the President's authority in this field to workplace conduct. For its part, this court will say only this: however extensive that power is, the federal-worker mandate exceeds it.

98 percent of federal workers were already vaccinated, but significant percentages remained unvaccinated in some departments (Agriculture: 11.7, VA: 11.5, DHS: 10, Energy: 9, BOP: 17.5, SSA: 9.7). A Fifth Circuit panel (Jerry Smith [Reagan] and Don Willett [Trump], with Stephen Higginson [Obama] dissenting) denied a stay pending appeal. Another Fifth Circuit panel then reversed (Stewart and Dennis [both Clinton], with Barksdale [GHWB] dissenting), finding that Brown had lacked jurisdiction because the mandate had not yet taken effect. The en banc Fifth Circuit upheld the injunction (10–6) in a decision by Judge Oldham (Trump), joined by Jones (Reagan), Smith (Reagan), Barksdale (GHWB), Elrod (GWB), Willett (Trump), Ho (Trump), Duncan (Trump), Engelhardt (Trump) and Wilson (Trump), with Stewart (Clinton), Dennis (Clinton), Southwick (GWB), Haynes (GWB), Graves (Obama) and Higginson (Obama) dissenting. It is striking that all six Trump appointees, both Reagan appointees and the sole GHWB appointee voted for the injunction, while both Obama and both Clinton appointees voted against it; the GWB appointees split, one to two.

The Supreme Court struck down OSHA's private employer vaccine mandate (6–3, along party lines) but upheld the CMS health care worker mandate (5–4, Roberts and Kavanaugh joining the liberals).[112] In the first case, Gorsuch wrote that COVID "is not an occupational hazard in most" workplaces:

> [Covid] can and does spread at home, in schools during sporting events, and everywhere else that people gather. That kind of universal risk is no different from the day-to-day dangers that all face from crime, air pollution, or any number of communicable diseases.

"Where the virus poses a special danger because of the particular features of an employee's job or workplace targeted regulations are plainly permissible." Even if federal law "really *did* endow OSHA with the power it asserts, that law would likely constitute an unconstitutional delegation of legislative authority." The dissenters asked who should decide worker safety: "An agency with expertise in workplace health and safety, acting as Congress and the President authorized? Or a court, lacking any knowledge of how to safeguard workplaces, and insulated from responsibility for any damage it causes?" In the CMS case, the dissenters objected:

> these cases are not about the efficacy or importance of COVID-19 vaccines. They are only about whether CMS has the statutory authority to force healthcare workers, by coercing their employers, to undergo a medical procedure they do not want and cannot undo.

The president of National Nurses United (the nation's largest nurses union, with nearly 225,000 members) said:

> at a time when we're closing in on 850,000 Americans having died in the worst global pandemic in a century, and when infections and hospitalizations are continuing to soar, it is the obligation of our public agencies to require and enforce essential public safety measures to protect the lives and health of all American workers.[113]

Gov. DeSantis called the CMS mandate "insane," "rooted in political [sic—"politics"], not medical science." Although Florida's Agency for Health Care Administration refused to monitor compliance, an AHCA spokesman warned: "if we do not comply with the CMS mandate, we could compromise our ability to serve our communities and provide care to patients under the Medicare and Medicaid programs." The Florida Hospital Association CEO said: "The Supreme Court ruling makes clear the authority that CMS has to implement and enforce its vaccine mandate." The Texas state hospital association was advising hospitals to follow the mandate. But the CEO of the American Health Care Association, representing nursing homes, warned: "When we are in the midst of another Covid surge, caregivers in vaccine hesitant communities may walk off the job because of this policy, further threatening access to care for thousands of our nation's seniors."

All 50 Republican senators formally challenged the mandates under the Congressional Review Act (knowing they would lose the Senate vote).[114] And joined by Democratic Sens. Manchin and Tester, they pushed through a proposal by Republican Sen. Braun to repeal the mandate (knowing it would lose in the House and be vetoed by Biden). Tester explained: "it's about certainty for businesses moving forward." (Actually, it aggravated uncertainty.) Braun predicted:

> If you keep plowing forward with it, and with everything that's been done to say that "Hey, this is falling flat across the country," that's his liability.

> I think it's just another bad subject that he's been doctrinaire about and not flexible.

Sen. McConnell declared: "The federal government, elites in Washington, cannot micromanage citizens' personal choices without a legitimate basis in the law and the Constitution. And that goes double for presidents going far beyond the bounds of their office and their authority." (He had supported vaccines but now, like DeSantis, saw mandates as a political wedge issue.) Sen. Capito said the mandate was "killing the American spirit of being able to make decisions about yourself." In September, Sen. Marshall had tried to revoke the funding for OSHA to enforce rules applicable to the private sector (a large part of what it does). Rep. Keller proposed a similar measure in the House with the full backing of GOP lawmakers. Neither had any chance of success.

Sen. Johnson declared: "we're opposed to the mandate. We don't want the federal government to be able to fund them in any way, shape or form."[115] 11 Republican senators vowed to block all federal funds, led by Marshall, who asked: "is Senator Schumer willing to shut down the economy over this?" The House Freedom Caucus urged McConnell to use "all procedural tools at your disposal to deny timely passage" of the budget bill. Sen. Cruz said: "we should use the leverage we have to fight against what are illegal, unconstitutional and abusive mandates from a president and an administration that knows they are violating the law." Sen. Lee concurred: "The only thing I want to shut down is Congress funding enforcement of an immoral, unconstitutional vaccine mandate." But Sen. Cornyn warned: "I don't think shutdowns benefit people." Sen. McConnell conceded: "we won't shut down." Sen. Rounds agreed: "the vast majority of Republicans would not like to see a shutdown, but . . . all it takes is one person." Sen. Capito called a shutdown "a useless pathway." Sen. Schumer said: "if there is a shutdown, it will be a Republican anti-vaccine shutdown." The Senate passed the stopgap budget, narrowly defeating an amendment to block the vaccine mandate on a 48–50 party-line vote (two Republicans absent). The House then passed the budget 221–212 (only Kinzinger joining the Democrats).

Sen. Johnson said:

> I've had every vaccination until this one because I had covid. The covid gods are not acknowledging natural immunity. They're not acknowledging vaccine injury. They're not acknowledging the fact that even if you're fully vaccinated, you can still get covid, you can still transmit covid, so what's the point of the mandates?[116]

About the same time, he exposed his appalling scientific ignorance. "Standard gargle, mouthwash, has been proven to kill the coronavirus. If you get it, you may reduce viral replication. Why not try all these things?" He cited a study finding that mouthwash provides "modest benefits" in lowering viral loads in saliva. There were no controls or peer review, and Listerine cautioned that its product "is not intended to prevent or treat COVID-19." YouTube had previously suspended Johnson's account for violating its medical misinformation policies. Later, he asked: "Why do we assume that the body's natural immune system isn't the marvel that it is? Why do we think that we can create something better than God in terms of combating disease?" (So much for modern medicine.) Johnson said on *The Charlie Kirk Show* on January 27, 2022, that there have been "over 22,000 deaths reported in association with the vaccines." While conceding "that doesn't prove causation," he invoked "story after story" of "all these athletes dropping dead on the field." His spokeswoman provided a link to a blogpost—"577 Athlete Cardiac Arrests, Serious Issues, 352 Dead, After COVID shot"—which had begun on a website tied to the far-right Austrian Freedom Party; the claim had been repeatedly debunked.

The Senate voted 49–44 (6 Democrats absent) to end Biden's vaccine mandate for health care workers at federally funded facilities (more political grandstanding since the House would not agree and Biden would veto it).[117] Sen. Marshall (a doctor) said: "This vaccine mandate is not about public health or science. The Biden administration's mandate is about fulfilling their desire to control every aspect of our lives." The Senate also voted 48–47 to end the national emergency declaration, though the White House said Biden would veto that.

New York required hospital and nursing home employees to be vaccinated by September 27, 2021, and home care, hospice and adult care workers by October 7, with no exceptions for religious objectors.[118] 16 percent of hospital workers and 15 percent of skilled nursing facility workers and adult care facility workers were not fully vaccinated. EDNY Judge Brian M. Cogan (GWB) denied an injunction to a Christian scientist, but WDNY Judge David N. Hurd (Clinton) issued a TRO against enforcing the mandate on those seeking religious exemptions; there were at least six other lawsuits. The Second Circuit (Walker [GHWB], Sack [Clinton] and Carney [Obama]) reversed the WDNY decision and upheld the EDNY decision. Supreme Court Justices Barrett, Kavanaugh and Roberts voted with the three liberals not to use the emergency docket to decide the case, as they had done after D Maine Judge Levy (Obama) and the First Circuit (Howard [GWB], Lynch [Clinton] and Barron [Obama]) declined to enjoin Maine's vaccine mandate for health care workers, which lacked a religious exemption. Justice Gorsuch wrote a 14-page dissent (joined by Alito). "The state's executive decree clearly interferes with the free exercise of religion—and does so seemingly based on nothing more than fear and anger at those who harbor unpopular religious beliefs." Justice Thomas also dissented. The Supreme Court subsequently declined to review the case over the same three dissents. The day the order took effect, 3,000 of the 8,000 unvaccinated NYC public hospital employees got vaccinations, with the result that 92 percent of all hospital and nursing home workers had received at least one dose, up from 82 percent of nursing home workers and 84 percent of hospital workers a week earlier. NYS Supreme Court Judge Laurence Love denied an injunction. EDNY Judge Cogan (GWB) also denied an injunction against a NYC requirement that public school employees be vaccinated. Supreme Court Justice Barrett had rejected an injunction request from Indiana University students, and Justice Sotomayor rejected one from NYC public school teachers. At least 90 percent of teachers, 95 percent of principals and 82 percent of other school staff were vaccinated. Republican State Assemblyman David J. DiPietro and five medical workers sued to block the vaccine mandate for health care workers. NYC fired 1,430 workers for refusing vaccinations; about 64 percent of them were in the Education Department. Mayor Eric Adams extended the mask mandate for children under 5 after NYS Supreme Court Judge Ralph Porizio (Staten Island) struck it down as "arbitrary, capricious and unreasonable."

Matt Troup, CEO and president of Conway Regional Health System in Arkansas, said he had "been compared to Hitler, been called a moron" for mandating employee vaccinations.[119] All 45 employees (out of the health system's 1,800) who sought religious exemptions had invoked the fact that fetal cell lines had been used to develop the vaccine. Conway required them to sign an agreement not to take any of the 28 other medications developed from fetal cell lines, including Tylenol, Motrin, Preparation H, Claritin, Enadryl and Tums.

21 states sued in MD Florida in Orlando to end the transportation mask mandate.[120] In a separate lawsuit brought by the Health Freedom Defense Fund in Tampa, MD Fla Judge Kathryn Kimball Mizelle (a Trump appointee and former Thomas clerk) enjoined the mandate (days before the scheduled oral argument). She held that "sanitation" in the Public Health Service Act 1944 meant "measures that clean something, not ones that keep something clean. Wearing a mask cleans nothing." (What about air the wearer and others breathe?) She did not address the words "other measures" in the act. She had rejected an effort by administration lawyers to transfer and consolidate this case with the one in Orlando, which had been assigned to an Obama appointee. The ABA had found Mizelle not qualified for lack of experience (only eight years in practice); 10 of the 22 nominees the ABA had rated not qualified in the 33 years since 1989 were nominated by Trump during his four-year term. After the CDC backed masks, the government appealed.

WD La Judge Robert R. Summerhays (Trump) enjoined the administration from reopening the border and ending the Trump policy of refusing to hear asylum requests under Title 42 (a public health law) because the government had failed to consider the cost to the states or to allow public comment under the APA.[121] Arizona AG Mark Brnovich, one of the plaintiffs, tweeted, "GREAT win for the rule of law today." The government said it would appeal.

After the CDC approved vaccines for children under five, 43 percent of parents said they would not vaccinate such children.[122] Republicans were three times as likely as Democrats to say they would "definitely not" vaccinate their children. But COVID hospitalization rates for infants were as high as those for seniors during the Omicron wave.

In November 2022, nearly all Republican governors and 13 Republican senators led by Sen. Lee sought to end the military's vaccine mandate.[123] Sen. Johnson said he would oppose the NDAA (an essential annual appropriation) unless the law ended the mandate, and Rep. McCarthy warned it "will not move" because "they're kicking out men and women who are serving." (DoD had reported in April that about 3,400 had been involuntarily separated; it granted few religious waivers. More than 97 percent of all DoD employees and more than 99 percent of active-duty service members were vaccinated.) HASC Chair Adam Smith said: "I was a very strong supporter of the vaccine mandate when we did it. But at this point in time, does it make sense to have that policy from August 2021?" Dr. Leana Wen wrote in her *Washington Post* column: "It's time the Pentagon ended its covid vaccine mandate for the military." But the National Security Council insisted that "vaccines are saving lives, including our men and women in uniform. So this remains very, very much a health and readiness issue for the force." And the Secretary of Defense wanted to retain the mandate. The White House said: "making sure our troops are ready to defend this country and prepared to do so . . . remains the president's priority and the vaccine requirement for covid does just that." Max Rose, an Army combat veteran, former congressman and former senior adviser on COVID to the Defense Secretary, wrote in a *New York Times* op ed:

> Congress and the White House should honor the military's decades-old practice of mandatory vaccinations—principally because it keeps those in uniform safe. Our elected officials shouldn't turn our military into pawns in the Covid culture war, complicating the decisions of combat commanders and damaging American national security.

But Congress passed the bill without the mandate (83–11 in the Senate, 350–80 in the House). Republicans planned to demand reinstatement of service members discharged for refusing the vaccine (although such an amendment failed in the Senate) and to investigate the administration for having imposed the mandate. The Pentagon formally ended the mandate but continued to encourage vaccination.

A Kaiser Family Foundation survey found that 35 percent of parents opposed all vaccine requirements for school attendance.[124] Among respondents who were or leaned Republican, the percentage wanting parents to be able to opt out more than doubled from 20 in 2019 to 44 in 2022; among those who were or leaned Democrat, by contrast, the percentage who endorsed vaccines increased from 86 to 88. Among all adults, the proportion believing parents should decide increased from 16 to 28 percent. The overall vaccination rate for kindergarteners dropped below 94 percent in the 2020–21 school year and again to 93 percent in the 2021–22 school year, with the largest declines in Mississippi, Georgia and Wisconsin. By the end of 2022, just 40 percent of adults had gotten the Omicron booster, which had been available since September; 40 percent of those who had gotten COVID vaccines said they did not need the booster. Social media continued to disseminate misinformation: in the month between Nov. 1 and Dec. 5, 2022, researchers found more than 500,000 such tweets, which had more than 16 million likes and 580,000 retweets. Since Musk took over Twitter, it disbanded its advisory council and reinstated Rep. Greene and Robert Malone (the anti-vax doctor who falsely claimed to have invented mRNA vaccines).

An analysis found that the least vaccinated decile of U.S. counties (less than 47.7 percent vaccinated) had a COVID death rate 3.41 times that of the most vaccinated decile (more than 78.6 percent vaccinated), and the decile with the highest proportion of votes for Trump (70.9–100 percent) had a rate three times that of the decile with the lowest proportion (0–25.2 percent).[125] Another study found the death rate was 11 percent higher in states that Republicans controlled and 26 percent higher where voters were conservative, after controlling for race, education, income and vaccination rates.

Anthony Fauci offered reflections on retiring after more than a half-century in public health.[126]

> I always speak the unvarnished truth to presidents and other senior government officials, even when such truths may be uncomfortable or politically inconvenient. . . . We also must acknowledge that our fight against Covid-19 has been hindered by the profound political divisiveness in our society. In a way that we have never seen before, decisions about public health measures such as wearing masks and being vaccinated with highly effective and safe vaccines have been influenced by disinformation and political ideology.

He deplored the threats and harassment he and his family suffered from "lowlife" people, including two jailed for "credible" attempts on his life. But these words just provoked Elon Musk to call for Fauci's prosecution, repeating the canard that he "lied to Congress and funded gain-of-function research that killed millions of people." And DeSantis (aping Trump?) said: "Grab that little elf and chuck him across the Potomac."

Although the Senate Health Committee voted 20–2 in March 2022 to create a Sept. 11–style panel to investigate the government's response to the pandemic, as part of the PREVENT Pandemics Act, the bill failed to pass the full Senate, despite lobbying by advocacy groups like Marked by Covid and Covid Survivors for Change.[127] Instead, the new Republican-dominated House Committee on Oversight and Accountability created a Select Subcommittee on the Coronavirus Pandemic to explore its origins and gain-of-function research.[128] Rep. Comer, the Committee chair, said disingenuously: "we're concerned about some government employees and these employees were hired long before the previous two presidents, so I don't think it's political at all." He also was interested in the "effectiveness of the vaccines and the concerns that people are starting to raise with respect to side effects." Philip Zelikow (who had been executive director of the Sept. 11 inquiry) led the Covid Crisis Group, which published its own report in spring 2023.[129]

At a roundtable including signers of the Great Barrington Declaration, Florida Gov. DeSantis announced the creation of a Public Health Integrity Committee, chaired by Surgeon General Ladapo and including some of the dissident scientists who joined the Declaration, to investigate and counter the recommendations of the CDC and FDA.[130] He also sought a grand jury investigation of "crimes and wrongdoing" related to the coronavirus vaccine, noting that myocarditis had been observed in some cases. He observed (without embarrassment): "In Florida, you know, it is against the law to mislead and to misrepresent, particularly when you're talking about the efficacy of a drug." His press office accused pharmaceutical companies and the Biden administration of advocating for vaccines "through relentless propaganda while ignoring real-life adverse events." Ladapo said the University of Florida would study autopsy results of "sudden deaths of individuals that received the COVID-19 vaccine in Florida." In February 2021, DeSantis had said it was "great" that Florida was getting "more vaccine." In December 2022 (contemplating a presidential run in 2024), he reversed course:

> These companies have made a fortune off this federal government imposing or at least attempting to impose mandates, and a lot of false statements. I think people want the truth and I think people want accountability, so you need to have a thorough investigation into what's happened with these shots.

Florida still had the eighth highest rate of COVID-19 cases/population and the 14th highest death rate. *The Washington Post* wrote: "Vaccines saved lives. DeSantis threatens that progress."[131] A model estimated that in the first year vaccines were available, they saved 15.5 million lives worldwide. An estimated 200,000 Americans died because they were unvaccinated during the Delta wave from mid-2021 to early 2022. Hostility to the COVID vaccine infected attitudes toward vaccination generally: the percentage of children vaccinated for MMR declined from 82 in October 2019 to 71 in December 2022.

In spring 2023, Republicans in Congress passed bills to repeal the coronavirus emergency, even though Biden announced he would end it on May 11.[132] They also continued to seek political advantage by attacking the vaccine. Rep. Roy said CDC Director Walensky admitted vaccines could not prevent transmission; in fact, she had been discussing the small number of breakthrough cases among the vaccinated. Rep. Massie denounced the "lie" that "vaccines can't cause any harm." Rep. Greene blamed vaccines for the shortage of health care workers, some of whom "want to trust their own natural immunity," and demanded "an IMMEDIATE investigation into Covid vaccines and the dramatic increase of people dying suddenly," claiming "I pretty much have the heartbeat of the base on this issue." Steve Bannon agreed that the "creation, approval, mandatory application, damage" from the vaccination "is a central issue for a vast majority of MAGA."

The concluding chapter reviews this narrative and places it in the broader context of ongoing Republican attacks on science.

Notes

AP	Associated Press
BMJ	*British Medical Journal*
CNN	Cable News Network
G	*Guardian*
MH	*Miami Herald*
MMWR	Mortality and Morbidity Weekly Report
NPR	National Public Radio
NYT	*New York Times*
WP	*Washington Post*
WSJ	*Wall Street Journal*

1 CCG (2023: 141).
2 See Parmet and Paul (2020, 2023); Hotez (2021).
3 Sha, "The snake-oil salesmen of the Senate," NYT (11.24.20); Iati, "Senate holds hearing on hydroxychloroquine, despite no evidence it works against covid-19," WP (11.20.20); Stolberg, "Anti-vaccine doctor has been invited to testify before Senate committee," NYT (12.7.20); Edmondson and Fandos, "A Wisconsin senator elevates fringe theories, questioning virus science," NYT (12.8.20); Rizzo, "Ron Johnson's unscientific take on the coronavirus vaccine," WP (3.15.21); Blake, " 'Here we go again with the theater': Fauci pushed back on Rand Paul's amateur epidemiology—again," WP (3.18.21).

4 CDC, "Science Brief: SARS-CoV-2 Infection-induced and Vaccine-induced immunity" (10 29.21). www.cdc.gov/coronavirus/2019-ncov/science/science-briefs/vaccine-induced-immunity.html.
5 Rizzo, "Ron Johnson's unscientific use of vaccine and death data," WP (5.12.21); Dawsey and Watson, "Republican leaders say they want to focus on the future, but Trump is far from done with the past," WP (6.6.21).
6 Barreda, "COVID-19: Dallas doctor's license suspended after saying he, staff do not wear masks," Salem Statesman Journal (12.4.20); Knowles, "A doctor derided mask-wearing. His medical license has been suspended," WP (12.6.20); Oregon Medical Board, In the Matter of Steven Arthur LaTulippe (5.6.21); https://omb.oregon.gov/Clients/ORMB/Public/VerificationDetails.aspx?EntityID=1451807.
7 Budryk, "Doctor that promoted false hydroxychloroquine claims arrested in connection with Capitol riot," The Hill (1.21.21); "Beverly Hills doctor who founded anti-vaccine group pleads guilty to joining Capitol riot," AP (3.3.22); Andrews, "Facebook and other companies are removing viral 'Plandemic' conspiracy video," WP (5.7.20); McBride, "Plandemic movie video removed by YouTube: watch," Heavy.com (5.6.20); Merlan, "The coronavirus truthers don't believe in public health," Vice (4.22.20); Frenkel, Decker and Alba, "How the 'Plandemic' movie and its falsehoods spread widely online," NYT (5.20.20); Wright (2021: 27); Chowkwanyun (2022: 330); Alberts, "Retraction," 334 *Science* 1636 (12.23.11); MacFarquhar, "Far-right extremists move from 'stop the steal' to stop the vaccine," NYT (3.26.21); Rabinowitz, "Doctor known for spreading Covid misinformation is sentenced to prison for role in US Capitol attack," CNN (6.16.22); Sommer, "COVID-denying medical group implodes over founder's extravagant spending," Daily Beast (11.14.22); "FSMB: spreading covid-19 vaccine misinformation may put medical license at risk" (7.29.21) www.fsmb.org/advocacy/news-releases/fsmb-spreading-covid-19-vaccine-misinformation-may-put-medical-license-at-risk/.
8 Bergengruen, "How 'America's Frontline Doctors' sold access to bogus COVID-19 treatments—and left patients in the lurch," Time (8.26.21); Brumfiel, "A doctor spread COVID misinformation and renewed her license with a mouse click," NPR (11.4.21); Lee, "America's Frontline Doctors plans to open clinics as California Medical Board investigates founder," The Intercept (12.20.21).
9 Blake, "Fox News and Trump are still pushing hydroxychloroquine. Here's what the data actually shows," WP (6.22.21).
10 www.cdc.gov/nchs/covid19/nhcs/intubation-ventilator-use.htm.
11 Lerer, "How Republican vaccine opposition got to this point," NYT (7.17.21); Blake, "Sherri Tenpenny's bizarre anti-vaccine testimony was a long time coming," WP (6.9.21); Frenkel, "The most influential spreader of coronavirus misinformation online," NYT (7.24.21); Frenkel and Hsu, "How local media spreads misinformation from vaccine skeptics," NYT (8.2.21); Dwoskin and Aaron, "The Trump administration bailed out prominent anti-vaccine groups during a pandemic," WP (1.18.21); Srikanth, "12 prominent people opposed to vaccines are responsible for two-thirds of anti-vaccine content online—report," The Hill (3.25.21); "Dr. Sherri Tenpenny—face masks are not effective against COVID-19. How masks are being used to control the population," Digital Freedom Platform (7.28.20); https://archive.ph/20210328014954/www.politifact.com/factchecks/2021/mar/04/sherri-tenpenny/covid-19-vaccine-does-not-cause-death-autoimmune-d/; "US doctor makes false claims about COVID-19 vaccines," AFP (4.28.21); Jankowicz, "Twitter bans anti-vaxxer who pushed the conspiracy theory that COVID-19 shots make people magnetic," Business Insider (9.12.21); Alba, "YouTube bans all anti-vaccine misinformation," NYT (9.29.21); Masson, "Ohio renews license of physician who says COVID-19

vaccines magnetize recipients," Becker Hospital Review (9.20.21); Draper (2022: 307–308).

12 Frenkel and Hsu, "How local media spreads misinformation from vaccine skeptics," NYT (8.2.21); Satija and Sun, "A major funder of the anti-vaccine movement has made millions selling natural health products," WP (12.20.19); Velasquez-Manoff (2022); Mercola, "About 'The Great Bird Flu Hoax'" (2009); Smith, "Dr Mercola: visionary or quack?" Chicago Magazine (1.31.12); "Anti-vaccine influencer Joseph Mercola removes Covid disinformation from his website," Coda Story (5.7.21); Alba, "YouTube bans all anti-vaccine misinformation," NYT (9.9.21); De Vynck, "YouTube is banning prominent anti-vaccine activists and blocking all anti-vaccine content," WP (9.29.21).

13 Velasquez-Manoff (2022).

14 Velasquez-Manoff (2022).

15 Risen, "Vladimir Zelenko, 48, dies; promoted an unfounded covid treatment," NYT (7.2.22); "Video makes false comparison between kids COVID and vaccine risks," Australian Associated Press (1.20.22); Burleigh (2021: 148).

16 "Fact Check-Indiana doctor makes false claims in viral video," Reuters (8.12.21); Alba and Frenkel, "Calls grow to discipline doctors spreading virus misinformation," NYT (8.27.21); Grullón Paz, "Elizabeth Warren asks Amazon to 'stop peddling misinformation about Covid vaccines and treatments,'" NYT (9.9.21).

17 Sawyer, Bloomgarden, Cooper, Nichols and Hickie, "State medical boards should punish doctors who spread false information about covid and vaccines," WP (9.21.21); "FSMB: spreading covid-19 vaccine misinformation may put medical license at risk" (7.29.21); https://phr.org/news/doctors-who-repeatedly-spread-covid-19-misinformation-and-disinformation-should-lose-medical-licenses-phr/; www.nolicensefordisinformation.org/; Myers, "Bill in California would punish doctor who spread COVID falsehoods," NYT (8.31.22); Myers, "Is spreading medical misinformation a doctor's free speech right?" NYT (11.30.22).

18 Myers, "A federal court blocks California's new medical misinformation law," NYT (1.26.23).

19 Kaplan, "Dr. Stephen Smith on effectiveness of hydroxychloroquine: 'I think this is the beginning of the end of the pandemic,'" Fox News (4.2.20); Korownyk, "Televised medical talk shows—what they recommend and the evidence to support their recommendations: a prospective observational study," 349 BMJ g7346 (12.17.14).

20 Gabriel, "Dr. Oz says he's running for Senate in Pennsylvania," NYT (12.1.21); Gabriel, "The Pennsylvania Senate candidate running as the Anti-Dr. Oz," NYT (12.10.21); Gabriel, "'Magic' weight-loss pills and covid cures: Dr. Oz under the microscope," NYT (12.26.21); Itkowitz, "Trump endorses Dr. Oz in Pennsylvania Senate race, a key battleground," WP (4.10.22); Goldschmidt, "Physicians to Columbia University: 'Dismayed' that Dr. Oz is on faculty," CNN (4.18.15); Izadi, "Dr. Oz responds after prominent physicians call for his firing from Columbia University," WP (4.18.15); Dell, "What's Wrong with Dr. Oz?" 112(5) Mo Med 332–333 (2015); www.breastcancerfoundation.org.nz/breast-awareness/risk-factors/factors-that-dont-cause-breast-cancer; Korownyk, "Televised medical talk shows—what they recommend and the evidence to support their recommendations: a prospective observational study," 349 BMJ g7346 (12.17.14); Luscombe, "Dr Oz dropped by Columbia amid pro-Trump Republican Senate run—report," G (5.1.22).

21 Knowles, "A doctor called coronavirus vaccines 'fake.' Now he sits on an Idaho regional health board," WP (9.17.21); D'Ambrosio, "Controversial Doc no longer with one of Idaho's largest health networks," Medpage Today (12.10.21); Dutton, "Idaho doctors, pathology board accuse Dr. Ryan Cole of endangering

public health," Idaho Capital Sun (12.16.21); Dutton, "Idaho's Dr. Ryan Cole defends his medical license, saying complaints are political attacks," Idaho Capital Sun (7.29.22); Dutton "Dr. Ryan Cole's journey from Boise to Nashville to France. His new focus? Monkeypox," Idaho Capital Sun (8.10.22).

22 Astor, "Vocal chiropractors split the profession on vaccines," NYT (7.16.21); Diamond, "Doctors, nurses and health groups call for mandatory coronavirus vaccinations for health workers," WP (7.26.21).

23 Dwoskin, "Facebook says post that cast doubt on covid-19 vaccine was most popular on the platform from January through March," WP (8.22.21); CCG (2023: 210).

24 Dwoskin, "Conspiracy theorists, banned on major social networks, connect with audiences on newsletters and podcasts," WP (127.22); Suliman, "Joni Mitchell pulls music from Spotify in stand with Neil Young against covid misinformation," WP (1.29.22); Timsit, "More musicians join Neil Young in demanding Spotify remove their content over covid misinformation," WP (1.20.22); Scott and Suliman, "White House wades into Spotify controversy as India.Arie, David Crosby, Stephen Stills and more artists pull music," WP (2.3.22); Gay, "Why I've decided to take my podcast off Spotify," NYT (2.3.22); Coyle, "Spotify to add advisories to podcasts discussing COVID-19," AP (1.30.22); Wakabayashi, "YouTube bars a right-wing host for making false covid claims," NYT (1.27.22); Jamison and Silverman, "Anti-vaccine activists see D.C. rally as a marker of recent gains," WP (1.22.22).

25 Medina, "Health officials warn people not to treat Covid with a drug meant for livestock," NYT (8.22.21); Goldberg, "Demand surges for deworming drug for covid, despite scant evidence it works," NYT (8.31.21); Lukpat, "New Mexico health officials link misuse of ivermectin to two Covid-19 deaths," NYT (9.26.21); Zuckerman, "Judge orders Cinci hospital to treat COVID-19 patient with ivermectin, despite CDC warnings," Ohio Capital Journal (8.30.21); Knowles and Bella, "A hospital refused to give ivermectin to a covid patient. Then a judge ordered doctors to administer it," WP (9.1.21); Taylor and May, "Ohio judge reverses order requiring covid patient to be given ivermectin," NYT (9.8.21); Kessler, "False meme: Nobel laureate did not say ivermectin 'cures' covid-19," WP (9.9.21); Alba, "Facebook groups promoting ivermectin as a Covid-19 treatment continue to flourish," NYT (9.28.21).

26 Jeong, "Texas court says hospital can't be forced to offer ivermectin to covid patient on ventilator," WP (11.19.21); Bennett, "'I am personally offended': Houston Methodist CEO denies doctor's claims about unvaccinated COVID patients," KHOU 11 (11.17.21); Gleeson, "Florida teacher at center of ivermectin lawsuit dies of COVID; husband says 'name a law after her,'" USA Today (11.17.21); Ramsey, "A registered nurse demanded her husband be treated for COVID-19. A judge refused," USA Today (9.17.21).

27 Epstein, "Luc Montagnier, Nobel-winning co-discoverer of H.I.V., dies at 89," NYT (2.11.21); Montagnier and Rubenfeld, "Omicron makes Biden's vaccine mandates obsolete," WSJ (1.9.22).

28 Kaplan, "Exit interview: C.D.C. head Redfield reflects on his time on the job," NYT (1.20.21).

29 Sonmez, "Fauci says he feels liberated to talk about science without repercussions under the Biden administration," WP (1.21.21); Shear, "Banished by Trump but brought back by Biden, Fauci aims to 'let the science speak,'" NYT (1.22.21); McNeil, "Fauci on what working for Trump was really like," NYT (1.25.21); Brewster, "CDC director: agency was 'muzzled' under Trump," Forbes (1.24.21).

30 Walensky, "Our pandemic despair is fading too quickly," NYT (6.27.23).

31 Kornfield, "Criticized by science community and Trump, Birx said she 'always' considered quitting," WP (1.22.21); Armey, "Deborah Birx said Trump was

being given 'parallel data' on Covid-19," WP (1.25.21); Bump, "Birx both exemplifies and blames the cherry-picking that spared the Trump presidency," WP (1.25.21); Diamond, "Election 'distracted' Trump team from pandemic response, Birx tells Congress, saying more than 130,000 people died unnecessarily," WP (10.27.21); Birx (2022: 360).

32 HSSCC (2022a: 4, 19–20).

33 Din, "Trump lashes out at Fauci and Birx after CNN documentary," Politico (3.29.21).

34 www.statista.com/statistics/1109004/coronavirus-covid19-cases-rate-us-americans-by-state/; Dawsey, "Trump slashes at McConnell as he reiterates election falsehoods at Republican event," WP (4.11.21).

35 Villegas, "Fauci pushes back on GOP criticisms, calling claims 'bizarre,'" WP (4.5.21).

36 Blake, "Rand Paul and the GOP effort to blame Fauci for the coronavirus," WP (5.12.21); Viser and Abutaleb, "Trump and his allies try to rewrite, distort history of pandemic while casting Fauci as Public Enemy No. 1," WP (6.6.21); Abutaleb and Harris, "Trump-era hunt for pandemic 'lab leak' went down many fruitless paths," WP (6.16.21).

37 www.statista.com/statistics/1109004/coronavirus-covid19-cases-rate-us-americans-by-state/.

38 Blake, "Jon Stewart goes all-in on the lab leak theory," WP (6.15.21).

39 Swisher, "Anthony Fauci on the lab leak theory and emailing Mark Zuckerberg," NYT (6.21.21).

40 Thebault, "In latest clash over Wuhan lab, Fauci tells Sen. Rand Paul: "You do not know what you're talking about,'" WP (7.20.21).

41 Farhi, "Four conservative radio talk-show hosts bashed coronavirus vaccines. Then they got sick," WP (9.1.21); Abutaleb and Reinhard, "Fauci swamped by angry calls over beagle experiments after campaign that included misleading image," WP (11.19.21); Bradford, "Fauci called a 'PUPPY KILLER' by Donald Trump Jr who is sell [sic] t-shirts bashing White House doc for cruel experiments," U.S. Sun (10.28.21).

42 Sheets and Bowden, "'You are distorting everything about me': Fauci tears into Rand Paul for using 'pandemic for political gain' with personal attacks," Independent (1.11.22); Zak and Roberts, "Anthony Fauci is up against more than a virus," WP (1.31.21).

43 Donald Trump Press Conference Announcement Transcript: Sues Facebook, Twitter, Google over Censorship Claims," Rev (7.21.21) www.rev.com/blog/transcripts/donald-trump-press-conference-announcement-transcript-sues-facebook-twitter-google-over-censorship claims.

44 Landay and Hosenball, "Republican report says coronavirus leaked from China lab; scientists still probing origins," Reuters (8.1.21); Cole, "Ex-CDC Chief says he was 'threatened' for believing COVID lab leak theory," Newsweek (8.10.21); Nakashima and Achenbach, "U.S. spy agencies rule out possibility the coronavirus was created as a bioweapon, say origin will stay unknown without China's help," WP (8.28.21); Achenbach, "Prominent scientist who said lab-leak theory of covid-19 origin should be probed now says evidence points to Wuhan market," WP (11.18.21); Taylor, "WHO covid origins report says 'lab leak' theory needs further investigation," WP (6.9.22); Achenbach, "Scientists hone argument that coronavirus came from Wuhan market," WP (7.26.22); Worobey et al., "The Huanan Seafood Wholesale Market in in Wuhan was the early epicenter of COVID-19 pandemic," 377 Science 951–59 (7.26.22).

45 Stolberg, "N.I.H. leader rebuts COVID lab leak theory at House hearing," NYT (2.9.23).

46 Gordon and Strobel, "Lab leak most likely origin of covid-19 pandemic, Energy Department now says," WSJ (2.26.23); Rasmussen and Popescu, "Available evidence still points to covid originating from spillover," WP (3.8.23); Stolberg and Mueller, "Hearing on covid's origins promises politics mixed with substance," NYT (3.8.23); Blake, "How the COVID lab leak became the American public's predominant theory," WP (3.17.23); Achenbach and Johnson, "Genetic data links raccoon dogs to covid origin; WHO seeks China cooperation," WP (3.18.23); Mueller, "W.H.O. accuses China of hiding data that may link COVID's origins to animals," NYT (3.18.23); Stolberg and Mueller, "Lab leak or not? How politics shaped battle over COVID's origin," NYT (3.20.23); Mueller, "Scientist revisits data on raccoon dogs and covid, stressing the unknowns," NYT (4.30.23).

47 Strobel and Gordon, "Covid emerged as Chinese lab faced biosafety issues, Senate Republican study finds," WSJ (4.17.23).

48 Barnes, "U.S. intelligence agencies remain divided over lab leak theory," NYT (6.24.23).

49 Linskey, Diamond and Pager, "Republicans seek to make vaccine passports the next battle in the pandemic culture wars," WP (3.31.21); Mazzei, Stolberg, Sullivan and Paz, "Florida's governor bans agencies and businesses from requiring 'vaccine passports,'" NYT (4.3.21); Sampson, "'Political buffoonery': cruise lines head for showdown with DeSantis over vaccine requirement ban," WP (5.30.21); "Global cruise industry contributes $7.97 billion to Florida's economy," www.globenewswire.com/news-release/2017/10/04/1140814/0/en/Global-Cruise-Industry-Contributes-7-97-Billion-to-Florida-s-Economy.html; Meckler and Strauss, "Florida offers school vouchers for families angry with mask mandates while judge temporarily blocks ban in Arkansas," WP (8.7.21); Mazzei, "As Covid surges in Florida, DeSantis refuses to change course," NYT (8.7.21); Fausset, "An Arkansas judge temporarily blocks the state's ban on mask mandates," NYT (8.7.21); Pietsch, Suliman and Knowles, "DeSantis's battle against mask, vaccine mandates approaches boiling point in Florida," WP (8.9.21); Knowles, "DeSantis sells 'Don't Fauci My Florida' merch as new coronavirus cases near highest in nation," WP (7.16.21).

50 Mello and Parmet (2021).

51 Filkins (2022).

52 Mervosh, "Florida's governor gives parents final say on masks for children in school," NYT (7.31.21); Bella and Kornfield, "Florida breaks record for new coronavirus cases as surge of infections rips through state," WP (8.1.21); Blake, "Ron DeSantis and the GOP's acquired immunity to correcting vaccine misinformation," WP (9.15.21); Shivaram, "Florida Gov. DeSantis taps a new surgeon general who doesn't support vaccine mandates," NPR (9.22.21); "Surgeon General asked to leave Tina Polsky's office after refusing to wear a mask," Florida Politics (10.24.21); Sarkissian, "Florida's surgeon general won't share Covid-19 vaccine status," Politico (10.27.21); "Florida surgeon general doesn't apologize, says he can't talk clearly with mask," Tampa Bay Times (10.27.21); Mazzei, "The doctor giving DeSantis's pandemic policies a seal of approval," NYT (2.23.22).

53 Guerrero, "UCLA sources: DeSantis's handpicked surgeon general mischaracterized his experience treating Covid-19 patients," MSNBC (11.10.21); Ladapo, "Coronavirus pandemic: We were caught unprepared. It is too late for shutdowns to save us," USA Today (3.24.21); Power, "UCLA sources: Joseph Ladapo did not treat COVID-19 patents," Florida Politics (11.9.21); Ladapo (2022); Filkins (2022).

54 Diamond, "Experts slam Florida Surgeon General's warning on coronavirus vaccines," WP (10.12.22); O'Donnell, "Florida health officials removed key data

from COVID vaccine report," Tampa Bay Times (4.7.23); "Florida officials cut key data from vaccine study," AP (4.8.23); Sarkissian, "Florida Surgeon General altered key findings in study on covid-19 vaccine safety," Politico (4.24.23); "Florida's Surgeon General played loose with facts about vaccine risk," WP (4.30.23).

55 Pietsch, Suliman and Knowles, "WHO calls for moratorium on booster vaccine shots through September, citing global disparity," WP (8.4.21); Villegas and Kornfield, "Some Florida school districts push ahead with mask mandates, defying DeSantis's threat to cut funds," WP (8.5.21); Suliman and Pietsch, "Oregon set to become third state to impose statewide indoor mask mandate," WP (8.11.21); Wang, "Public health experts urge local mask and vaccine requirements as schools reopen across the country," WP (8.9.21); Kornfield, "Florida school districts with mask mandates may be investigated and punished, state says," WP (8.18.21); Delkic, "A Florida school board defies the governor's mask ban," NYT (8.16.21); Committee to Protect Health Care, "Florida Physicians: Repeal anti-mask laws, protect FL children" (8.14.21); Sargent, "The latest GOP anti-mask lunacy is stirring a backlash. New polling reveals it," WP (8.17.21); Kornfield, "Florida school districts with mask mandates may be investigated and punished, state says," WP (8.18.21).

56 Strauss, "Florida Gov. DeSantis faces growing revolt from school districts imposing mask mandates," WP (8.19.21); Stolberg and Green, "The Biden administration will use a federal civil rights office to deter states from banning masks in classrooms," NYT (8.19.21); Strauss, "Vaccine mandates ordered in New York City, New Jersey Schools, as masking battle escalates in Florida," WP (8.24.21); Strauss, "More than half of Florida's students now go to schools mandating masks in defiance of DeSantis," WP (8.25.21); Kornfield, "Fla. judge rules DeSantis administration cannot restrict school districts' mask mandates," WP (8.27.21); Meckler, "Biden administration opens civil rights investigations over bans on school mask mandates," WP (8.30.21); Green and Slotnik, "The U.S. Education Department is investigating five states over their mask mandate bans," NYT (8.31.21); Rozsa, "Florida judge rules against DeSantis again, allows schools to require masks," WP (9.8.21); Slochek, "Biden administration offers direct grants in fight with Florida over school mask mandates," MH (9.9.21); Fitzsimons, "DeSantis files emergency appeal after judge says Florida must allow school mask mandates," NBC News (9.9.21); Rosza and Strauss, "Florida school mask fights heat up again as appeals court backs DeSantis and Biden administration opens civil rights investigation," WP (9.11.21); "Ron DeSantis reaches a new low of cynicism and recklessness," WP (9.15.21); Diaz, "Florida's Board of Education approves cutbacks to 8 school districts over mask mandates," NYT (10.6.21); Marcos and Slotnik, "American and Southwest Airlines reject the Texas order banning vaccine mandates," NYT (10.12.21).

57 Rozsa, "DeSantis brings back Florida lawmakers to crack down on pandemic mandates," WP (11.15.21); Mazzei, "As. G.O.P. fights mask and vaccine mandates, Florida takes lead," NYT (11.18.21); Pietsch, "Disney World halts vaccine requirement for workers after Florida restricts employer mandates," WP (11.21.21).

58 Filkins (2022); Wang, "Fla. Gov. Ron DeSantis upbraids students for wearing masks, calling it 'covid theater,'" WP (3.2.22); Rozsa, "Florida's top health official says healthy children should not get coronavirus vaccine," WP (3.8.22).

59 Rampell, "Red states are now paying people not to get vaccinated," WP (11.29.21); Gregg, "5 GOP-led states extend unemployment aid to workers who lose jobs over vaccine mandates," WP (12.27.21); Baker and Ivory, "Threats, resignations and 100 new laws: why public health is in crisis," NYT (10.18.21);

Meckler and Strauss, "Florida offers school vouchers for families angry with mask mandates while judge temporarily blocks ban in Arkansas," WP (8.7.21); Mazzei, "As covid surges in Florida, DeSantis refuses to change course," NYT (8.7.21); Fausset, "An Arkansas judge temporarily blocks the state's ban on mask mandates," NYT (8.7.21); "Get vaccinated. Get masked. It's the only way out of this," NYT (8.6.21); Paul, "Jennifer Aniston and other celebrities endorse vaccines. Experts say their pleas may not help," WP (8.8.21).

60 Thebault, "Texas Gov. Abbott says state is 'very close' to herd immunity. The data tells a different story," WP (4.11.21); Montgomery, Heyward and Sandoval, "Abbott criticized for ban on covid mandates as cases soar in Texas," NYT (8.9.21); Paybarah, "Local officials in Texas can temporarily require masks, two judges rule," NYT (8.11.21); Kannapell, "Texas takes its ban on school mask mandates to the state Supreme Court," NYT (8.15.21); Anders and Hauptman, "Texas Supreme Court sides with Gov. Abbott, temporarily blocking mask mandates," WP (8.16.21); Hauser, "The Texas State Supreme Court upholds governor's mask mandate ban, for now," NYT (8.16.21); DePasquale and Hard, "Texas drops enforcement of its governor's ban on mask mandates," NYT (8.20.21); Kornfield and Bella, "Texas Supreme Court rejects Abbott's ban on school mask mandates—for now," WP (8.20.21); Anders and Hauptman, "Texas Supreme Court sides with Gov. Abbott temporarily blocking mask mandates," WP (8.15.21); Thebault, Paul, Jeong, Timsit, Rosenberg and Marimow, "Federal judge overrules Texas ban on mask mandates in schools," WP (11.11.21); McGill, "Appeals court upholds Texas block on school mask mandate," AP (7.27.22); Saul, "Campuses are virus incubators, but these colleges can't require vaccines," NYT (8.13.21); Wang, "Texas Gov. Abbott issues executive order prohibiting cities from requiring masks, vaccines," WP (7.30.21); Montgomery, "Gov. Greg Abbott bars mandates for vaccinations and masks in Texas," NYT (7.31.21); DePasquale, "A Texas court affirms a ruling against the governor's ban on mask mandates," NYT (11.23.21).

61 www.nytimes.com/interactive/2021/us/texas-covid-cases.html.

62 DePasquale, "A Texas court affirms a ruling against the governor's ban on mask mandates," NYT (11.23.21).

63 Waldman, "How the GOP crusade against vaccines could get even more dangerous," WP (7.14.21); Rojas, "Top Tennessee vaccine official says she was fired over shots for teens," NYT (7.13.21); Bella and Villegas, "Tennessee resumes most vaccine outreach to minors paused after GOP backlash," WP (7.23.21); Paybarah and Levin, "Tennessee's governor allows parents to opt out of mask mandates at school," NYT (8.17.21); Renkl, "In the South, we are fighting Covid. And our own elected officials," NYT (8.23.21); Tennessee Medical Association, "TMA Response to Threats Toward Physicians and Need to Receive Vaccination" (8.17.21); Mattise and Sainz, "DA won't prosecute for governor's student mask opt-out order," AP (8.17.21); Petri, "Two more federal judges rule against the Tennessee governor's ban on mask mandates," NYT (9.26.21); Dzhanova, "The governor of Tennessee signed a sweeping bill into law that prohibits businesses from mandating COVID-19 vaccinations and imposes limits on schools," Business Insider (11.14.21).

64 Ma, "ACLU sues over South Carolina ban on school mask mandates," AP (8.24.21); Castronuovo, "Federal judge temporarily blocks South Carolina's ban on school mask mandates," The Hill (9.28.21); Nirappil, "Kentucky schools overwhelmingly keep mask mandates after Republicans scrapped state requirement," WP (9.21.21).

65 Healy, "Arizona banned school mask mandates. Now some kids are sick and parents are angry," NYT (9.1.21); Arizona Education Association, "AEA and

Education Groups file lawsuit against governor's mask ban" (8.13.21); Rappeport, "Arizona could lose relief funds for undermining school mask mandates," NYT (10.6.21); Rappeport, "The Treasury Department threatens to keep relief funds from Arizona for using it to fight school mask rules," NYT (1.14.22); Rappeport, "Arizona sues to stop Treasury from recouping relief funds," NYT (1.22.22).

66 Sellers and Stanley-Becker, "As coronavirus surges, GOP lawmakers are moving to limit public health powers," WP (7.26.21); Mazzei, "Wearing masks indoors again? Some states are a vehement no," NYT (7.29.21); Decker, "Which states ban mask mandates in schools, and which require masks?" Education Week (8.20.21); Iati, "Judge continues to prohibit New York state from banning religious exemptions to vaccine mandate," WP (10.13.21).

67 Bellware, "GOP lawmaker who once spurned masks urged people to take covid-19 seriously after eight-month illness," WP (8.1.21); Slotnik and Hassan, "The U.S. surpasses 40 million known coronavirus cases," NYT (9.7.21); Diamond, Mueller, Baumhardt and Myers, "'I feel defeated': Mask and vaccine mandates cause new divides as officials try to head off virus surge," WP (8.15.21); Bump, "More Republicans support opposition to government vaccine mandates than support open carry," WP (10.21.21); Leonhardt, "U.S. covid deaths get even redder," NYT (11.8.21).

68 Goldstein, "Anger over masks mandates, other covid rules, spurs states to curb power of public health officials," WP (12.25.21); "Fighting omicron means facing reality. Slogans don't help," WP (1.5.22); Natanson and Asbury, "Seven school boards sue to stop Gov. Youngkin's mask-optional order on the day it takes effect," WP (1.24.22); Natanson, "More than half of Virginia school districts are defying Youngkin's mask-optional order," WP (1.27.22); Singh, "Virginia governor sued again over order to make masks optional in schools," Reuters (2.1.22); Natanson, Weiner and Jouvenal, "Judge temporarily halts Youngkin order making masks optional in Va. schools after lawsuit from school boards," WP (2.4.22); Jouvenal, Lumpkin and Natanson, "Virginia's public colleges and universities can't require coronavirus vaccine, new GOP attorney general finds," WP (1.29.22).

69 Graham, "Vaccine resisters seek religious exemptions. But what counts as religious?" NYT (9.11.21).

70 Talbot and Clark, "'Best $500 I ever spent': GOP lawmakers flout mask rules, risk fine on House floor," NBC News (5.18.21); Fandos, "The U.S. House of Representatives will once again require masks in the chamber," NYT (7.28.21); Sotomayor and Wagner, "House Republicans refuse to follow new mask mandate, leading Pelosi to call McCarthy a 'moron' for his comments," WP (7.28.21); Fandos and Weisman, "In the Capitol, revival of mask mandate ignites partisan recriminations," NYT (7.29.21); Edmondson, "House Democrats quash a G.O.P. effort to end the chamber's mask mandate," NYT (5.20.21); "Mask up (again) and get vaccinated. Now is not the time to let up against covid," WP (7.29.21); Fandos, "The U.S. House of Representatives will once again require masks in the chamber," NYT (7.28.21); Alfaro, "Rep. Marjorie Taylor Greene hit with four more fines for breaking House rule by refusing to wear a mask," WP (11.2.21); Broadwater, "2 Georgia Republicans rack up fines for defying House's mask mandate," NYT (12.29.21); Diamond, Knowles and Pager, "Vaccine hesitancy morphs into hostility, as opposition to shots hardens," WP (7.15.21).

71 McLean and Mueller, "More than one-quarter of Congress has had COVID-19," The Hill (3.9.22).

72 Stolberg and Alba, "Surgeon General assails tech companies over misinformation on covid-19," NYT (7.15.21); Viser, Lerman and Pager, "'They're killing

people': Biden aims blistering attack at tech companies over vaccine falsehoods," WP (7.16.21); Kang, "Facebook tells Biden: 'Facebook is not the reason' vaccination goal was missed," NYT (7.17.21); Knox, "Nearly 30 groups urge Facebook, Instagram, Twitter to take down vaccine disinformation," WP (7.19.21); Sargent, "A vile new Trump-GOP claim about vaccines suggests trouble ahead," WP (7.19.21); Pietsch, "Twitter suspends Rep. Marjorie Taylor Greene for spreading covid-19 misinformation," WP (7.20.21); Weisman and Stolberg, "As Virus Resurges, G.O.P. lawmakers allow vaccine skepticism to flourish," NYT (7.20.21); Grynbaum, Hsu and Kanno-Youngs, "On Fox News, vaccination pleas intensify but skepticism persists," NYT (7.20.21); Diamond and Pager, "'Patience has worn thin': Frustration mounts over vaccine holdouts," WP (7.24.21); Lerer, "How Republican vaccine opposition got to this point," NYT (7.17.21); Blake, "Sherri Tenpenny's bizarre anti-vaccine testimony was a long time coming," WP (6.9.21); Hsu, "Despite outbreaks among the unvaccinated, Fox News hosts smear shots," NYT (7.21.21); Weiland, "In Louisiana, vaccine misinformation has public health workers feeling 'stuck,'" NYT (7.26.21); Stanley-Becker, "Charlies Kirk's pro-Trump youth group stokes vaccine resistance as covid surges again," WP (7.29.21); Sides et al. (2022: 250–251); Gadarian et al. (2022: 256); CCG (2023: 217).

73 www.cdc.gov/nchs/covid19/mortality-overview.htm.

74 Sides et al. (2022: 252–253); Gadarian et al. (2022: 256–258, 262–265, 272, 286).

75 Downie, "New covid variant. Same Republican denialism," WP (11.29.21); Gazit et al., "Comparing SARS-CoV-2 natural immunity to vaccine-induced immunity: reinfections versus breakthrough infections," MedRxiv (8.25.21) www.medrxiv.org/content/10.1101/2021.08.24.21262415v1; Bozio et al., "Laboratory-confirmed COVID-19 among adults hospitalized with COVID-19-like illness with infection-induced or MRNA vaccine-induced SARS-Cov-2 immunity—nine states, January-September 2021," 70(44) MMWR 1539–1544 (11.5.21) www.cdc.gov/mmwr/volumes/70/wr/mm7044e1.htm; Hals, "U.S. judge upholds COVID-19 vaccine requirement for those with 'natural immunity,'" Reuters (10.1.21).

76 "Tracking Coronavirus in Florida: latest map and case count," NYT (5.7.22).

77 "Tracking Coronavirus in Mississippi: latest map and case count," NYT (5.7.22).

78 Hals, "U.S. judge upholds COVID-19 vaccine requirement for those with 'natural immunity,'" Reuters (10.1.21).

79 Mettler, Johnson, Moyer, Contrera, Davies, Silverman, Hermann and Jamison, "Anti-vaccine activists march in D.C.—a city that mandates coronavirus vaccination—to protest mandates," WP (1.23.22); Zak and Roberts, "Anthony Fauci is up against more than a virus," WP (1.31.21); Jeong, "Robert F. Kennedy Jr. slammed for saying the unvaccinated have less freedom than Anne Frank did," WP (2.25.22); Nagourney, "A Kennedy's crusade against covid vaccines anguishes family and friends," NYT (2.26.22); Alba, "The latest covid misinformation star says he invented the vaccines," NYT (4.2.22); Frenkel, "Platforms drop Kennedy-led account," NYT (8.19.22); Abutaleb and Paletta (2021: 369); Gabriel, "Robert Kennedy Jr., a noted vaccine skeptic, files to run for president," NYT (4.6.23); Epstein, McFadden and Qiu, "Robert Kenney Jr., with Musk, pushed right-wing ideas and misinformation," NYT (6.6.23).

80 Gabriel, "Robert Kennedy Jr., a noted vaccine skeptic, files to run for president," NYT (4.6.23); Stolberg, "Robert F. Kennedy Jr., soon to announce White House run, sows doubts about vaccines," NYT (4.18.23).

81 Stolberg, "Republicans, wooing Trump voters, make Fauci their boogeyman," NYT (2.7.22).

82 Sotomayor, Alemany and DeBonis, "Growing number of Republicans urge vaccinations amid delta surge," WP (7.21.21); Weisman and Stolberg, "As virus resurges, G.O.P. lawmakers allow vaccine skepticism to flourish," NYT (7.20.21); Grynbaum, Hsu and Kanno-Youngs, "On Fox News, vaccination pleas intensify but skepticism persists," NYT (7.20.21); Shear, Weisman and Stolberg, "U.S. 'not out of the woods yet,' says C.D.C. chief," NYT (7.23.21); Weisman, "In the Capitol, the Delta variant spreads worry and partisanship," NYT (7.24.21); Diamond and Pager, "'Patience has worn thin': Frustration mounts over vaccine holdouts," WP (7.24.21); Kessler, "Scalise's misleading clip job claiming 'vaccine misinformation' by Democrats," WP (8.5.21); Rizzo, "Rand Paul's false claim that masks don't work," WP (12.2.21); Azar, "I was the architect of Operation Warp Speed. I have a message for all Americans," NYT (8.3.21).

83 www.worldometers.info/coronavirus/country/sweden/.

84 www.statista.com/statistics/1102257/cumulative-coronavirus-cases-in-the-nordics/.

85 Mervosh, "The largest U.S. teachers' union announces support for vaccination or testing for educators," NYT (8.13.21); Fitzsimmons and Wong, "N.Y.C. union leaders say mayor's covid mandate took them by surprise," NYT (7.28.21); Otterman and Goldstein, "New York City's biggest police union sues over city's vaccine mandate," NYT (10.26.21); Jeong, "Judge denies NYC police union's request to halt vaccine mandate," WP (10.28.21); Miller, "6 firefighters suspended for taking truck to threaten NY Senate staff over vaccine mandate," NBC News (10.29.21); Peiser, "Staten Island protesters foreshadow fight against children's vaccine mandates, warning of possible violence," WP (11.2.21); Goldstein and Otterman, "9,000 unvaccinated N.Y.C. workers put on unpaid leave as mandate begins," NYT (11.2.21).

86 Fitzsimmons, "New York City sets vaccine mandate for religious and private school workers," NYT (12.2.21).

87 Kramer, "New York City announces first-in-the-nation vaccine mandate for private companies," CBS News (12.6.21); Stempel, "Judge to review New York City vaccine mandate for public sector," Reuters (12.8.21); Ferre-Sadurni and McKinley, "New York businesses ordered to require masks indoors or vaccine proof," NYT (12.11.21); Cheng, "New York State, seeking to save its indoor mask mandate, moves to appeal court ruling," WP (2.25.22); Ferre-Sadurni and Ashford, "New York State's mask policy is back in effect after a judge grants a stay," NYT (2.26.22).

88 Goldstein and Scheiber, "As more teachers' unions push for remote schooling, parents worry. So do Democrats," NYT (1.8.22); Smith, "Chicago schools will reopen as teachers and the city reach a deal over virus safeguards," NYT (1.11.22).

89 Shear, Stolberg and Karni, "Biden rekindles vaccination push with new orders," NYT (7.30.21); Diamond, Mueller, Baumhardt and Myers, "'I feel defeated': Mask and vaccine mandates cause new divides as officials try to head off virus surge," WP (8.15.21); Pietsch, "Chicago police union urges officers to 'hold the line' over vaccine mandate. Mayor says 'bring it on,'" WP (10.14.21); Jimenez, "More than a third of Chicago police officers defy city vaccine mandate," CNN (10.18.21); Smith, "A judge blocks Chicago from enforcing its vaccine mandate for police officers," NYT (11.2.21).

90 Pietsch and Timsit, "Fauci urges police officers to get vaccinated as union protests heat up," WP (10.18.21); Bella, "Thousands of LAPD employees plan to seek vaccine exemptions; police officials sue city over mandate," WP (9.16.21); Vera and Campbell, "Federal judge dismisses LAPD employees lawsuit against Covid-19 vaccine mandate," CNN (1.10.22); Hassan, "The L.A. sheriff rejects

the county's vaccine mandate for his officers, saying too many would quit," NYT (10.9.21); Paybarah, "Latest vaccine policy in Los Angeles County is aimed at a defiant sheriff," NYT (2.9.22); Medina, "Vaccine hesitancy, an issue among police officers, is also evident among firefighters," NYT (10.10.21); Medina, "Across the U.S., clashes intensify between city officials and the police over vaccination issues," NYT (10.18.21); Kindy, "Boosted by the pandemic, 'constitutional sheriffs' are a political force," WP (11.2.21).

91 Jacobson v. Massachusetts, 197 U.S. 11 (1905).

92 Lamothe, Knowles, Pietsch, Suliman and Goldstein, "Pentagon will seek mandate for vaccination for all active-duty military personnel by mid-September," WP (8.10.21); Horton, "Air Force is first to face troops' rejection of vaccine mandate as thousands avoid shots," WP (10.29.21); Horton, "Marine Corps compliance with vaccine mandate on course to be military's worst," WP (11.22.21); Horton, "Vaccine holdouts in U.S. military approach 40,000 even as omicron variant fuels call for boosters," WP (12.11.21); Baldor, "Air Force discharges 27 for refusal to get COVID vaccine," AP (12.14.21); Castronuovo, "GOP senators seek to block dishonorable discharges for unvaccinated troops," The Hill (9.21.21); Williams, "Oklahoma Gov. asks Pentagon to drop vaccine mandate for National Guardsmen," The Hill (11.2.21); Fenwick, "Oklahoma's governor puts an opponent of vaccine mandates in charge of National Guard," NYT (11.13.21); Horton and Lamothe, "Oklahoma National Guard rejects Pentagon's coronavirus vaccine mandate," WP (11.14.21); Forgey, "Pentagon: Oklahoma Guard must comply with vaccine mandate," Politico (11.15.21); Horton and Demirjian, "Pentagon warns National Guard troops could be forced out for vaccine refusal after Oklahoma rejects mandate," WP (11.17.21); Steinhauer, "The U.S. Army secretary to National Guard members who resist vaccines: Prepare for discipline," NYT (11.19.21); Steinhauer, "The Defense Department says Oklahoma National Guard must get vaccinated," NYT (11.29.21); Williams, "Oklahoma sues to exempt National Guard from Pentagon vaccine mandate," The Hill (12.3.21); Jeong and Horton, "Federal court denies Oklahoma Gov. Kevin Stitt's attempt to stop military vaccine mandate," WP (12.29.21); Williams, "Oklahoma National Guard says unvaccinated airmen can't participate in drills," The Hill (12.30.21).

93 Williams, "Federal judge blocks Air Force from booting service member over vaccine refusal," The Hill (2.15.22); Liptak, "Supreme Court rules against Air Force officer who refused vaccine," NYT (4.19.22); Baldor, "Three Air Force cadets who refused vaccine won't be commissioned," AP (5.21.22).

94 Steinhauer, "Five Republican governors seek vaccine exemptions, escalating a fight with the Pentagon," NYT (12.15.21); Steinhauer, "Vaccine holdouts in Army and Navy will be dismissed, military says," NYT (12.17.21); Williams, "Marines kick out more than 100 for refusing COVID-19 vaccine," The Hill (12.16.21); Sneed, "Texas Gov. Abbott sues Biden over requirement that National Guard be vaccinated," CNN (1.5.22); Williams, "Texas governor seeks to block vaccine mandate for National Guard members," The Hill (2.8.22); Steinhauer, "The defense secretary tells Republican governors: National Guard troops must be vaccinated," NYT (2.1.22).

95 Shammas, Kornfield, Pannett and Suliman, "Army says it will begin discharging unvaccinated soldiers," WP (2.3.22); Doornbos, "Navy ousts first sailors for refusing coronavirus vaccine," Stars and Stripes (1.6.22); Lamothe, "Judge grants relief to Navy SEALs who refused coronavirus vaccine, sued Biden administration," WP (1.4.22); Albeck-Ripka, "A federal judge blocks the Defense Dept. from punishing Navy forces who refuse the vaccine," NYT (1.4.22); Kime, "Pentagon asks Supreme Court to rule in Navy SEALs' COVID-19 vaccination

refusal case," Military.com (3.9.22); Austin v. U.S. Navy SEALS, 142 S.Ct. 1301 (2022); Barnes, "Supreme Court won't stop Biden administration from deployment decisions involving vaccinated Navy SEALs," WP (3.26.22); Toropin, "A Florida judge won't let the Navy remove a rule-breaking, vaccine-refusing ship commander," Military.com (3.8.22); "US Navy refuses to deploy warship over unvaccinated CO," American Military News (3.9.22).

96 Stack, "Houses of Worship struggle back, and tread lightly on vaccines," NYT (8.26.21); Gay, "A trove of intelligence reports reveal New York's fight against vaccine disinformation," NYT (10.31.21); Thomson, "The pandemic's wrongest man," The Atlantic (4.1.21); Monroe and Savillo, "Fox has undermined vaccines nearly every day in the last six months," MediaMatters (10.5.21).

97 Ivory and Baker, "Public health officials in the U.S. need federal protection from abuse and threats, a national group says," NYT (10.20.21); Anthes, "'They see us as the enemy': school nurses battle covid-19, and angry parents," NYT (11.16.21); Sellers, "Much has changed since the start of the pandemic. But the nation's public health system remains fractured," WP (1.3.22); Benner, "Republicans assail Garland over Justice Department schools memo," NYT (10.28.21); Benner, "F.B.I. set plan to track threats against school boards and teachers," NYT (11.17.21); Mark, "A man gave a Nazi salute at a school board meeting to oppose mask rules. Ted Cruz defended it as a form of protest," WP (10.28.21); Bush, "Almost 2 in 5 Covid-19 researchers have faced harassment, survey finds," NBC News (3.24.22); Broadwater, "House G.O.P. subpoenas Biden officials for investigating school-related threats," NYT (2.4.23).

98 Vakil, "Trump tells Navarro to 'protect executive privilege' in House COVID-19 probe," The Hill (11.20.21); Diamond, "Navarro defies house subpoena in coronavirus probe," WP (12.12.21).

99 https://ourworldindata.org/covid-deaths#what-is-the-cumulative-number-of-confirmed-deaths.

100 Blake, "The right's emerging hoax-ification of the omicron variant," WP (11.29.21).

101 www.cdc.gov/flu/about/burden/past-seasons.html; Stolberg, "The White House, warning of a fall surge, plans for how to provide vaccines if there's no more Covid aid," NYT (5.6.22).

102 Barr, "Fauci says Fox News host Jesse Watters should be fired for 'ambush' and 'kill shot' comments," WP (12.21.21).

103 Paybarah and McCarthy, "Donald Trump said he got a booster shot and his supporters booed," NYT (12.21.21); "Every shout-out for shots is valuable. Even the one from Trump," WP (12.24.21); Grynbaum, "Fox News host's incendiary Fauci comments follow a network pattern," NYT (12.25.21); Wagner, "Trump abruptly ends NPR interview after he is pressed on baseless election fraud claims," WP (1.12.22); Harwell, "Since Jan. 6, the pro-Trump Internet has descended into infighting over money and followers," WP (1.3.22); Knowles and Beachum, "Some GOP leaders are scornful or silent about booster shots seen as key to fighting omicron," WP (1.4.22); Weiland, "As White House presses for booster shots, Americans are slow to get them," NYT (10.15.22).

104 Linskey, Abutaleb, Kim and Rein, "Biden announces sweeping new vaccine mandates for businesses, federal workers," WP (9.9.21); Rosenberg, "White House vaccine rule would require companies and workers to comply by Jan. 4," WP (11.4.21); "Biden is right: Vaccine refusal 'has cost all of us,'" NYT (9.11.21); Timsit and Pietsch, "Republican governors threaten to sue over Biden's sweeping vaccine mandates," WP (9.10.21); Timsit, "GOP governors threaten to sue over mandates; Biden says, 'have at it,'" Wp (9.11.21); Healy, Fausset and Goodman, "President tells rivals to "have at it,'" NYT (9.11.21); Stolberg, "G.O.P. seethes

at Biden mandate, even in states requiring other vaccines," NYT (9.13.21); Sonmez, Sotomayor and Alfaro, "GOP condemnation of Biden coronavirus mandate fuels concern other vaccine requirements could be targeted," WP (9.13.21); Boot, "The hyperbolic GOP reaction to Biden's vaccine mandate shows why it's necessary," WP (9.10.21).

105 Suliman and Jeong, "Biden accuses Republican governors of risking lives as 24 states threaten legal action," WP (9.17.21); Jeong, "Texas Gov. Greg Abbott bans coronavirus vaccine mandates, including for private businesses," WP (10.12.21); Marcos and Slotnik, "American and Southwest Airlines reject the Texas order banning vaccine mandates," NYT (10.12.21); Weisgerber, "Pentagon orders Texas contractors to mandate vaccines for employees, despite governor's ban," Defense One (10.14.21); Jeong, "Alabama Gov. Kay Ivey joins states pushing back against Biden administration's vaccine mandates," WP (10.26.21).

106 Levin, "Florida sues Biden administration over contractor vaccine mandate," Bloomberg (10.28.21); Levin, "11 states sue the Biden administration over its vaccination mandate for large companies," NYT (11.5.21); Quinn, "10 states sue Biden administration over COVID-19 vaccine requirement for health care workers," CBS News (11.11.21); Rosenberg, "GOP-appointed judges freeze Biden vaccine requirement after federal lawsuit," WP (11.6.21); Hirsch and Grullon Paz, "A court temporarily blocks Biden's vaccine mandate," NYT (11.7.21); Rosenberg and Marimow, "Federal appeals court halts Biden administration's vaccine requirement, delivering policy a major blow," WP (11.13.21); Hals, "Court lottery gives Biden administration a chance to revive COVID vaccine mandate," Reuters (11.16.21); Savage, "Challenges to workplace vaccine mandate moved to appeals court in Cincinnati," NYT (11.17.21); Pietsch, "Disney World halts vaccine requirement for workers after Florida restricts employer mandates," WP (11.21.21); Hirsch and Maheshwari, "Why the retail industry is fighting vaccine mandates," NYT (11.25.21); Diamond, "Dozens of health groups urge businesses to voluntarily adopt Biden's vaccine rule," WP (11.19.21); Diamond, "Dozens of health groups urge businesses to voluntarily adopt Biden's vaccine rule," WP (11.19.21).

107 Marimow, "Biden's vaccine-or-testing policy for private companies will be reviewed by three-judge panel," WP (12.16.21); Southern Baptist Theological Seminary v. OSHA; Marimow, "Appeals court reinstates Biden's vaccine policy for businesses, setting up a likely showdown at the Supreme Court," WP (12.18.21); Hirsch and Goldberg, "The U.S. Labor Department extends its deadline for large companies to mandate vaccines," NYT (12.18.21); Hals and Singh, "U.S. judge upholds United Airlines' COVID-19 vaccine mandate for employees," Reuters (11.9.21).

108 Rosenberg and Suliman, "Judge temporarily blocks Biden administration vaccine mandate for health-care workers in 10 states," WP (11.30.21).

109 Louisiana v. Becerra, 577 F.Supp.3d 483 (WD La 11.30.21), modified, 20 F4th 260 (5th Cir. 2021); Hals, "Courts block two Biden administration COVID vaccine mandates," Reuters (11.30.21); Sneed, "Trump-appointed judges question role of vaccines in fight against Covid as they block mandates," CNN (12.10.21); Baylor Scott and White Health v. McCullough (Dallas County Texas District Court 7.29.21); Impelli, "Jay Bhattacharya, Stanford doctor, calls lockdowns the 'biggest public health mistake we've ever made,'" Newsweek (3.8.21); McGill and Liebe, "Health worker vaccine mandate blocked in half the states," AP (12.15.21); Sneed, "Health care worker vaccine mandate can be enforced in half the country, appeals court says," CNN (12.15.21); Texas v. Becerra (ND Tex 12.15.21).

110 Commonwealth of Kentucky v. Biden, 571 F.Supp.3d 715 (ED Ky 2021); Vakil, "Appeals Court upholds decision to temporarily block vaccine mandate for

contractors in three states," The Hill (1.6.22); Grullón Paz, "Here's the latest on what courts have said about Biden's vaccine mandates," NYT (12.8.21); Cheng, "Boeing drops vaccine mandate for U.S. workers, joining Amtrak and other major federal contractors," WP (12.18.21).

111 Rosenberg and Rein, "Federal judge in Texas blocks Biden's vaccine requirement for government workers," WP (1.22.22); McGill, "Vaccine mandate for federal workers blocked by 2nd court," AP (2.10.22); Feds for Medical Freedom v. Biden, 581 F.Supp.3d; 826 (S.D. Tex. 2022), stay denied pending appeal, 25 F.4th 354 (5th Cir. 2022), reversed, 30 F.4th 503 (5th Cir. 2022); Lukpat and Hassan, "A federal appeals court upholds Biden's vaccine mandate for federal workers," NYT (4.8.22); Yoder, "White House tells agencies to delay vaccine mandate after court win," WP (4.8.22); McGill, "Opponents of federal vaccine mandate seek rehearing," AP (5.23.22); McGill, "Court revives block of vaccine mandate for federal workers," AP (6.27.22); McGill, "Court blocks COVID-19 vaccine mandate for US government workers," ABC News (3.23.23).

112 National Federation of Independent Business v. Department of Labor; Ohio v. Department of Labor; Biden v. Missouri; Becerra v. Louisiana; Barnes, "Supreme Court blocks Biden's workplace vaccine rules, allows requirement for health-care workers," WP (1.13.22).

113 Burch and Abelson, "Hospitals confront the fallout from Supreme Court ruling on vaccine mandate," NYT (1.16.22).

114 Diamond, "Dozens of health groups urge businesses to voluntarily adopt Biden's vaccine rule," WP (11.19.21); Romm, "Senate votes to repeal key Biden administration vaccine and testing policy," WP (12.8.21); Cochrane, "Senate votes to scrap Biden vaccine mandate as Republicans eye 2022," NYT (12.9.21).

115 Romm, DeBonis and Kim, "Government nears possible shutdown as Republicans take aim at vaccination and testing mandates," WP (12.2.21); Cochrane, "Senate Republicans threaten shutdown over vaccine mandate," NYT (12.1.21); Romm and DeBonis, "Congress passes stopgap spending bill, averting shutdown despite GOP revolt on vaccine requirements," WP (12.3.21).

116 Jeong, "A GOP senator suggested gargling mouthwash to kill the coronavirus. Doctors and Listerine are skeptical," WP (12.9.21); Bump, "Ron Johnson somehow isn't clear on why post-illness immunity is worse than no-illness immunity," WP (1.5.22); Kessler, "How the falsehood of athletes dying of coronavirus vaccines spread," WP (2.1.22).

117 Cochrane, "In symbolic vote, Senate rejects vaccine mandate for health workers," NYT (3.3.22); Ollstein, "Senate votes to end Covid-19 emergency declaration, Biden threatens veto," Politico (3.3.22).

118 Shapiro and Bromwich, "A federal appeals court delays New York City's vaccine mandate for teachers," NYT (9.26.21); Ramos, "New York weighs using the National Guard to replace unvaccinated health care workers," NYT (9.26.21); Otterman and Goldstein, "New York hospitals face possible mass firings as workers spurn vaccines," NYT (9.26.21); Otterman and Goldstein, "Deadline looming, thousands of health care workers in New York get vaccinated," NYT (9.28.21); Shapiro and Weiser, "New York City can proceed with vaccine mandate for educators and staff, judges ruled," NYT (9.28.21); Otterman and Goldstein, "Thousands of N.Y. health care workers get vaccinated ahead of deadline," NYT (9.29.21); Goldstein and Otterman, "Who is suing over New York's vaccine mandate?" NYT (9.30.21); Sharp, "Maine's Covid-19 mandate appealed to U.S. Supreme Court," AP (10.15.21); John Does v. Mills, 566 F.Supp.3d 34 (D Me 2021), aff'd, 16 F.4th 20 (1st Cir. 2021); Barnes, "Supreme Court won't block vaccine mandate for Maine health-care workers with religious objections," WP (10.30.21); We the Patriots USA v. Hochul (2nd Cir. 11.4.21); Barnes, "Supreme Court won't stop vaccine mandate for New York health care

workers," WP (12.14.21); Liptak, "Supreme Court allows vaccine mandate for New York health care workers," NYT (12.14.21); Barron, "Deadline day for unvaccinated municipal employees in N.Y.C.," NYT (2.11.22); Price, "NYC fires more than 1,000 workers over vaccine mandate," AP (2.14.22); Hurley, "U.S. Supreme Court rejects challenge to Maine COVID-19 vaccine mandate," Reuters (2.22.22); Fitzsimmons, "New York City keeps mask mandate for kids under 5 as cases rise," NYT (4.2.22); Marimow and Barnes, "Supreme Court lets vaccine mandate stand, tosses rulings on guns, abortion," WP (7.1.22).

119 Maloy, "Many are searching for vaccine mandate loopholes. These are the people trying to stop them," WP (10.2.21).

120 Aratani, "21 states sue Biden administration to end transportation mask mandate," WP (3.30.22); Laris, "Federal judge voids mask mandate for airplanes, in other transportation settings," WP (4.18.22); Savage and Murphy, "Federal judge strikes down mask mandate for planes and public transit," NYT (4.19.22); Waldman, "Mask ruling shows Trump's toxic judicial legacy is poisoning America," WP (4.20.22); Aratani Simmons, Gahan and Oldham, "Justice Dept. to appeal mask mandate ruling if CDC says it's needed," WP (4.20.22); Diamond and Marimow, "Biden administration to appeal ruling striking down transit mask mandate," WP (4.20.22); Abutaleb, Sampson and Marimow, "How a single judge's ruling upended national covid policy," WP (4.22.22); Franklin, "DOJ asks federal appeals court to reverse order lifting travel mask mandate," NPR (6.1.22).

121 Sacchetti, "Federal judge blocks Biden administration from ending Title 42," WP (4.20.22).

122 Langmaid, "More than 40% of parents of young kids say they will not get their child a covid-19 vaccine, survey finds," CNN (7.26.22); Lin II and Money, "COVID hospitalization rates in babies as bad as for seniors amid Omicron wave, study shows," LAT (11.30.22).

123 Mitchell, "GOP governors, senators take aim at Pentagon COVID-19 vaccine mandate," The Hill (11.30.22); Edmonson and Ismay, "Congress poised to repeal covid vaccine mandate for troops in military bill," NYT (12.6.22); Romm, "Congress eyes end to military coronavirus vaccine mandate," WP (12.5.22); Klein and Foran, "White House calls removed Covid-19 vaccine mandate a 'mistake' but won't say if Biden will sign NDAA," CNN (12.7.22); Wen, "It's time the Pentagon ended its covid vaccine mandate for the military," WP (12.9.22); Rose, "An unvaccinated military puts our national security at risk," NYT (12.15.22); Demirjian, "Senate passes defense bill that arms U.S. allies, ends vaccine mandate," WP (12.15.22); Mitchell, "Pentagon officially drops COVID-19 vaccine mandate," The Hill (1.10.23).

124 Hoffman, "Opposition to school vaccine mandates has grown significantly, study finds," NYT (12.16.22); Sun, "Growing vaccine hesitancy fuels measles, chickenpox resurgence in U.S.," WP (12.26.22); Hsu, "As Covid-19 continues to spread, so does misinformation about it," NYT (1.2.23); Stobbe, "US kindergarten vaccination rate dropped again, data shows," AP (1.12.23).

125 Gaba, "September Update: COVID Death Rates By Partisan Lean & Vaccination Rate" (9.11.22) https://acasignups.net/22/09/11/september-update-covid-death-rates-partisan-lean-vaccination-rate; Johnson, "Can politics kill you? Research says the answer increasingly is yes," WP (12.16.22).

126 Fauci, "A message to the next generation of scientists," NYT (12.11.22); Suliman, "Fauci slams 'lowlife' trolls harassing his wife, children over covid," WP (12.12.22); Sargent, "Musk's ugly attack on Fauci shows how right-wing info warfare works," WP (12.12.22); Wallace-Wells, "Dr. Fauci looks back: 'something clearly went wrong,'" NYT (4.30.23).

127 Stolberg, "Two decades after 9/11 inquiry, a similar plan for Covid stalls in Congress," NYT (12.13.22).
128 Romm, "House GOP to embark on sweeping probe of covid origin, U.S. response," WP (1.10.23).
129 CCG (2023).
130 Rozsa, "DeSantis forms panel to counter CDC, a move decried by health professionals," WP (12.13.22); Frisaro, "DeSantis seeks grand jury investigation of COVID-19 vaccines," AP (12.13.22); Arnsdorf, "DeSantis reverses himself on coronavirus vaccines moves to right of Trump," WP (12.17.22); www.statista.com/statistics/1109004/coronavirus-covid19-cases-rate-us-americans-by-state/.
131 "Vaccines saved lives. DeSantis threatens that progress," WP (12.19.22).
132 Swan and Broadwater, "House votes to end covid precautions as G.O.P. uses pandemic in political attacks," NYT (2.1.23); Qiu, "Republicans assail vaccine mandates with misleading claims," NYT (2.1.23); Zaslav, Mattingly and Raju, "Senate votes to end Covid-19 emergency, 3 years after initial declaration," CNN (3.29.23).

4

A PERMANENT WAR ON SCIENCE?

The COVID-19 pandemic presented the greatest domestic challenge Trump faced during his presidency. His response was a catastrophic failure.[1] Australia, which resembles the U.S. in demographic profile, degree of urbanization and global exposure through travel and trade, had a COVID-19 death rate one-tenth as large.[2] Had the U.S. effectively implemented Australia's policies, it could have saved more than 900,000 lives. Instead, Trump demanded a miraculous quick fix for which he could claim sole credit, like the "solutions" he embraced or advocated for other problems: immigration (Build the Wall), hostile nuclear powers (bromances with Putin, Xi and Kim, ending the agreement with Iran), protracted military conflict (nuke 'em, bomb ISIS families, assassinate leaders, demolish cultural treasures) and civil unrest (send in the cavalry). He admitted to Bob Woodward that he "always wanted to play [the pandemic] down" because "my job is to reassure people and not scare them." He maintained falsely that the coronavirus was no more serious than the seasonal flu, whose vaccines should work just as well against COVID. He joined with Xi in baselessly promising that COVID would disappear with warm weather. He surrounded himself with sycophants wholly bereft of medical or public health training—Navarro (a dissident economist with a fierce animus against China, who claimed expertise because "I understand how to read statistical studies"), Kushner (Trump's son-in-law and fellow real estate entrepreneur), Azar (a lawyer and former pharmaceutical company executive) and Pence (the ultimate yes-man)—just as he did in other areas (e.g., Stephen Miller advising on immigration law with no legal qualifications, lawyers woefully ignorant of election law, see Abel 2024a, 2024b). He relied on personal experience and anecdotes from unqualified people like Laura Ingraham (a Fox host), Larry Ellison (a wealthy IT entrepreneur), Rudy Giuliani

DOI: 10.4324/9781032629124-4

(a former U.S. Attorney and NYC mayor) and even Jack Nicklaus (a golf pro and hero to Trump, a fanatical amateur). Trump (and advisers like Kudlow and Mnuchin) consistently prioritized the economy (which he conflated with stock market indices) over public health.

Trump's errors began on day one. He blamed China for the coronavirus (and kept reinforcing that association by referring to it as the Wuhan or China virus or Kung flu—racial epithets far easier for the public to remember than SARS-CoV-2), seeking to exploit the xenophobia he constantly stoked by attacking immigrants and restricting foreign trade. He claimed to have solved the pandemic by closing U.S. borders—but only after COVID was already well established in the U.S., rendering that piece of political theater epidemiologically meaningless. (Pence had to overrule the top CDC doctor, who pointed out its futility, and order Director Redfield to do this.) And Trump repeatedly declared premature victory by minimizing the number of cases and confidently predicting their decline or disappearance (reenacting Bush's infamous proclamation of *Mission Accomplished* five weeks into the eight-year Iraq war). Trump boasted about the number of COVID tests at a time when few actually were available—and then performed a characteristic volte-face, blaming what he criticized as excessive tests for the rising number of cases (while seeking to exclude U.S. cruise ships from case counts). He minimized the significance of fatality rates by associating them with the elderly—who were going to die anyway.

Trump sought to control any information that might undermine his Panglossian picture of the pandemic by silencing scientists within the administration, prohibiting the CDC from speaking to the media. He muzzled Messonnier and muted Bright (just as he attacked whistleblowers and foreign policy officials who criticized his "perfect" phone call with Zelensky, see Abel 2025). He sought to prevent hospitals from reporting data. He smeared scientists who opposed him as tools of a mythic "deep state" (just as he defamed critics in the DoS, DoJ, DHS, FBI and CIA, see Abel 2024a). He accused doctors of objecting to HCQ because it was cheaper than remdesivir (although doctors may not profit from prescribing medications). Having sidelined the experts, Trump uncritically embraced misinformation from buddies (including Rudy Giuliani) and supportive right-wing media, especially Fox News (which he watched addictively). Then claiming expertise he totally lacked, he pushed drugs like HCQ, convalescent plasma, ivermectin, sunlight and even bleach, with predictably tragic results. The administration recruited its own medical "experts": mavericks like Paul Alexander and Scott Atlas, who eagerly sought the president's ear and the public gaze by offering false promises that "herd immunity" could be achieved quickly and cheaply (disregarding the inevitable deaths in vulnerable populations, severe consequences of intubation and the estimated 28 percent of cases that become long COVID).[3] Alexander also sought to "edit" the sacrosanct

MMWRs. These scientific shills were professional outsiders, without relevant expertise (Atlas was a neuroradiologist) or institutional position (Atlas was at the right-wing Hoover Institution, uncomfortably located on the campus of Stanford University, whose medical school condemned him; McMaster University disavowed Alexander, its alumnus and erstwhile adjunct, leaving him with no visible institutional affiliation). These two opportunists claimed that science thrived on disagreement. But they were hardly paradigm-changing pioneers like Galileo, Darwin or Einstein. And they operated by assertion, not by providing statistically meaningful evidence obtained from double-blind randomized controlled trials and subjected to peer review—practices that both men eschewed. Other self-styled "experts" had questionable credentials. Steven Hatfill, Navarro's medical adviser, obtained an undergraduate medical degree in Rhodesia only after failing his first exams and then did a one-year internship at a rural South African hospital during apartheid. His Ph.D. thesis was rejected by Rhodes University, which did not stop him from falsely claiming that degree, as well as three fictitious master's degrees from Oxford, or lying that he had served in U.S. Special Forces. (Hatfill wisely sought to conceal his role in the administration.) Sen. Paul, a nonpracticing ophthalmologist, posed as an expert on contagious diseases when attacking Fauci, one of the nation's leading epidemiologists.

Parroting Atlas, Trump said scientists simply had "different views," as though these were preferences for ice cream flavors, from which laypeople could pick and choose: chacun à son goût; de gustibus non est disputandum. Attorney General Barr, with supreme confidence, dismissed science as "nonsense." Some conservative Supreme Court Justices have displayed a similar contempt for expertise (other than in law). In a case alleging that electoral districting favored one party, Chief Justice Roberts casually rejected a quantitative test offered to evaluate the claim as "sociological gobbledygook."[4] In his concurrence in a case striking down affirmative action, Justice Thomas criticized his colleague Justice Jackson for "unquestioningly acced[ing] to the view of elite experts" and using "broad observations about statistical relationships between race and select measures of health, wealth and well-being."[5]

Many of the doctors who defied the scientific consensus (such as Stephen Smith, Stella Immanuel, Vladimir Zelenko, Simone Gold, Jane Orient, Steven LaTulippe, Judy Mikovits, Lee Meritt, Sherry Tenpenny, Andrew Wakefield, Joseph Mercola, Daniel Stock and Garrett Soldano) were medically marginal figures, courting celebrity for profit, some abandoning practice to become obscenely rich snake oil salesmen (while risking the wrath of the FDA). Many belonged to tiny dissident splinter groups they themselves had formed, like AAP and AFLDS. Some of the self-styled experts were not even doctors: Gregory Rigano, Adrian Bye. But a few boasted elite credentials: Oz, Atlas, his Stanford colleague John Ionnidis, the three authors of the Great Barrington Declaration (with tenured positions at Harvard, Oxford and

Stanford) and Joseph Ladapo (with a Harvard MD and Ph.D. and faculty positions at UCLA and University of Florida). In this, they resembled the Ivy League lawyers who engineered Trump's legally indefensible efforts to overturn the 2020 election (see Abel 2024a), as well as the OLC lawyers in the Bush administration who justified torture, indefinite detention without trial, extraordinary rendition, targeted killing and electronic surveillance.[6] Whereas professional bodies can and do discipline doctors for mistreating individual patients, they could do little about those who exploited their medical credentials to misinform the general public, even though the latter behavior had far greater potential to harm. (The same distinction applied to what lawyers did in and out of court in challenging the 2020 election, see Abel 2025.) Social media greatly amplified those unfiltered voices, indifferent to their scientific validity, leaving laypeople free (indeed compelled) to choose their own response to the pandemic.

Trump bragged about pressuring the proudly independent FDA to quickly authorize HCQ (though it later withdrew the EUA), Regernon, convalescent plasma and, most importantly, the vaccines. Alexander and Caputo (the latter with no medical expertise) rewrote CDC guidances and sought to tamper with the sacrosanct MMWRs and then cover this up by destroying the smoking gun emails. Caputo asked Alexander to concoct a fictitious (and conveniently inflated) figure for the number of deaths caused by pandemic regulations (like the votes Trump asked Georgia Secretary of State Raffensperger to "find" in order to deliver that state's electors, see Abel 2024a). (Trump also sought to distort the census by including a citizenship question that would suppress noncitizen responses, see Abel 2024b; and his February 2020 State of the Union message misrepresented the GDP, unemployment, wages, median household income, job gains from trade agreements, length of the border wall and border crossings.)[7] Trump repeatedly subordinated scientific protocols to political priorities, determined to reopen the country by Easter, secured approval of convalescent plasma before the Republican National Convention in September and sought to have vaccines approved before the November election. The FDA, CDC and NIH resisted, rightly fearing their scientific reputations would be fatally compromised. Even Big Pharma, which stood to profit handsomely from FDA approval of their vaccines, unanimously backed a federal bureaucracy that assured the public the drugs they took were safe and efficacious.[8]

Some medical experts, however, were alarmingly complicit. Birx praised Trump for being "so attentive to the scientific literature and the details and the data" and lauded "his ability to analyze and integrate data," despite the fact that he consistently ignored or disparaged both data and science. And she stood by mutely as he promoted ingesting bleach, claiming she could not question the word of the commander-in-chief (though she had left the military a decade earlier). When Trump misrepresented statistics about the efficacy of convalescent plasma, NIH Director Collins was similarly complaisant; and FDA Director Hahn and his subordinate, Marks, compounded the errors, which were only corrected later by outside scientists. CDC Director Redfield also sometimes succumbed to pressure from Trump. (Redfield and Birx may have been chosen, or retained, partly because they are evangelical Christians; and their acquiescence may be due, in part, to the fact that Redfield, like Birx, had spent years in the military, retiring as colonel in 1996, and was accustomed to following orders.) Few officials resigned: Olivia Troye (Pence's representative on the COVID task force), Miles Taylor (DHS chief of staff), Kyle McGowan (CDC chief of staff), Max Kennedy Jr. (RFK's grandson) and Steven Bright; but most spoke out only after resigning (if at all). It was members of the independent scientific community who denounced political interference most vocally (some institutions for the first time): former government officials, doctors, other scientists, scientific journals and professional associations.

Politics constantly compromised science. Trump refused to wear a mask out of concern for his image when dealing with "presidents, prime ministers, dictators, kings, queens" (he did not discriminate among celebrities), eagerness to pander to the prejudices of his base and determination to affront the media—taking refuge in typical gibberish: "maybe [masks are] great, and maybe they're just good. Maybe they're not so good." He exploited COVID as an opportunity to augment federal authority by attacking blue state pandemic precautions, conveniently ignoring the traditional Republican commitment to decentralizing power. Red states followed suit, preempting the local pandemic regulations of their own blue cities and counties. Conservatives attacked regulations for infringing religious liberty (appealing to the evangelical base). The administration sought to reopen schools, wooing working parents desperate for childcare while disregarding the fears of teachers (whom they dismissed as union members likely to vote Democratic). Trump gave Caputo $300 million for a CDC campaign brazenly entitled "Helping the President Will Help the Country" (though Caputo had a mental breakdown before he could spend it).

Trump and conservatives viciously attacked Fauci, seeking to make him (rather than their own errors) the target of public anger about the pandemic and public health measures. Trump openly resented Fauci's independence and greater popularity. As the former host of *The Apprentice*, whose favorite tagline was "You're fired," the president found Fauci's civil service protection insufferable. Conservatives kept reviving the baseless claim that the Wuhan Institute of Virology had created the coronavirus, so they could accuse Fauci of having funded that lab's research. Despite these unrelenting attacks, Fauci refused to quit, feeling an obligation to keeping being the "skunk at the picnic." Republicans responded by treating him like a skunk. Months after Fauci retired, Rep. Ronny Jackson (who had withdrawn his nomination as DVA

Secretary because, as Trump's White House physician, he abused alcohol, improperly prescribed drugs to White House staff and created a hostile work environment) declared that "Covid numbers were being inflated" because Democrats needed COVID to achieve their political goals and "people like Fauci needed Covid to GET RICH!"[9] In June 2023, the DeSantis campaign attacked Trump on Twitter by using false images of the former president hugging and kissing Fauci.[10]

Given the virulence of attacks by Trump and other Republicans on the CDC and Fauci, it is unsurprising (if deeply regrettable) that trust in the Centers fell from 69 percent in April 2020 to 44 percent in January 2022.[11] After two years of the pandemic, confidence in public health officials (such as those in the CDC), state and local elected officials and President Biden had declined 43–52 percent. The fact that only 34 percent of Americans trusted their health care system, compared to 76 percent of Australians, may partly explain why COVID deaths per population were ten times higher in the U.S. than Down Under. (Age-adjusted excess mortality was 51.5 percent lower in Europe than the U.S. from the last quarter of 2020 through the first half of 2021 and 83 percent lower in the last half of 2021. COVID mortality per capita was almost ten times greater in the U.S. than in Japan. As of March 16, 2023, the U.S. had 341 deaths per 100,000 people, compared with 255 in France, 203 in Germany and 135 in Canada.)[12] Polls in 2021 found that almost half of respondents wrongly believed the CDC was concealing information about the side effects of vaccines and exaggerating the number of deaths, and more than a third wrongly believed HCQ and ivermectin were effective treatments.[13] Just 6 percent of Republicans believed that eight items of covid misinformation were untrue (compared to 38 percent of Democrats), 18 percent believed you could get COVID from the vaccine, 14 percent that it caused infertility and 27 percent that pregnant women should not be vaccinated. 80 percent of Republicans but only 36 percent of Democrats said people should be absolutely free to refuse a vaccine. Party political differences about other pandemic prevention measures were equally stark. Mask mandates for unvaccinated schoolchildren were supported by 88 percent of Democrats but opposed by 69 percent of Republicans. In September 2021, 62 percent of all Americans but only 32 percent of Republicans supported face mask and social distancing guidelines. Unsurprisingly, behavior was correlated with attitudes. In October 2021, 60 percent of the unvaccinated were Republicans, but only 17 percent were Democrats (by contrast, 43 percent of Americans identified as Republican and 46 percent as Democrat). In January 2022, 62 percent of Democrats had been vaccinated with a booster compared to 32 percent of Republicans. Between March and August 2020, Republicans (but not Democrats) displayed declines in the intent to get both the COVID vaccine and a flu shot, as well as in favorable attitudes toward vaccines. The percentage of children who had received the other usual vaccines (required by most schools) declined from 95 to 94 after January 2020. In mid-November 2022, only 10 percent of those eligible had received the Omicron booster, which was free and plentiful and had been available since the beginning of September; just 68 percent of Americans were vaccinated for COVID as of March 2023, making the U.S. 69th in order of countries worldwide. These differences were tragically reflected in differences in COVID death rates/100,000 people in October 2021 within the U.S.: 25 in counties that had heavily supported Trump but just 7.8 in those heavily blue. The National Bureau of Economic Research found in September 2022 that excess deaths were 76 percent higher among Republicans than among Democrats, a gap that had increased sevenfold since vaccines were available.

After leaving office, Trump faced the dilemma of how to deal with anti-vaxxers, who inflamed suspicion of and hostility to a federal government now dominated by Democrats while attacking what the ex-president claimed as his greatest achievement. Anti-vaxxers embraced multiple contradictions: rejecting the COVID vaccine while accepting many others (smallpox, MMR, diphtheria, tetanus, pertusis and polio); eagerly relying on medical science to treat COVID but not to prevent it; and championing the choice of parents not to mask or vaccinate their school-age children while denying that of parents who wanted to protect their own children, especially those with compromised immune systems, as well as other vulnerable members of their household (not to mention the choice of teachers and other school employees to be safe). Resistance also emerged in the military, police and firefighters (generally Trump's strongest supporters), which was surprising given those services' equally long history of mandatory vaccinations (smallpox, typhoid and yellow fever during World War II; influenza, hepatitis A and B and human papillomavirus more recently) and their strong tradition of following orders.

More generally, anti-vaxxers invoked libertarian values while refusing to acknowledge that those who contracted COVID exposed others to an increased risk of infection and imposed on everyone the costs of treatment and disability (which were spread through private insurance and government benefits). As John B. Finch allegedly said during an anti-alcohol campaign in the 1880s: "my liberty to swing my fists extends only as far as the other person's nose." Resistance to masks, social distancing, school and business closures and vaccines displaced the deeply painful feelings provoked by the epidemic—fear of illness, disability and death; bereavement; economic hardship; and anger at disrupted lives and lost freedom—onto the government, reframing public health measures as authoritarian rather than caring. In this, resisters sought to don the mantle of that ever-popular Republican icon, Ronald Reagan, who famously pronounced in his 1981 inaugural address that "government is not the solution to our problem, government is the problem," upping the ante five years later with an equally quotable slogan: "The top 9 most terrifying words in the English Language are: 'I'm from the government, and I'm here to help.' "[14] Trump supporters were particularly susceptible to that message because they were more likely to be dependent on the government and to deal with their resentment of that dependence through denial. Republicans amplified these feelings by highlighting public health limitations on religious observance, which was both more common and more highly valued among Trump supporters (thereby reviving the battle between religion and science).

Such resistance encouraged right-wing politicians to engage in irresponsible posturing by refusing to wear masks, be vaccinated or disclose having done so, representing such infantile behavior as courageous acts of defiance. Some also raised money from these stunts—often far exceeding the fines levied in Congress (just as Trump raised money following the FBI search of Mar-a-Lago and his indictment for withholding classified documents, see Abel 2025). And Senate Republicans grandstanded by mounting two challenges to Biden's vaccine mandates (both pointless since they would be defeated in the House and vetoed by the president) and threatening to shut down the government because the mandates "micromanage citizens' personal choices."

The Republican politicization of science also provoked significant backlash. Most employees (at least in blue states) wanted themselves and fellow workers to be vaccinated. Large employers supported the federal vaccine mandates (and imposed their own) in order to maintain a healthy workforce (especially during a time of labor scarcity) and minimize the business costs of worker illness (sick pay, lower productivity). Conservatives who had suffered personal medical crises (e.g., Sen. McConnell's childhood polio) or knew those struggling with COVID often favored vaccines. State court judges, even in red states like Florida, Texas and Arkansas, upheld pandemic restrictions and deferred to professionals about medical decisions (especially in big cities, which tended to vote Democrat).

Federal judges' decisions about government responses to the pandemic bifurcated dramatically along party political lines (using the party of the appointing president as a proxy measure for the judge's political preference) (see Table 4.1)[15] (like those about the Trump administration's immigration actions, see Abel 2024a).

Among the 162 votes I identified, 97 percent of Democratic appointees deferred to science, compared with just 32 percent of Republican appointees, a highly significant difference (see Table 4.2).

The difference between decisions by Trump appointees (80 percent against science) and other Republican appointees (59 percent) also was significant, though less strong (see Table 4.3).

All Obama appointee decisions favored science, as did 92 percent of those by Clinton appointees. Justice Thomas, by contrast, voted against science every time. Several decisions by Republican appointees stand out. The Supreme Court bizarrely declared that OSHA could not require employers

TABLE 4.1 Pandemic cases: Analysis of judges' decisions by appointing president

Appointing President	*For Science*	*Against Science*
Obama	34	0
Clinton	22	2
Trump	8	33
GWB	20	22
GHWB	2	10
Reagan	4	4
Ford	0	1

TABLE 4.2 Pandemic cases: Analysis of judges' decisions by party of appointing president

Appointing President	*For Science*	*Against Science*
Democrat	56	2
Republican	33	70

Chi-square = 61.4966 $p < 0.00001$

TABLE 4.3 Pandemic cases: Analysis of decisions by judges appointed by Trump and other Republican presidents

Appointing President	*For Science*	*Against Science*
Trump	8	33
Other Republicans	26	37

Chi-square = 5.3432 $p = .020803$

to protect workers against COVID because it "is not an occupational hazard in most workplaces" since it could be contracted elsewhere; but that is true of many, indeed most, workplace risks. MD Fla Judge Kathryn Kimball Mizelle (Trump), whom the ABA had found not qualified for lack of experience, ruled that "sanitation" did not include masks (which sought to protect wearers from contaminated air and prevent wearers with COVID from infecting others).[16] Several judges cavalierly dismissed the judgments of the highest military officials. Enjoining the Air Force from discharging a member who refused the vaccine, MD Ga Judge Tilman Self III (Trump) asked with false naivete: "what real interest can our military leaders have in furthering a requirement that violates the very document they swore to support and defend?" Granting 35 sailors a preliminary injunction against the vaccine, ND Texas Judge Reed O'Connor (GWB) said the "loss of religious liberties outweighs any forthcoming harm to the Navy." MD Fla Judge Steven

Merryday (GHWB) prohibited the Navy from reassigning or demoting a commander who refused the vaccine, finding him "triumphantly fit and slim and strong . . . robustly healthy . . . young." WD La Judge Terry Doughty (Trump) enjoined the vaccine mandate for health care workers, relying on an assertion that "the virus has achieved an immune escape from COVID-19 vaccines," which was advanced by a doctor who had been disavowed by the hospital that had employed him because of his heterodox medical opinions.

Republicans exploited these sharp political divisions among judges by seeking, with distressing success, to litigate in front of GOP appointees. Texas Attorney General Paxton filed 14 of his 26 lawsuits against the Biden administration in divisions within two districts that were staffed by a single Trump appointee: Kacsmaryk in ND Texas Amarillo and Tipton in SD Texas Victoria; other Republican lawsuits were filed in ND Texas Wichita Falls, staffed by O'Connor (GWB).[17] Similarly, the Attorneys General of Missouri and Louisiana sued Biden administration officials for allegedly stifling social media, filing in WD Louisiana in order to appear before another Trump appointee (Doughty).[18] A survey of 239 partisan multistate cases over the last three administrations found that Doughty had heard 9 of the 25 challenges to the Biden administration, more than any other judge, and had been assigned to hear 80–100 percent of cases filed in his division during that period.[19] 82 percent of cases in the Fifth Circuit were filed in the three districts staffed by Kacsmaryk, Tipton and Doughty; all but one of the 17 were assigned to Republican appointees. Most of the 27 multistate cases that Republican Attorneys General brought against the Obama administration were filed in ND and SD Texas, where O'Connor heard the largest number (striking down free preventive medical treatment under Obamacare). Democrats followed a similar strategy, seeking sympathetic judges by filing 59 percent of their lawsuits against Trump in SDNY and ND Ca.

The Republican assault on science had profound ramifications, extending far beyond the more than 100 million Americans who contracted COVID and the more than one million who died from it to encompass an entire nation struggling with the pandemic.[20] It amplified the already profound divergence between attitudes toward science among supporters of the two political parties. In 1975, 72 percent of Republicans and 67 percent of Democrats expressed faith in science, a difference of just five percent. In July 2021, confidence had declined to 45 percent among Republicans while increasing to 79 percent among Democrats, a gap of 34 percent. Party affiliation explained much more of this difference than did education (which only slightly increased confidence among Democrats). Party preference also correlated with specific beliefs: that the effects of global warming have already occurred (82 percent of Democrats compared with just 29 percent of Republicans, the latter having declined from 40 percent before Trump); that God had created humans in their present form within the last 10,000 years (34 and

52 percent, respectively). The proportion of Americans who believed in the right-wing conspiracy theories of QAnon rose from 14 to 17 percent between March and October 2021, while the proportion who rejected them declined from 40 to 34 percent; those who trusted OANN and Newsmax were nearly five times as likely to believe in QAnon; and 70 percent of QAnon believers thought the 2020 election had been stolen. Herschel Walker, the College Football Hall of Famer unsuccessfully backed by Trump for Georgia's Senate seat, voiced extreme versions of these beliefs shortly before the primary: "at one time, science said man came from apes. . . . If that is true, why are there still apes?" "Let me tell you science can't do" in vitro fertilization "because there has to be a God." (In August 2020, he promoted a "mist" that could "kill any covid on your body.") Party affiliation also correlated with having quite a lot of confidence or more in higher education (56 percent Democrats versus 33 percent Republicans) and the belief that higher education is too liberal (1 versus 32 percent) and does not let students think for themselves (6 versus 21 percent). Between March and August 2020, party affiliation had a stronger correlation than the local COVID case count with beliefs and actions concerning the pandemic and government policies on masks and social distancing.[21]

Apparently convinced (perhaps for the earlier reasons) that the culture wars, like the pandemic, could be exploited for political gain, Republicans broadened their attack to other forms of expert knowledge. Christopher Rufo, a senior fellow at the conservative Manhattan Institute, who frequently appeared on Fox News, made this strategy explicit on Twitter.[22]

> We have successfully frozen their brand—"critical race theory"—into the public conversation and are steadily driving up negative perceptions. We will eventually turn it toxic, as we put all of the various cultural insanities under that brand category. The goal is to have the public read something crazy in the newspaper and immediately think "critical race theory."

Trump invited Rufo to the White House and promptly issued an executive order canceling all diversity training in the federal government. After Florida Gov. DeSantis appointed Rufo to the Board of Trustees of New College of Florida, a progressive institution, it fired the college president and sought to cancel the contracts of all faculty and staff. DeSantis was exultant: "We don't want students to go through, at taxpayer expense, and graduate with a degree in Zombie studies." When the right-wing Claremont Institute and the Idaho Freedom Foundation claimed that "social-justice" ideology had infected that state's public universities, the legislature cut $2.5 million in funding from social justice programming and prohibited public education from directing "students to personally affirm, adopt or adhere" to critical race theory. (Competing with DeSantis for the 2024 Republican presidential nomination, Trump vowed to "eliminate all diversity, equity and inclusion programs across the entire federal government," which Biden had restored.)[23]

The Republican campaign extended to K-12 schools (none of which taught critical race theory). The Oklahoma State Board of Education demoted the Tulsa Public Schools to "accredited with warning" after a teacher complained that the district's training materials "shame white people"; the Board did the same to Mustang Public Schools (near Oklahoma City) after it self-reported that an exercise had made students uncomfortable on account of race or sex. 37 states were considering (and 14 had enacted) limits on teaching race and discrimination in public schools. From January to August 2022, at least 137 bills had been introduced in state legislatures to restrict teaching on race, gender, LGBTQ and American history, up from 54 in all of 2021. At least 17 states were considering legislation requiring teachers to post all instructional material online so parents could object. The Florida Commissioner of Education rejected 41 percent of proposed math books, most intended for primary schools, because of "references to Critical Race Theory (CRT), inclusions of Common Core, and the unsolicited addition of Social Emotional Learning (SEL) in mathematics." There were 40 bills to impose similar restrictions in higher education. Texas Lt. Gov. Dan Patrick (seeking re-election) declared: "I will not stand by and let looney Marxist UT professors poison the minds of young students with Critical Race Theory."

Libraries were targeted as well. In fall 2021, the American Library Association (ALA) reported an "unprecedented" increase in book challenges, whose numbers had reached the highest level since its records began 20 years earlier: 681 attempts to ban or restrict access to 1,651 different books in the first eight months of that year, compared with 200–400 annually in 2018–20.[24] Those numbers increased again in 2022: 1,269 attempts to ban 2,571 titles, up from 1,858 titles the previous year; seven states passed laws restricting library holdings and loans. Almost all the books affected were by or about people of color or LGBTQ people. Pen America said at least 50 groups were trying to remove books. Librarians were attacked by local politicians and reported to law enforcement, leading some to quit. Exposing the absurdity of these bans, one parent forced the Davis (Utah) School District to withdraw the Bible from elementary and middle schools for its "pornographic or indecent" content. (The embarrassed district reversed that decision within weeks.)[25] Five Republicans seeking the 2024 presidential nomination—Trump, DeSantis, Haley, Hutchinson and Ramaswamy—addressed the "Joyful Warriors National Summit" of Moms for Liberty, which claimed 100,000 members in 44 states and aggressively sought book bans.[26]

Like the attacks on scientists described earlier, these campaigns also had consequences.[27] A poll found that only 64 percent of respondents believed in the honesty of grade school teachers, down from 75 percent in 2020 and an all-time low; only 28 percent had "a great deal" or "quite a lot" of confidence in public schools, the second lowest figure since the question first was asked in 1973. The decline was greatest among Republicans. A November 2022 Pew Research Center survey found that 72 percent of Democrats believed colleges and universities had a positive effect on how thing were going, but 76 percent of Republicans said they affected the country negatively.[28] Just as misinformation fueled acts of violence (such as the attempted kidnapping of Michigan Gov. Whitmer and the January 6 insurrection), so it incited Jeremy Hanson to write the dictionary publisher Merriam-Webster: "There is no such thing as 'gender identity.' The imbecile who wrote this entry should be hunted down and shot" and the company headquarters "shot up and bombed." He was charged with interstate communication of threats to commit violence.

These attacks also prompted resistance.[29] Faculty at the University of Texas and more than a dozen other institutions vowed to reject restrictions of academic freedom. The Penguin Random House CEO donated $500,000 to create a fund to oppose book banning. One poll found widespread opposition to banning books that criticized U.S. history (87 percent), contained ideas with which people disagreed (85 percent) or discussed race or slavery (87 percent). In another, more than 70 percent of Americans expressed concern about restrictions on books in schools and favored teaching about the "ongoing effects of slavery and racism." Library patrons sued to block book removals. Thousands of educators protested virtually and in person against censorship, and thousands of others pledged to "refuse to lie to young people about U.S. history and current events—regardless of the law." The National Education Association (the nation's largest labor union) warned that "some lawmakers want to play politics with truth." The Ohio State University Senate voted almost unanimously to declare:

> There are no "two sides" to racism any more than there are two sides to the Holocaust or the roundness of the earth; there are only truths that must be taught well so that we might ensure better futures for all citizens.

More than six dozen scholarly and educational groups, including the American Historical Association, American Association of University Professors, American Federation of Teachers and Association of American Colleges and Universities, declared that "the clear goal of these efforts is to suppress teaching and learning about the role of racism in the history of the United States. The ideal of informed citizenship necessitates an educated public."

Gov. DeSantis's obvious 2024 presidential ambitions made Florida a central battleground.[30] The University of Florida ordered three faculty members not to serve as expert witnesses in a lawsuit challenging new voting restrictions and a fourth not to testify in a lawsuit challenging the governor's order withholding funds from schools that enforced mask mandates. ND Florida

Judge Mark E. Walker (Obama) enjoined the university order, comparing it to Hong Kong University removing a sculpture commemorating Tiananmen Square out of fear of Chinese government retaliation. But Board of Trustees Chairman Morteza Hosseini said faculty members performing such outside work might be neglecting their duties, misusing university funds and taking advantage of their positions "to improperly advocate personal political viewpoints to the exclusion of others." "[O]ur legislators are not going to put up with the wasting of state money and resources, and neither is this board." The legislature passed what DeSantis called the "Stop WOKE Act," regulating what schools, universities and workplaces could teach about race and identity. Other laws modified tenure, removed Florida universities from national and regional accreditation reviews and mandated annual "viewpoint diversity surveys."

In February 2023, Florida denied high school credit for the Advanced Placement Black history course, saying it "lacks educational value."[31] The College Board revised the curriculum, claiming it had done so in response to feedback from high school teachers and university faculty before Florida had acted. The Florida Department of Education replied that it had begun complaining in July 2022, but the Board denied having engaged in any discussions with the state. Nevertheless, it eliminated references to intersectionality, critical race studies, Kimberle Crenshaw, BLM, queer studies, bell hooks, Audre Lorde, Angela Davis, Alice Walker and Henry Louis Gates Jr. DeSantis also threatened to eliminate <u>all</u> AP classes (although nearly 200,000 Florida students had taken 366,000 AP tests in 2021). Arkansas, Virginia, North Dakota and Mississippi were also reviewing the African American AP curriculum.

The Florida legislature passed the Parental Rights in Education Bill, regulating the teaching of sexual orientation and gender identity in grades K-3 and requiring that lessons for older students be "age appropriate."[32] DeSantis's spokeswoman said it "would be more accurately described as an Anti-Grooming Bill. If you're against the anti-Grooming bill, you are probably a groomer or at least you don't denounce the grooming of 4- to 8-year-old children" to identify as gay or lesbian. "Silence is complicity." At a campaign rally, Trump agreed that teaching "far left gender theories to our children" was "truly child abuse, plain and simple." Under pressure from employees and "guests," Disney suspended all political donations (not just those to Florida politicians). Government officials in New York, Chicago and Los Angeles condemned the law, invited businesses to relocate and banned government travel to Florida. The state retaliated by terminating the special tax status it had granted Disney World 55 years earlier. Biden warned:

> Already, there have been reports that "Safe Space" stickers are being taken down from classrooms. Teachers are being instructed not to wear rainbow

> clothing. LGBTQ+ teachers are being told to take down family photos of their husbands and wives—cherished family photos like the ones on my own desk.

The Florida Education Department advised districts to disregard a Biden administration guidance that federal law prohibited discrimination based on sexual orientation and gender identity (reprising the South's massive resistance to the Supreme Court's desegregation decision nearly 70 years earlier). Perhaps fearing he was being outflanked in the culture wars by his strongest challenger for the Republican nomination, Trump promised to "keep men out of women's sports," end teacher tenure and cut aid to schools that teach "critical race theory, gender ideology, or other inappropriate racial, sexual or political content onto [sic] our children." "As the saying goes, personnel is policy and at the end of the day if we have pink-haired communists teaching our kids we have a major problem."

Republicans opened another front in the culture wars by attacking transgender youth.[33] The president of the conservative American Principles Project said that after the Supreme Court declared same-sex marriage a constitutional right in 2015, "we knew we needed to find an issue that the candidates were comfortable talking about. And we threw everything at the wall" to see what sticks. After the 67,000-member American Academy of Pediatrics (AAP) supported same-sex parenting, a small group broke away to form the American College of Pediatricians (ACP, a deliberately confusing name), which began lobbying in 2021 for laws against gender-affirming care. Between January 2021 and April 2023, at least 20 states enacted anti-trans laws, 14 in the latest four months, despite a statement by the AAP and the AMA that "there is a consensus in the field, and amongst these signatories, that gender-affirming medical care is important and beneficial for many transgender youth." The Missouri Attorney General (seeking re-election in 2024) invoked the Merchandising Practices Act to require 18 months of therapy before any transgender care (for adults as well as youths). Not wanting to be left out, Trump declared in April 2023 that if re-elected, he would direct the FDA to investigate whether transgender hormone treatments increased the risk of violence (a moral panic for which there was no evidence).

Texas joined at least 18 other states to ban puberty blockers and hormone therapy for those under 18, threatening to suspend the licenses of medical professionals who provided either treatment.[34] (All these were red states: Montana, Idaho, Utah, Arizona, North Dakota, South Dakota, Nebraska, Indiana, Kentucky, West Virginia, Tennessee, Mississippi, Georgia and Florida.)[35] Gov. Abbott (who had won re-election in 2022 and was said to be considering a 2024 presidential run) told the Department of Family and Protective Services to launch child abuse investigations of health care professionals who provided puberty-suppressing drugs and hormones to transgender teenagers. (This campaign blithely inverted the argument conservatives had been making that individuals should be able to decide how to respond to COVID.) Abbott's senior campaign adviser, Dave Carney, called the issue "a 75, 80 percent winner." A University of Texas Southwestern Medical Center clinic treating transgender youths closed under pressure from Abbott's office. 21 states had introduced similar bills.

These actions also provoked opposition. Adm. Rachel Levine, DHHS assistant secretary for health and the highest-ranking pediatrician in the Biden administration, said: "Our nation's leading pediatricians support evidence-based, gender-affirming care for transgender young people." Dr. Jack Turban (chief fellow in child and adolescent psychiatry at Stanford Medical School) warned: "Texas officials are spreading blatant falsehoods about medical care for transgender young people." A woman with a transgender daughter sued after being placed on leave by the Department of Family and Protective Services; Travis County District Court Judge Amy Clark Meachum issued a TRO against Abbott's rule. Biden said Abbott's "actions callously threaten to harm children and their families just to score political points."

> Respected medical organizations have said that access to gender-affirming care for transgender children can benefit mental health, lower suicide rates, and improve other health outcomes. Children, their parents, and their doctors should have the freedom to make the medical decisions that are best for each young person—without politicians getting in the way.

More than 60 major businesses, including Johnson & Johnson, Macy's, Apple, Meta, Google, Levi Strauss, Gap, Ikea and REI, took digital ads and a full-age ad in *The Dallas Morning News* to protest Abbott's action.

In Louisiana, Republican state Sen. Fred Mills, a pharmacist, cast the deciding vote in the Health and Welfare Committee to block a bill banning transition care for transgender minors.[36]

> I relied on science and data and not political or societal pressures. I prioritized the value of the physician-patient relationship, I put my trust that the physicians in Louisiana know better than I do how to treat these children, and I decided that this is such a small unique subset of medical needs of the entire population that I should not take away approved and appropriate medicinal options.

After another committee approved the bill and the legislature passed it, Democratic Gov. John Bel Edwards vetoed it, despite the veto-proof margin.

Florida Surgeon General Ladapo (who had questioned COVID-19 vaccines) issued a memo advising doctors against prescribing puberty blockers or hormone therapy for transgender youths and declaring that social gender transition (including nonmedical procedures and changes of name, pronouns or clothing) should "not be a treatment option for children or adolescents."[37] This contradicted a DHHS Guidance on gender transition and the best practices of the AMA, AAP and American Psychiatric Association. The AMA called such measures a "government intrusion into the practice of medicine that is detrimental to the health of transgender and gender-diverse children and adults." The Endocrine Society (18,000 specialists) asked the state to withdraw the recommendation and "allow physicians to provide evidence-based care." "Our Clinical Practice Guideline adheres to these [Institute of Medicine] national standards and cites more than 260 scientific studies." Ladapo dismissed the studies for their "low-quality evidence, small sample sizes, and medium to high risk of bias" and (following the Trump script) accused DHHS of "injecting political ideology into the health of our children." Led by Ladapo, the Florida Board of Medicine voted 6–3 (5 absent) to prohibit doctors from providing puberty blockers and hormones or surgery to those under 18 unless they were already receiving such treatment. The Board was appointed by DeSantis, and eight members had donated to his political campaigns. The Florida Board of Osteopathic Medicine followed suit. At least ten states prohibited Medicaid from paying for gender-affirming care for anyone.

After Iowa passed a law banning gender-affirming care for transgender youth, Gov. Reynolds denounced the "radical left," who "believe that children should be encouraged to pick their gender and the parents, well, they're just in the way."[38] Overriding Democratic Gov. Beshear's veto, Kentucky legislators banned access to gender-affirming health care for transgender children, restricted school bathrooms and lockers, prohibited teachers from discussing sexual orientation and gender identity and let teachers use birth names and pronouns against a student's wishes.[39] The bill's sponsor was running for lieutenant governor. The state's GOP spokesman said: "Today may well be remembered as the day Andy Beshear lost his bid for reelection." (In April 2023, Beshear's approval rating was up 4 percent from the previous year, making him the most popular Democratic governor in the U.S. and the fifth most popular governor.)[40] Ten other states had passed similar bans.

The Alabama legislature fought on both fronts of this culture war: restricting what students could be taught about gender and sexuality and criminalizing medical care for transgender young people.[41] Signing the bill, Gov. Ivey said: "I believe very strongly that if the Good Lord made you a boy, you are a boy, and if he [sic] made you a girl, you are a girl." (This echoed earlier religious sloganeering against same-sex marriage: "the Bible says it's Adam and Eve, not Adam and Steve.") Sen. Cruz accused Biden of supporting the "genital mutilation of children." Rep. Greene asserted: "communist groomers" wanted to "allow a for-profit medical industry to chop off these confused children's genitals."

Trump quickly jumped on what he believed was a bandwagon, releasing his "Plan to Protect Children from Left-Wing Gender Insanity" by promising to bar federal agencies from promoting "the concept of sex and gender transition at any age" and require the government to recognize the gender assigned at birth as the only gender.[42] His Republican competitors piled on. Mike Pence declared he would support a national ban on gender affirming care for transgender minors. Ron DeSantis launched his presidential campaign at the Eternity Church in Iowa, where Pastor Jesse Newman (who spoke at the event) had called homosexuality a sin and Pride flags "rainbow sex cult flags." The DeSantis campaign solicited donations by showing Biden in front of a Pride flag, with the message: "When did we start accepting this as the norm?"[43] A campaign social media post said, "To wrap up 'Pride Month,' let's hear from the politician who did more than any other Republican to celebrate it," and featured Trump saying in 2016, "I will do everything in my power to protect our L.G.B.T.Q. citizens," and supporting transgender people choosing a bathroom. It contrasted that with a media headline: "Pride event in St. Cloud canceled after DeSantis signs 'Protection of Children Act' into law." Nikki Haley asked rhetorically: "How are we supposed to get our girls used to the fact that biological boys are in their locker rooms? And then we wonder why a third of our teenage girls seriously contemplated suicide last year."[44] (She offered no evidence for a causal connection.)

After media reported that the female shooter who had killed three children and three teachers at a Nashville school used male pronouns, Donald Trump Jr. commented falsely: "there is a clear epidemic of trans/non-binary mass shooters."[45] His father and Rep. Greene both blamed hormone therapy (though there was no evidence that the shooter had received it). Tucker Carlson showed a photo of the shooter with the title "Trans Killer" and the statement: "we are witnessing the rise of trans violence." A post by a member of Turning Point USA claiming that "the modern trans movement is radicalizing activists into terrorists" garnered 10 million views and a "!" tweet from Elon Musk. During the school shooting in Uvalde, Sen. Cruz tweeted that the shooter was a "transsexual leftist illegal alien" (he was none of those).

Drag performances became yet another site of contestation. At its Pride Day celebration, the Dodgers hosted Sisters of Perpetual Indulgence, an LGBT group whose members dress as Catholic nuns. Mike Pence called it "deeply offensive," and Sen. Tim Scott (another aspirant) denounced the event as "shameful and disgusting." By the middle of 2023, at least 26 bills had been introduced in state legislatures to restrict drag performances.[46]

President Biden responded to all of this by condemning "prejudiced people" who indulged in a "totally, thoroughly unjustified, ugly" "appeal to fear."[47] "LGBTQ Americans, especially children, you're loved, you're heard. And this administration has your back." "You enrich every part of American life. You are some of the bravest and most inspiring people I've ever known, and I've known a lot of good folks." In a proclamation designating June as Pride Month, Biden decried these "hateful laws."

> These bills and laws attack the most basic values and freedoms we have as Americans. The right to be yourself. The right to make your own health decisions. The right to raise your children. . . . if it were you, you'd want the space to figure it out with your family and your doctor.
>
> Books about LGBTQI+ people are being banned from libraries. Transgender youth in over a dozen States have had their medically necessary health care banned. Homophobic and transphobic vitriol spewed online has spilled over into real life, as armed hate groups intimidate people at Pride marches and drag performances, and threaten doctors' offices and children's hospitals that offer care to the LGBTQI+ community.

Federal judges also pushed back against these laws. Three had been appointed by Democratic presidents. ND Fla Judge Robert I. Hinkle (Clinton) issued a preliminary injunction against Florida's ban on gender-affirming therapy, finding that "gender identity is real" and the statute "prohibits . . . treatments even when medically appropriate."[48] He ridiculed the state's claim that professional associations endorsing such care had acted for political reasons: "if ever a pot called a kettle black, it is here. The statute and the rules were an exercise in politics, not good medicine." ED Ark Judge James Moody (Obama) also enjoined his state's ban.[49] "Rather than protecting children or safeguarding medical ethics, the evidence showed that the prohibited medical care improves the mental health and well-being of patients and that, by prohibiting it, the state undermined the interests it claims to be advancing." WD Ky Judge David J. Hale (Obama) similarly issued a TRO against that state's law. Surprisingly, two Trump appointees did the same. SD Ind Judge James Patrick Hanlon enjoined most of that state's ban on transition care for minors.[50] And MD Tn Judge Eli J. Richardson (Trump) also did so, taking comfort from the actions of other federal judges.[51]

> The court realizes that today's decision will likely stoke the already controversial fire regarding the rights of transgender individuals in American society on the one hand, and the countervailing power of states to control certain activities within their borders and to use that power to protect minors. The court, however, does not stand alone in its decision.

Federal judges appointed by presidents of both parties also were critical of limitations on drag shows. WD Tn Judge Tommy Parker (Trump) enjoined that state's ban, declaring that it "reeks of constitutional maladies of vagueness." The legislature "carelessly, if not intentionally," enacted a measure "for the inappropriate purpose of chilling constitutionally free speech." It "targets the viewpoint of gender identity" by grouping "male and female impersonators" with exotic dancers, topless dancers and strippers. MD Fla Judge Gregory A. Presnell (Clinton) enjoined his state's restriction as a violation of the First Amendment.[52]

Here, too, hate speech and governmental actions had broader consequences.[53] Armed Proud Boys and neo-Nazis demonstrated outside drag events. Boston Children's Hospital received bomb threats after caring for transgender children. The Department of Justice charged at least three men for threats and attacks; there were 12 times as many such incidents in 2022 as in 2020. In June 2023, the A.D.L. and GLAD reported more than 350 anti-LGBTQ incidents over an 11-month period.[54] A Gallup poll found that acceptance of same-sex relationships declined from a high of 71 percent in 2022 to 64 percent in 2023; among Republicans, it fell twice as much (15 percent) to 41 percent, the lowest level since 2014. According to a Pew survey in fall 2022, 55 percent of Republicans felt that same-sex marriage was bad for society. After Dylan Mulvaney (a transgender influencer with more than 10 million followers on TikTok) posted a video on Instagram mentioning that Budweiser had put her face on a tallboy can of Bud Light to celebrate the 365th-day milestone of her *Days of Girlhood* series, which chronicled her gender transition, she suffered stalking and personal attacks; and a boycott of Bud Light cut its sales by 29 percent, while Anheuser-Busch stock fell by more than 15 percent.[55]

The Supreme Court decision overruling Roe v. Wade opened yet another front in the war on medical expertise.[56] The Alliance for Hippocratic Medicine (whose eponym must be turning in his grave) promptly sued to nullify the FDA's approval two decades earlier of the abortion drug mifeprostone, filing in ND Texas to ensure the case would be heard by Judge Kacsmaryk, a proudly anti-abortion Trump appointee. (As deputy general counsel of the Christian conservative law firm First Liberty, he had written a law review article against "abortifacient drugs designed to kill unborn children" shortly before his confirmation hearing but removed his name prior to publication so he would not have to report it to the Senate Judiciary Committee.) He performed just as expected, issuing a nationwide injunction.[57] He invoked a Finnish study, whose author objected that the judge purposely misrepresented its analysis. He relied on flawed research by the Charlotte Lozier Institute, an anti-abortion group. He asserted that chemical abortions caused "negative change" in patients—based on several dozen anonymous blog posts from the abortionchangesyou.com website. An American College of Obstetricians and Gynecologists (ACOG) meta-analysis of hundreds of studies of women who had abortions found that "serious side effects occur in less than 1% of patients, and major adverse events . . . in less than 0.3% of patients." ACOG, the AMA, the Society for Maternal-Fetal Medicine and other professional organizations filed an amicus brief calling the risk of death from mifepristone "almost non-existent" and lower than that from wisdom tooth extractions, colonoscopies and Viagra. (There had been fewer than 28 reported deaths, just 0.0006 percent of the more than 5 million women who had taken the drug.) The AMA president denounced Kacsmaryk's decision as "one of the most brazen attacks yet against reproductive health," which "could also upend the Food and Drug Administration's drug regulatory process" and "throw our health care system into chaos." Announcing an immediate appeal, the Justice Department said the ruling had deprived "patients of access to this safe and effective treatment, based on the court's own misguided assessment of the drug's safety." More than 400 pharmaceutical executives signed a letter declaring that the judge "ignores decades of scientific evidence and legal precedent" and warning that "any medicine is at risk for the same outcome." The trade organization Pharmaceutical Research and Manufacturers of America also supported "the agency's ability to regulate." *The Washington Post* said Kacsmaryk's opinion was "more rooted in ideology than law" and based on "dubious studies by anti-abortion activists." A former FDA principal deputy commissioner denounced the "shocking and irresponsible action." The Fifth Circuit (Englehardt and Oldham [both Trump] and Haynes [GWB]) temporarily stayed part of the ban (because the statute of limitations for challenging the FDA's original approval had expired) but upheld the injunction against the administration's 2016 ruling, which allowed the drug to be prescribed until 10 weeks after gestation (rather than seven) and delivered by mail. The Biotechnology Innovation Organization said both courts had "substituted their own idiosyncratic views of clinical benefit and safety for the legislatively required, gold-standard benefit-risk analysis performed by FDA's medical and scientific professionals." In a separate case brought by a dozen Democratic state Attorneys General, ED Washington Judge Thomas O. Rice (Obama) ordered the FDA to expand access to mifeprostone. After the DoJ sought Supreme Court review of the Texas case "to defend the FDA's scientific judgment," the Court stayed the Fifth Circuit ruling until it decided on the merits.

In the end, science (and academic research more generally) preserved its integrity in the face of the Trump administration's efforts to politicize it. The gold standard of double-blind clinical trials (followed by the FDA and NIH) and peer review of research and publications ensured that scientific findings by career civil servants were subjected to rigorous review before being implemented in response to the pandemic. Most scientists recognized that their reputations depended on faithful adherence to those professional norms. But there have always been some with paper credentials (even from elite institutions) willing, even eager, to sell their cultural capital for visibility, influence and money, as revealed by the decades-long struggles to regulate tobacco, carcinogenic chemicals, automobiles, firearms and now carbon emissions.

Such "scientists" cynically exploit the skeptical ethos indispensable to the advancement of knowledge, making bold pronouncements without offering any evidence to support them. Although there are penalties for falsifying data, plagiarizing or lying on a resume, there are none for vaccine or climate change deniers. Federal courts generally defended the judgments of professional experts, although there were striking differences between judges appointed by Democratic and Republican presidents, especially Trump. But Republican politicians continue to exploit populist resentment of expertise by denying or disregarding science.

Today, nearly a century after the 1925 Scopes trial—when more than a third of Democrats and more than half of Republicans still believe in creationism—scientists, educators, librarians and other experts are still fighting politicians who seek to prevent them from exercising their professional judgment.[58] Christians often quote the statement St. John attributed to Jesus: "the truth will set you free." Many universities (including Harvard, Yale, Johns Hopkins, University of Michigan and Southern Methodist University) feature "veritas" in their mottos. Regardless of whether our belief in the centrality of truth is religious or secular, we can all agree that denying the distinction between truth and falsity is fatal to liberal democracy.

Notes

CNN	Cable News Network
G	*Guardian*
NPR	National Public Radio
NYT	*New York Times*
WP	*Washington Post*
WSJ	*Wall Street Journal*

1 CSIS et al. (2023).
2 Cave, "How Australia saved thousands of lives while covid killed a million Americans," NYT (5.15.22).
3 Burns, "Long COVID: What Do the Latest Data Show?" Kaiser Family Foundation (1.26.23).
4 Gill v. Whitford, 138 S.Ct. 1916 (2018); see Fowler, "Chief Justice Roberts and other judges have a hard time with statistics. That's a real problem," WP (10.31.17); Enos et al. (2017).
5 Students for Fair Admissions v. Harvard (USSC 2023); VanSickle, "In affirmative action ruling, Black Justices take aim at each other," NYT (7.1.23).
6 Abel (2018a: ch. 4).
7 Kiely et al., "State of the Union: President Trump stretched and distorted facts about economy, jobs," USA Today (2.5.20).
8 Cf. Kolko (1965) (interdependence of railroads and regulation).
9 Diamond, "Covid is still a leading cause of death as the virus recedes," WP (4.17.23).

10 Nehemas, "DeSantis campaign uses apparently fake images to attack Trump on Twitter," NYT (6.9.23).
11 Lopez, "Behind Biden's poll doldrums, a persistent virus," NYT (5.7.22); Chung and Olson, "The pandemic has eroded Americans' trust in experts and elected leaders alike, a survey finds," NYT (7.7.22); Dielsman et al., "Pandemic preparedness and COVID-19: an exploratory analysis of infection and fatality rates, and contextual factors associated with preparedness in 177 countries, from Jan. 1, 2020, to Sept. 30, 3031," The Lancet (2.1.22); Cave, "How Australia saved thousands of lives while Covid killed a million Americans," NYT (5.15.22); Diamond, Mueller, Baumhardt and Myers, "'I feel defeated': Mask and vaccine mandates cause new divides as officials try to head off virus surge," WP (8.15.21); Bump, "The pandemic did what the anti-vax movement couldn't: Powered skepticism of vaccine rules," WP (2.17.22); Bump, "Republicans are still a bigger obstacle to vaccination than Black Americans," WP (9.16.21); Bump, "More Republicans support opposition to government vaccine mandates than support open carry," WP (10.21.21); Krugman, "The viral lies that keep killing us," NYT (1.4.22); Jones, "U.S. political party preferences shifted greatly during 2021," Gallup (1.17.22) https://news.gallup.com/poll/388781/political-party-preferences-shifted-greatly-during-2021.aspx; Leonhardt, "Irrational skepticism vs. Power of boosters," NYT (2.1.22); but see Sreedhar and Gopal, "Behind low vaccination rates lurks a more profound social weakness," NYT (12.4.21) (arguing the real difference is class); Fridman et al. (2021); Blake, "A pollster tested 8 pieces of covid misinformation. On 6 of 8, more Republicans said they were true than false," WP (11.9.21); Velasquez-Manoff (2022); Amour and Abbott, "Loads of covid-19 boosters are going unused this fall and here's why," WSJ (11.17.22); Wallace-Wells, "Dr. Fauci looks back: 'something clearly went wrong,'" NYT (4.30.23); Cohn, "Americans are frustrated with the pandemic. These polls show how much," NYT (2.8.22); Holder, "Tracking coronavirus vaccinations around the world," NYT (3.13.23); Kirzinger et al., "KFF COVID-19 Vaccine Monitor: The Increasing Importance of Partisanship in Predicting COVID-19 Vaccination Status," Kaiser Family Foundation (11.16.21); Wood and Brumfiel, "Pro-Trump counties now have far higher COVID death rates. Misinformation is to blame." NPR (12.5.21); but see Lazarus et al., "A Survey of COVID-19 vaccine acceptance across 23 countries in 2022," 29 Nature Medicine 366–75 (2023) (acceptance in U.S. slightly above global average).
12 CCG (2023: 9–10, 172, 218–219); Johns Hopkins Coronavirus Resource Center, Mortality Analyses https://coronavirus.jhu.edu/data/mortality.
13 Indiana University Media Report, "Nearly Half of Survey Respondents Believe Vaccine Misinformation" (7.14.21); Krankovic, "Most Republicans Who Have Heard of Ivermectin as a COVID-19 Treatment Think It May Be Effective" YouGovAmerica (9.2.21); Hamel et al., "KFF COVID-19 Vaccine Monitor: Media and Misinformation," Kaiser Family Foundation (11.8.21).
14 www.reaganfoundation.org/ronald-reagan/reagan-quotes-speeches/inaugural-address-2/; www.reaganfoundation.org/ronald-reagan/reagan-quotes-speeches/news-conference-1/.
15 Parmet and Paul (2020); Mok and Posner (2021).
16 Weiss, "Federal judicial nominee lacks enough experience, ABA says in letter explaining 'not qualified' rating," American Bar Association Journal (10.14.20).
17 Vladeck, "Don't let Republican 'judge-shoppers' thwart the will of voters," NYT (2.5.23); Stolberg and Abelson, "Federal judge strikes down Obamacare requirement for free preventive care," NYT (3.31.23).
18 Myers, "Free speech v. disinformation comes to a head," NYT (2.10.23).

19 Wheeler, "Republicans find home court for Biden suits in western Louisiana," Bloomberglaw (12.20.22); Stein, "The Justice Department's fight against judge shopping in Texas," WP (3.20.23).
20 https://news.gallup.com/poll/352397/democratic-republican-confidence-science-diverges.aspx; https://news.gallup.com/poll/343025/global-warming-attitudes-frozen-2016.aspx; https://news.gallup.com/poll/145286/Four-Americans-Believe-Strict-Creationism.aspx; Smith, "Belief in QAnon has strengthened in US since Trump was voted out, study finds," G (2.24.22); Milligan, "A quarter of Republicans believe central views of QAnon conspiracy movement," U.S. News (2.24.22); Griffiths, "GOP Senate candidate Herschel Walker suggests evolution isn't real: 'Science said man came from apes . . . If that is true, why are there still apes?'" Business Insider (3.16.22); https://news.gallup.com/poll/216278/why-republicans-down-higher.aspx.
21 Makridis and Rothwell (2020a, 2020b).
22 Meckler and Dawsey, "Republicans, spurred by an unlikely figure, see political promise in targeting critical race theory," WP (6.21.21); Zerofsky (2022); Bikales, "Okla. downgrades school district over complaint it shamed White people," WP (7.31.22); Saul, Mazzei and Gabriel, "DeSantis takes on education establishment, and builds his brand," NYT (2.1.23).
23 Huynh, "Trump, crossing paths with DeSantis, tries to outflank him," NYT (7.1.23).
24 Harris and Alter, "Book ban efforts spread across the U.S.," NYT (1.31.22); Natanson, "Schools nationwide are quietly removing books from their libraries," WP (3.22.22); Harris and Alter, "Book banning efforts surged in 2021. These titles were the most targeted," NYT (4.4.22); Harris and Alter, "With rising book bans, librarians have come under attack," NYT (7.7.22); Fortin and Heyward, "Teachers tackle Black history month, under new restrictions," NYT (2.12.22); Mervosh, "Back to school in DeSantis's Florida, as teachers look over their shoulders," NYT (8.27.22); Natanson, "School book bans and challenges, at record highs, are rising again," WP (9.19.22); Young and Friedman (America 2022); Friedman and Johnson (2022); Meckler, "New transparency bills would force teachers to post instructional materials," WP (3.2.22); Strauss and Bever, "Florida rejects math books with 'references' to critical race theory," WP (4.16.22); McGee, "UT faculty members demand answers after Dan Patrick says Liberty Institute intended to fight critical race theory," KXAN (2.16.22); Flaherty, "Texas Lt. Governor slams 'looney Marxist' professors, CRT," Inside Higher Ed (2.18.22); Anderson and Svrluga, "College faculty are fighting back against state bills on critical race theory," WP (2.19.22); Harris and Alter, "A fast-growing network of conservative groups is fueling a surge in book bans," NYT (12.13.22); Alter and Harris, "Attempts to ban books doubled in 2022," NYT (3.27.23).
25 McDaniel, "Protester opposed to book bans gets Bible pulled from some Utah schools," WP (6.3.23); Flower and Mossburg, "Utah school board unanimously reversed its decision to remove the Bible off school shelves after appeals," CNN (6.21.23).
26 Weisman, "Moms for Liberty's school board antagonism draws G.O.P. heavyweights," NYT (6.29.23); Natanson and Knowles, "Moms for Liberty didn't exist 3 years ago. Now it's a GOP kingmaker," WP (6.30.23).
27 Natanson, "Trust in teachers is plunging amid a culture war in education," WP (9.6.22); Liptak, "Man charged with threatening Merriam-Webster over gender definitions," NYT (4.22.22).
28 Svrluga, "Conservatives seek control over public universities with state bills," WP (6.3.23).

29 Harris, "Publishing C.E.O. donates $500,000 to fight book bans," NYT (2.17.22); Sargent, "A surprising poll about GOP book bans should light a fire under Democrats," WP (2.23.22); Gowen, "Texas residents sue county for removing books, firing librarian," WP (4.25.22); Natanson, "Teens fight for the right to read with 'banned-book clubs' and lawsuits," WP (5.11.22); Strauss, "Teachers across the country protest laws restricting lessons on racism," WP (6.13.21); Schuessler, "Scholarly groups condemn laws limiting teaching on race," NYT (6.17.21); Harris and Alter, "Authors and students sue over Florida law driving book bans," NYT (6.21.23); Natanson and Knowles, "Moms for Liberty didn't exist 3 years ago. Now it's a GOP kingmaker," WP (6.30.23).

30 Wines, "Judge issues stinging free speech ruling against University of Florida," NYT (1.22.22); Svrluga and Rozsa, "In Florida, DeSantis's plans for colleges rattle some academics," WP (7.1.22); Atterbury, " 'Positively dystopian': Florida judge blocks DeSantis' anti-woke law for colleges," Politico (11.17.22); Brasch, "Judge nixes higher education portions of Florida's Stop WOKE Act," WP (11.17.22); Rosza, "A Black professor defies DeSantis law restricting lessons on race," WP (1.21.23).

31 Meckler, "Florida rejects AP Black history class, saying it 'lacks educational value,' " WP (1.20.23); Mazzei and Hartocollis, "Florida rejects A.P. African American studies class," NYT (1.19.23); Fawcett and Hartocollis, "Florida gives reasons for rejecting A.P. African American studies class," NYT (1.22.23); Hartocollis and Faucett, "The College Board strips down its A.P. curriculum for African American studies," NYT (2.1.23); Anderson and Rosza, "Amid attacks from DeSantis, AP African American studies course is updated," WP (2.1.23); Goldstein, "Inside the College Board's revised African American studies curriculum," NYT (2.2.23); Anderson, "College Board faces storm of criticism over AP African American studies," WP (2.3.23); Saul, Mazzei and Gabriel, "DeSantis takes on education establishment, and builds his brand," NYT (2.1.23); Meckler, "Florida details months of complaints about AP African American studies course," WP (2.9.23); Shapira, "College Board accuses Florida Department of Education of 'slander,' " WP (2.13.23); Hartocollis, Goldstein and Saul, "The College Board's rocky path, through Florida, to the A.P. Black studies course," NYT (2.13.23); Mazzei, "How a progressive Florida college became DeSantis's latest target," NYT (2.14.23); Anderson, "DeSantis threatens to rid Florida of advanced placement classes," WP (2.14.23); Gates, "Who's afraid of Black history?" NYT (2.17.23); Meckler and Natanson, "More states scrutinizing AP Black studies after Florida complaints," WP (2.18.23); Anderson, "Did politics scrub 'systemic' from AP African American studies plan?" WP (2.19.23).

32 Craig, "Florida legislature passes bill to restrict LGBTQ topics in elementary schools," WP (3.8.22); Itkowitz, "Trump endorses Dr. Oz in Pennsylvania Senate race, a key battleground," WP (4.10.22); Ables, "Disney suspends political donations in Florida after bill restricting LGBTQ discussion," WP (3.14.22); Rosza, "DeSantis takes on Disney in a culture war with national implications," WP (4.13.22); Rozsa, "DeSantis proposes dissolving special tax status for Disney World," WP (4.20.22); Rozsa, "Florida legislature passes bill repealing Disney's special tax status," WP (4.21.22); Strauss, "Florida law limiting LGBTQ discussions takes effect—and rocks schools," WP (7.2.22); Rozsa, "Florida teachers race to remake lessons as DeSantis laws take effect," WP (7.31.22); Edsall, "This is Trump's 'magic' trick," NYT (3.1.23).

33 Ghorayshi, "Texas governor pushes to investigate medical treatments for trans youth as 'child abuse,' " NYT (2.24.22); Ghorayshi, "Texas youth gender clinic closed last year under political pressure," NYT (3.10.22); Turban, "Texas officials are spreading blatant falsehoods about medical care for transgender kids," WP (3.2.22); Parks, "ACLU files lawsuit over Texas governor's order to treat

gender-affirming care for kids as child abuse," WP (2.3.22); Paul and Parks, "Judge partially blocks Texas Gov. Greg Abbott's order to treat gender-affirming care as child abuse," WP (3.2.22); Parks, "Texas judge suspends Gov. Greg Abbott's order to treat gender-affirming care as child abuse," WP (3.12.22); Wagner, "Biden accuses Texas Gov. Abbott of 'government overreach at its worst' for investigating parents of children transitioning genders," WP (3.3.22); Haberman, "Businesses assail Texas move to classify care for trans teens as 'child abuse,'" NYT (3.11.22); Astor, "G.O.P. state lawmakers push a growing wave of anti-transgender bills," NYT (1.26.23); Hsu, "Judge curbs Fla. probe into U.S. medicine's trans treatment standards," WP (1.27.23); Sasani, "Utah bans transition care for transgender youth," NYT (1.30.23); Kindy, "GOP targets drag shows with new bills in at least 14 states," WP (2.14.23); Albeck-Ripka, "Tennessee bans drag shows on public property," NYT (3.3.23); Rojas, Cochrane, Sasani and Paulson, "Tennessee law limiting 'cabaret' shows raises uncertainty about drag events," NYT (3.5.23); Klein, "If you read the G.O.P.'s anti-trans policies, you'll see what it really wants," NYT (3.7.23); Cochrane, "Judge temporarily blocks Tennessee law that restricts drag performances," NYT (4.1.23); Paris, "Bans on transition care for young people spread across U.S.," NYT (4.15.23); Nagourney and Peters, "How a campaign against transgender rights mobilized conservatives," NYT (4.16.23); Chen, "Missouri to restrict medical care for transgender adults, citing consumer protection law," NYT (4.15.23); Wells, "Trump, in legal peril, draws cheers at NRA convention; Pence draws boos," WP (4.15.23); Kindy, "Historic surge in bills targeting transgender rights pass at record speed," WP (4.17.23); Weber, Gilbert and Lorenz, "Documents show how conservative doctors influenced abortion, trans rights," WP (6.15.23); Hassan, "States passed a record number of transgender laws. Here's what they say," NYT (6.29.23).

34 Bisset and Hennessy-Fiske, "Texas becomes largest state to ban gender-affirming care for minors," WP (6.3.23).

35 Paris, "See the states that have passed laws directed at young trans people," NYT (6.7.23).

36 Rojas, "Louisiana lawmakers pass ban on transition care for transgender minors," NYT (6.7.23); Rojas, "Governor vetoes Louisiana's ban on transition care for transgender minors," NYT (7.1.23).

37 Branigin, "Florida memo on gender dysphoria contradicts leading medical guidance," WP (4.21.22); Ghorayshi, "Florida restricts doctors from providing gender treatments to minors," NYT (11.5.22).

38 Gowen, "Iowa's sharp right turn: from centrist state to 'Florida of the North,'" WP (3.21.23).

39 Wan, "Kentucky lawmakers pass major anti trans law, overriding governor's veto," WP (3.30.23); Robertson and Londoño, "G.O.P. lawmakers override Kentucky governor's veto of anti-trans law," NYT (3.30.23).

40 Shreve, "Poll: Beshear ranks fifth most popular governor in U.S. ahead of re-election bid," Spectrum News 1 (4.19.23).

41 Rojas and Mzezewa, "Alabama lawmakers approve ban on medical care for transgender youth," NYT (4.8.22); Klemsrud, "Equal rights plan and abortion are opposed by 15,000 at rally," NYT (11.20.77); Constance R. Sullivan-Blum "'It's Adam and Eve, not Adam and Steve': What's at Stake in the Construction of Contemporary American Christian Homophobia" (January 2009) https://doi.org/10.1215/9780822391395-004.

42 Byler, "Trump is exploiting an anti-trans turn in public opinion," WP (2.21.23).

43 Arnsdorf, Dawsey and Knowles, "Republican opposition to LGBTQ rights erupts in backlash to Pride month," WP (6.30.23); Nehemas and Haberman, "DeSantis, seeking attention, uses L.G.B.T.Q. issues to attack Trump," NYT (7.2.23).

44 Qiu, "Fact-checking Nikki Haley on the campaign trail," NYT (6.18.23).

45 Kessler, "The data is clear: there is no 'clear epidemic' of transgender mass shooters," WP (3.30.23); Nirappil, "The right exploits Nashville shooting to escalate anti-trans rhetoric," WP (3.30.23).
46 Anders, "Tennessee drag ban is unconstitutional, federal judge rules," WP (6.3.23); Cochrane, "Tenn. anti-drag law is ruled unconstitutional," NYT (6.4.23).
47 Wagner, "Biden decries rash of 'cruel' state laws targeting rights of LGBTQ+ individuals," WP (6.9.23); Rogers, "At Pride event Biden vows to protect rights of L.G.B.T.Q. Americans," NYT (6.11.23); Weisman, "Moms for Liberty's school board antagonism draws G.O.P. heavyweights," NYT (6.29.23); Natanson and Knowles, "Moms for Liberty didn't exist 3 years ago. Now it's a GOP kingmaker," WP (6.30.23).
48 Rojas and Ghorayshi, "Judge sides with families fighting Florida's ban on gender care for minors," NYT (6.7.23).
49 Branigin, "Arkansas federal judge blocks first ban on gender-affirming care," WP (6.21.23).
50 Smith, "Judge mostly blocks Indiana ban on transition care for minors," NYT (6.17.23).
51 Betts and Cochrane, "Judges block transgender care bans for minors in Kentucky and Tennessee," NYT (6.29.23).
52 Massei, "Judge rules against Florida law restricting drag shows," NYT (6.24.23).
53 Astor, "Transgender Americans feel under siege as political vitriol rises," NYT (12.12.22).
54 Astor, "Report cites more than 350 anti-L.G.B.T.Q. incidents over 11 months," NYT (6.22.23); Arnsdorf, Dawsey and Knowles, "Republican opposition to LGBTQ rights erupts in backlash to Pride month," WP (6.30.23).
55 Creswell, "Cheaper than water? Retailers try to unload Bud Light," NYT (6.30.23).
56 Dobbs v. Jackson Women's Health Organization (USSC 2022).
57 Stein, Marimow and Kitchener, "Justice Department appeals Texas abortion pill ruling," WP (4.10.23); "The abortion pill should remain available while courts deliberate," WP (4.11.23); Jewett and Belluck, "Abortion ruling could undermine the F.D.A.'s drug-approval authority," NYT (4.10.23); Belluck and Jewett, "Drug company leaders condemn ruling invalidating F.D.A.'s approval of abortion pill," NYT (4.11.23); Sharfstein, "I worked at the F.D.A. The abortion pill decision is dangerous," NYT (4.11.23); Stein, Marimow and Masih, "Appeals court temporarily keeps abortion pill available but limits access," WP (4.13.23); Belluck, "Court says abortion pill can remain available but imposes temporary restrictions," NYT (4.13.23); Stein, Marimow and Masih, "U.S. asks Supreme Court to restore full access to abortion pill," WP (4.14.23); Weber, McGinley, Ovalle and Sellers, "Unpacking the flawed science cited in the Texas abortion ruling," WP (4.14.23); Kitchener, Barnes and Marimow, "The controversial article Matthew Kacsmaryk did not disclose to the Senate," WP (4.15.23); Barnes and Marimow, "The Supreme Court temporarily restores full access to key abortion medication," WP (4.15.23); Resneck, "This could be one of the most brazen attacks on Americans' health yet," NYT (4.21.23); Totenberg, "Supreme Court blocks lower court decision in case on FDA approval of abortion pill," NPR (4.21.23).
58 https://news.gallup.com/poll/145286/Four-Americans-Believe-Strict-Creationism.aspx; Lepore, "The Parent Trap," New Yorker (3.21.22).

REFERENCES

Abel, Richard L. 2018a. *Law's Wars: The Fate of the Rule of Law in the US "War on Terror."* New York: Cambridge University Press.

_____. 2024a. *How Autocrats Abuse Power: Resistance to Trump and Trumpism.* Abingdon: Routledge.

_____. 2024b. *How Autocrats Seek Power: Resistance to Trump and Trumpism.* Abingdon: Routledge.

_____. 2025. *How Autocrats Are Held Accountable: Resistance to Trump and Trumpism.* Abingdon: Routledge.

Abutaleb, Yasmeen and Paletta, Damian. 2021. *Nightmare Scenario: Inside the Trump Administration's Response to the Pandemic That Changed History.* New York: HarperCollins.

Arendt, Hannah. 1951. *The Origins of Totalitarianism.* New York: Schocken Books.

Bailey, Brian J. 1998. *The Luddite Rebellion.* New York: NYU Press.

Baker, Peter and Glasser, Susan. 2022. *The Divider: Trump in the White House, 2017–2021.* New York: Doubleday.

Ball, James. 2017. *Post-Truth: How Bullshit Conquered the World.* London: Biteback

Barr, William P. 2022. *One Damn Thing After Another: Memoirs of an Attorney General.* New York: William Morrow.

Bender, Michael C. 2021. *"Frankly, We Did Win This Election": The Inside Story of How Trump Lost.* New York: Grand Central Publishing.

Birx, Deborah. 2022. *Silent Invasion: The Untold Story of the Trump Administration, Covid-19 and Preventing the Next Pandemic Before It's Too Late.* New York: HarperCollins.

Borrell, Brendan. 2021. *The First Shots: The Epic Rivalries and Heroic Science Behind the Race to the Coronavirus Vaccine.* Boston: Mariner Books.

Boston Women's Health Book Collective. 1973. *Our Bodies, Ourselves.* New York: Simon & Schuster.

Brown, Michael J. 2020. *Hope & Scorn: Eggheads, Experts, & Elites in American Politics.* Chicago: University of Chicago Press.

Burgin, Angus. 2022. "The Crisis of Truth in the Age of Trump," in Julian E. Zelizer (ed.), *The Presidency of Donald Trump: A First Historical Assessment*. Princeton, NJ: Princeton University Press.

Burleigh, Nina. 2021. *Virus: Vaccinations, the CDC and the Hijacking of America's Response to the Pandemic*. New York: Seven Stories Press.

Carpenter, Amanda. 2018. *Gaslighting America: Why We Love It When Trump Lies to Us*. New York: HarperCollins.

Chowkwanyun, Merlin. 2022. "The 60/40 Problem: Trump, Culpability, and COVID-19," in Julian E. Zelizer (ed.), *The Presidency of Donald Trump: A First Historical Assessment*. Princeton, NJ: Princeton University Press.

Covid Crisis Group (CCG). 2023. *Lessons from the Covid War: An Investigative Report*. New York: Public Affairs.

CSIS (Center for Strategic and International Studies) Global Health Policy Center, Brown University Pandemic Center and COVID Collaborative. 2023. *American Democracy and Pandemic Security: Strengthening the U.S. Pandemic Response in a Free Society*. Providence, RI: CSIS.

D'Ancona, Matthew. 2017. *Post-Truth: The New War on Truth and How to Fight Back*. New York: Random House.

Dean, John W. and Altemeyer, Bob. 2020. *Authoritarian Nightmare: Trump and His Followers*. Brooklyn: Melville House.

Draper, Robert. 2022. *Weapons of Mass Delusion: When the Republican Party Lost Its Mind*. New York: Penguin Press.

Edwards, George C. III 2021. *Changing Their Minds? Donald Trump and Presidential Leadership*. Chicago: University of Chicago Press.

Enos, Ryan D., Fowler, Anthony and Havasy, Christopher S. 2017. "The Negative Effect Fallacy: A Case Study of Incorrect Reasoning by Federal Courts," 14 *Journal of Empirical Legal Studies* 618–647.

Epstein, Steven. 1998. *Impure Science: AIDS, Activism and the Politics of Knowledge*. Berkeley: University of California Press.

Esper, Mark. 2022. *A Sacred Oath: Memoirs of a Secretary of Defense during Extraordinary Times*. New York: HarperCollins.

Farkas, Johan and Schou, Jannick. 2019. *Post-Truth, Fake News and Democracy: Mapping the Politics of Falsehood*. New York: Routledge.

Filkins, Dexter. 2022. "Party Crasher," *New Yorker* (June 27).

Fridman, Ariel, Gerson, Rachel and Gneezy, Ayelet. 2021. "COVID-19 and Vaccine Hesitancy: A Longitudinal Study," *PLoS One* e0250123.

Friedman, Jonathan and Johnson, Nadine Field. 2022. Banned in the USA: The Growing Movement to Censor Books in Schools. Washington, D.C.: Pen America.

Gadarian, Shana Kushner, Goodman, Sara Wallace and Pepinsky, Thomas B. 2022. *Pandemic Politics: The Deadly Toll of Partisanship in the Age of COVID*. Princeton, NJ: Princeton University Press.

Haberman, Maggie. 2022. *Confidence Man: The Making of Donald Trump and the Breaking of America*. New York: Penguin Press.

Hanage, William P. et al. 2020. "COVID-19: US Federal Accountability for Entry, Spread, and Inequities—Lessons for the Future," 35 *European Journal of Epidemiology* 995–1006.

Hayden, Michael V. 2018. *The Assault on Intelligence: American National Security in an Age of Lies*. New York: Penguin Press.

Hofstadter, Richard. 2020. "On the Unpopularity of Intellect," in *Uncollected Essays, 1956–1965*. New York: Library of America.

Holmes, Stephen. 2018. "How Democracies Perish," in Cass R. Sunstein (ed.), *Can It Happen Here? Authoritarianism in America*, 387–427. New York: HarperCollins.

Hotez, Peter J. 2021. "America's Deadly Flirtation with Antiscience and the Medical Freedom Movement,"131 *Journal of Clinical Investigation* e149072.

House Permanent Select Committee on Intelligence (HPSCI). 2022. (The report has no title, but the subject is the Intelligence Committee's Response to the COVID-19 Pandemic) (December 15). Washington, D.C.: HPSCI.

House Select Subcommittee on the Coronavirus Crisis (HSSCC). 2022a. *The Atlas Dogma: The Trump Administration's Embrace of a Dangerous Herd Immunity via Mass Infection Strategy (June)*. Washington, D.C.: HSSCC.

_____. 2022b. *A "Knife Fight" with the FDA: The Trump White House's Relentless Attacks on FDA's Coronavirus Response* (August). Washington, D.C.: HSSCC.

_____. 2022c. *"It Was Compromised": The Trump Administration's Unprecedented Campaign to Control CDC and Politicize Public Health during the Coronavirus Crisis* (October). Washington, D.C.: HSSCC.

Illich, Ivan. 1971. *Deschooling Society*. New York: Harper & Row.

_____. 1973. *Tools for Conviviality*. New York: Harper & Row.

_____. 1974. *Medical Nemesis: The Expropriation of Health*. New York: Harper & Row.

Jones, Rebecca. 2020. *Unconfirmable: How Trump's Nominees Are Failing or Evading Senate Confirmation but Holding Office Anyway*. Washington D.C.: Program on Government Oversight.

Karl, Jonathan. 2021. *Betrayal: The Final Act of the Trump Show*. New York: Dutton.

Kessler, Glenn. 2020. "Trump and Coronavirus: 'Their New Hoax,' " in Glenn Kessler, Salvador Rizzo and Meg Kelly (eds.), *Donald Trump and His Assault on Truth: The President's Falsehoods, Misleading Claims and Flat-Out Lies*. New York: Scribner.

Kessler, Glenn, Rizzo, Salvador and Kelly, Meg. 2020. *Donald Trump and His Assault on Truth: The President's Falsehoods, Misleading Claims and Flat-Out Lies*. New York: Scribner.

Kolko, Gabriel. 1965. *Railroads and Regulation, 1877–1916*. Princeton, NJ: Princeton University Press.

Ladapo, Joseph. 2022. *Transcend Fear: A Blueprint for Mindful Leadership in Public Health*. New York: Skyhorse Publ.

Lemire, Jonathan. 2022. *The Big Lie: Election Chaos, Political Opportunism, and the State of American Politics after 2020*. New York: Flatiron Books.

Leonnig, Carol and Rucker, Philip. 2021. *I Alone Can Fix It: Donald J. Trump's Catastrophic Final Year*. New York: Penguin Press.

Lewis, Michael. 2021. *The Premonition: A Pandemic Story*. New York: W.W. Norton.

Makridis, Christos and Rothwell, Jonathan T. 2020a. "Politics is wrecking America's pandemic response" (Sept. 17) Washington, D.C.: Brookings Institution www.brookings.edu/blog/up-front/2020/09/17/politics-is-wrecking-americas-pandemic-response/

_____. 2020b. "The Real Cost of Political Polarization: Evidence from the COVID-19 Pandemic" *SSRN Electronic Journal*. www.brookings.edu/blog/up-front/2020/09/17/politics-is-wrecking-americas-pandemic-response/

Martin, Jonathan and Burns, Alexander. 2022. *This Will Not Pass: Trump, Biden, and the Battle for America's Future*. New York: Simon & Schuster.

McIntyre, Lee. 2018. *Post-Truth*. Cambridge, MA: MIT Press.

_____. 2022. "Post-Truth as a Precursor to Authoritarianism," in Austin Sarat, Lawrence Douglas and Martha Merrill Umphrey (eds.), *Law and Illiberalism*. Amherst: University of Massachusetts Press.

Meadows, Mark. 2021. *The Chief's Chief*. St. Petersburg, FL: All Seasons Press.

Mello, Michelle M. and Parmet, Wendy E. 2021. "Public Health Law after Covid-19," 385 *New England Journal of Medicine* 1153–1155.

Mok, Kenny and Posner, Eric A. 2022. "Constitutional Challenges to Public Health Orders in Federal Courts during the COVID-19 Pandemic," 102 *Boston University Law Review* 1729.

Nichols, Tom. 2017. *The Death of Expertise: The Campaign against Established Knowledge and Why It Matters*. New York: Oxford University Press.

Orwell, George. 1949. *1984*. London: Secker & Warburg.

Parmet, Wendy E. 2023. *Constitutional Contagion: Covid, the Courts, and Public Health*. New York: Cambridge University Press.

Parmet, Wendy E. and Paul, Jeremy. 2020. "COVID-10: The First Post-truth Pandemic," 110 *American Journal of Public Health* 945–946.

_____. 2023. "Post-Truth Won't Set Us Free: Health Law, Patient Autonomy, and the Rise of the Infodemic," in I. Glenn Cohen, Abbe R. Cluck, Katherine Kraschel and Carmel Shachar (eds.), *COVID-19 and the Law: Disruption, Impact, and Legacy*. New York: Cambridge University Press.

Patterson, Thomas E. 2019. *How America Lost Its Mind: The Assault on Reason That's Crippling Our Democracy*. Norman: University of Oklahoma Press.

Prado, C.G. (ed.) 2018. *America's Post-Truth Phenomenon: When Feelings and Opinions Trump Facts and Evidence*. New York: Praeger.

Rizzo, Salvador. 2020a. "Boasts to the Base: 'You're the Super-Elite!' " in Glenn Kessler, Salvador Rizzo and Meg Kelly (eds.), *Donald Trump and His Assault on Truth: The President's Falsehoods, Misleading Claims and Flat-Out Lies*. New York: Scribner.

Rosenblum, Nancy L. and Muirhead, Russell. 2020. *A Lot of People Are Saying: The New Conspiracism and the Assault on Democracy*. Princeton, NJ: Princeton University Press.

Rucker, Philip and Leonnig, Carol. 2020. *A Very Stable Genius: Donald J. Trump's Testing of America*. New York: Penguin.

Sadurski, Wojciech. 2022. *A Pandemic of Populists*. New York: Cambridge University Press.

Sides, John, Tausanovitch, Chris and Vavreck, Lynn. 2022. *The Bitter End: The 2020 Presidential Campaign and the Challenge to American Democracy*. Princeton, NJ: Princeton University Press.

Skowronek, Stephen, Dearborn, John A. and King, Desmond (eds.), 2021. *Phantoms of a Beleaguered Republic: The Deep State and the Unitary Executive*. Oxford: Oxford University Press.

Smith, Adam. 1776. *An Inquiry into the Nature and Causes of the Wealth of Nations*. London: Strahan & Cadell.

Stelter, Brian. 2020. *Hoax: Donald Trump, Fox News, and the Dangerous Distortion of Truth*. New York: One Signal Publishers.

Trump, Donald and Schwartz, Tony. 1987. *The Art of the Deal.* New York: Random House.

Trump, Donald and Zanker, Bill. 2007. *Think BIG and Kick Ass in Business and Life.* New York: Harper Collins.

U.S. House Committee on Science, Space, and Technology (USHCSST). 2021. *Brain Drain: Quantifying the Decline of the Federal Scientific Workplace.* Washington, D.C.: USHCSST.

U.S. Senate Committee on Health, Education, Labor and Pensions (USSCHELP). Minority Oversight Staff. 2022. *An Analysis of the Origins of the COVID-19 Pandemic: Interim Report* (October). Washington, D.C.: U.S. Senate.

U.S. Senate Homeland Security and Governmental Affairs Committee (USSHSGAC). 2022. *Historically Unprepared: Examination of the Federal Government's Pandemic Preparedness and Initial COVID-19 Response.* Washington, D.C.: USSHSGAC.

Velasquez-Manoff, Moises. 2022. "The Anti-Vaccine Movement's New Frontier," *New York Times* (May 29).

Wolff, Michael. 2018. *Fire and Fury: Inside the Trump White House.* New York: Picador.

Woodward, Bob. 2020. *Rage.* New York: Simon & Schuster.

Woodward, Bob and Costa, Robert. 2021. *Peril.* New York: Simon & Schuster.

Woolhandler, Steffie et al. 2021. "Public Policy and Health in the Trump Era," 397 *The Lancet* 705–53.

Wright, Lawrence. 2021. *The Plague Year: America in the Time of Covid.* New York: Alfred A. Knopf.

Young, Jeremy C. and Friedman, Jonathan. 2022. *America's Censored Classrooms.* Washington, D.C.: Pen America.

Zerofsky, Elisabeth. 2022. "Right Minds: The Claremont Institute Helped Shape a Trumpian Vision for American Conservatism. The Revolution It Started Is Far from Finished," *New York Times* (August 7).

INDEX

Kolibri 360 GmbH
Ferdinand-Jühlke-Straße 7
99095 Erfurt, Deutschland
produktsicherheit@kolibri360.de